ALEX

HAMILTON'S

London

HANNAH RYAN

For Americophiles everywhere.

CONTENTS

KEY FIGURES

Alexander Hamilton

(b. 1755 or 1757, Saint Kitts and Nevis - 1804, New York City, New York)

Alexander Hamilton exhibited intellectual potential at an early age. Educated at King's College in New York, he served as aide-de-camp to General George Washington, the first Treasury Secretary, and the Commanding General of the United States Army. In 1789, he founded the Federalist Party and later died at the hands of Aaron Burr following a bloody duel in Weehawken, New Jersey, in 1804.

Elizabeth Schuyler Hamilton

(b. 1757, Albany, New York – 1854, Washington D.C.)

Born into the prominent Dutch Schuyler family in upstate New York, Eliza married Hamilton in 1780 and they had eight children together. After Hamilton's death she fought tirelessly to preserve his memory. In later life she became a philanthropist and co-founded the first private orphanage in New York City.

Angelica Schuyler Church
(b. 1756, Albany, New York - 1814, New York City, New York)

Eliza Hamilton's older sister, Angelica Schuyler married Englishman John Barker Church in 1777 and lived with him in Paris and London, as well as in their various homes in New York and Boston. A vivacious hostess, she was known to charm just about anyone she met and is the subject of a debate about whether she and Hamilton were having an affair. She lived in London for thirteen years between 1785 and 1797.

John Barker Church
(b. 1748, Lowestoft, England - 1818, London, England)

Husband of Angelica Schuyler, John Barker Church was a businessman who left England in mysterious circumstances. He served as an envoy to France and later returned to England with Angelica where he became a member of parliament. A good friend and loyal brother-in-law to Hamilton, he fought a bloodless duel with Hamilton's killer, Aaron Burr, over a business dispute in 1799.

John Adams
(b. 1735, Braintree, Massachusetts
- 1826, Quincy, Massachusetts)

A Harvard-educated lawyer, John Adams was one of the most ardent proponents for American independence. He served as an envoy to France, Minister Plenipotentiary to Britain, and as the first vice-president and second president. Although both Federalists, Adams and Hamilton famously detested each other, and their feud is a defining facet of both of their careers. He spent three years in London between 1785 and 1788.

Abigail Adams
(b. 1744, Weymouth, Massachusetts – 1818, Quincy, Massachusetts)

The wife of John Adams, Abigail supported her husband's dislike of Alexander Hamilton. She is remembered as a 'Founding Mother' of the United States and a supporter of women's rights in the spheres of education and property. A modern woman in many respects, the ample discourse she left is a treasure-trove for historians. She lived in London with John in the 1780s.

Thomas Jefferson

(b. 1743, Shadwell, Virginia - 1826, Charlottesville, Virginia)

Thomas Jefferson was the principal architect of the Declaration of Independence. A scientist, inventor, philosopher, and politician, he served as the second vice-president and third president of the United States. The feud between Jefferson and Hamilton was, in part, responsible for the birth of political parties in the United States. He visited London for six weeks in the spring of 1786.

Benjamin Franklin

(b. 1706, Boston, Massachusetts - 1790, Philadelphia, Pennsylvania)

A world-renowned polymath, Benjamin Franklin remains an enduring icon of the Revolutionary Period. A gifted man from humble origins, Franklin made his fortune as a printer before branching out into civics, philosophy, and science. He spent sixteen years in London during the American Revolution, before serving as the first Minister Plenipotentiary to France.

Benedict Arnold

(b. 1741, Norwich, Connecticut -
1801, London, England)

An infamous turncoat, Benedict
Arnold was once a hero in the
Continental Army. However, he
felt he was not receiving the credit
he deserved for his significant
military feats. Resultingly, he
masterminded a plan to sell the
fortification of West Point to the
British, however, the plot was
discovered when his British
acquaintance, John André, was
captured. He and his family fled
to London after the War of
Independence ended.

Margaret 'Peggy' Shippen Arnold

(b.   1760,   Philadelphia,
Pennsylvania - 1804, London,
England)

The wife of Benedict Arnold,
Peggy was a Philadelphia socialite
believed to have been an integral
cog in Arnold's plan to sell West
Point to the British. If she was
involved, payments she received
from George III when the
Arnolds moved to London make
her the highest paid British spy of
the American Revolution.

John Jay
(b. 1745, New York City, New York - 1829, Bedford, New York)

John Jay was a New York-born lawyer and King's College alumnus. He was a friendly face to Alexander Hamilton and the two Federalists worked together, along with James Madison, on the Federalist Papers. He founded the New York Manumission Society and served as the first Chief Justice as well as negotiating the Treaty of Paris. He spent several months in London between 1794 and 1795 while negotiating the Jay Treaty.

John Laurens
(b. 1754, Charleston, South Carolina - 1782, Combahee River, South Carolina)

Born to Henry Laurens, co-owner of the largest slave-trading house in North America, John Laurens was an ardent anti-slavery advocate. He spent much of his youth in Europe where he was educated in both Geneva and London. He was good friends with Hamilton, and some have even questioned whether the pair had a sexual relationship. He lived in London in the 1770s.

Aaron Burr
(b. 1756, Newark, New Jersey -
1836, Staten Island, New York)

Descended from several illustrious families, Aaron Burr studied at Princeton College and fought in the War of Independence. He served as a senator and Attorney General in New York before holding the office of vice-president during Thomas Jefferson's first presidential term. In 1804, he killed Alexander Hamilton in a duel and was later tried and acquitted for the Burr Conspiracy. He lived in Europe for four years between 1808 and 1812 and spent ample time in London.

TIMELINE

- **1755 *or* 1757**: Alexander Hamilton is born on January 11 in Charlestown on the island of St Kitts and Nevis.

- **1757**: Benjamin Franklin is sent to London as a colonial agent for the Pennsylvania Assembly.

- **1760**: King George II dies at Kensington Palace in London.

- **1761**: King George III is crowned at Westminster Abbey.

- **1764**: The Sugar Act is imposed by the British government and is followed in close succession by the Currency Act.

- **1765**: The Stamp Act and the Quartering Act.

- **1767**: The Townsend Acts.

- **1770**: The Boston Massacre.

- **1772 *or* 1773**: Alexander Hamilton arrives in New York City.

- **1773**: The Boston Tea Party.

- **1775**: Shots are fired at Lexington and Concord.

- **1775**: Benjamin Franklin returns from Britain permanently.

- **1777**: Angelica Schuyler marries John Barker Church.

- **1780**: Alexander marries Eliza at the Schuyler Mansion in Albany.

- **1781**: The Battle of Yorktown. General Charles Cornwallis surrenders to George Washington.

- **1782**: Alexander and Eliza's first child, Philip, is born.

- **1783**: Benjamin Franklin, John Jay, John Adams, and Henry Laurens negotiate the Treaty of Paris with representatives from Britain.

- **1785**: The Churches depart New York for London.

- **1785**: John Adams is appointed as the first United States Minister Plenipotentiary to Great Britain.

- **1786**: Thomas Jefferson visits London.

- **1787**: The Constitutional Convention is held in Philadelphia.

- **1787**: Alexander Hamilton, James Madison, and John Jay write the Federalist Papers defending the new Constitution.

- **1788**: The Adams family arrive home from London.

- **1789**: George Washington is inaugurated as president. John Adams is vice-president.

- **1789**: Thomas Jefferson returns from France.

- **1790**: Benjamin Franklin dies aged eighty-four.

- **1791:** Alexander Hamilton has an affair with Maria Reynolds.

- **1794:** John Jay travels to London to negotiate the Jay Treaty.

- **1797:** The Churches return to New York.

- **1797:** John Adams is elected president.

- **1799:** John Barker Church duels with Aaron Burr.

- **1800:** Thomas Jefferson is elected as the third president.

- **1801:** Philip Hamilton is killed in a duel with George Eacker.

- **1804:** Alexander Hamilton dies in a duel with Aaron Burr.

- **1807:** Aaron Burr is arrested for the Burr Conspiracy.

- **1808:** Aaron Burr leaves America for Europe.

- **1808:** James Madison is elected as the fourth president.

- **1811**: George Frederick, the Prince of Wales, is named Prince Regent.

- **1812:** The War of 1812 breaks out between Britain and America.

- **1814:** Angelica Schuyler Church dies aged fifty-eight. She is buried in Trinity Church in Lower Manhattan.

- **1815:** John Quincy Adams is named U.S. Minister to Britain.

- **1816:** James Monroe is elected as the fifth president.

- **1818:** Abigail Adams dies in Massachusetts aged seventy-three.

- **1818:** John Barker Church dies in London aged sixty-nine.

- **1820:** King George III dies at Windsor Castle aged eighty-one.

- **1821:** King George IV is crowned at Westminster Abbey.

- **1825:** John Quincy Adams is elected as the sixth president.

- **1826:** John Adams and Thomas Jefferson die on the same day, aged ninety and eighty-three respectively. They died on the fiftieth anniversary of the signing of the Declaration of Independence.

- **1830:** King George IV dies at Windsor Castle aged sixty-seven.

- **1837:** Queen Victoria, Her Majesty Queen Elizabeth II's great-great-grandmother, becomes monarch aged eighteen.

- **1854:** Eliza Hamilton dies in Washington D.C. aged ninety-seven. She is buried next to Alexander Hamilton in Trinity Church graveyard in Lower Manhattan.

Author's Note

_____

For ease of reading, in regard to quotations, the author has modernised spelling and punctuation, corrected spelling mistakes and, in instances where a quote uses French or Latin, a translation has been provided.

PROLOGUE

BETSEY CRIES "ATLANTIC!"

On the last day of January 1791, Treasury Secretary Alexander Hamilton wrote to his London-based sister-in-law, Angelica Schuyler Church, "I must endeavour to see Europe one day."[1] Earlier in the month, he had proposed an excise tax on spirits distilled within the United States, a law that would lead to a three-year uprising in Western Pennsylvania called the Whiskey Rebellion and leave a tarnish on his political record. But, sat in the initial U.S. capital of Philadelphia on that below-freezing Monday afternoon, his mind was elsewhere. Over the past six years, his letters to his wife's sister had been saturated with the desirous sentiments of the Hamilton family to see Europe. By 1791, Hamilton was increasingly yearning to cross the Atlantic to meet Angelica in the city she had been living in for over half a decade. And it was not just the politician who wanted to see London, however, but his beloved wife, Elizabeth. Writing in October 1791, the couple's desire to travel had reached a crescendo and Hamilton told Angelica that "Betsey according to your hint cries 'Atlantic.'"[2] Yet, Hamilton's hunger to see for himself the Old World he had fought to cut ties from was never to be satisfied. Killed at the age of forty-seven (or forty-nine), he could not have known that when he stepped off the ship that carried his teenage self from St. Croix to New York in the 1770s, it would be the first and last time he would ever make an international journey. And Eliza, as much as she too pined to see Europe, would never leave the confines of the mid-Atlantic states. Yet, a cohort of the Hamiltons' surrounding milieu did stride along London's cobbled, manure-strewn streets; in fact, some of the most prominent figures in the life of Alexander Hamilton spent elongated periods of time in the city, which was then the centre of the western world. They shopped in the city's gilded consumer paradises; frequented museums and eateries; made appearances at the royal court; and met with some of the metropolis's most notable residents. This anthology seeks to tell the story of Alexander Hamilton's links to London through those travels of his family, friends, and foes. Although many of them had not met Hamilton by the time they arrived in the capital, the marks they would leave on Hamilton's story would be consequential and, in some cases, epoch-making. Resultingly, this is a handbook for any fan of the treasury secretary, or historian of the Revolutionary Era more generally, to follow the journeys taken and the spots visited by the names associated with the politician, and to document Anglo-American – and Anglo-Hamiltonian – connections.

Alexander Hamilton's life was, for over two centuries, largely forgotten by all but historians and economists, and possibly those who take interest in the faces on American currency. Lacking the bravado surrounding his contemporaries, such as George Washington or Thomas Jefferson, Hamilton had faded into the background. Even though he is the face of the $10 bill, the only person alongside Benjamin Franklin – until Harriet Tubman replaces Andrew Jackson as the face of the $20 bill - to feature on American tenner who was not a United States President; constructed the intricate basis of the American economy; and was integral in

Washington's inner circle during the War of Independence, his legacy grew to be reminiscent of a supporting actor in the Revolution and Confederation periods. After his premature death at the hands of Vice-President Aaron Burr, Hamilton fell victim to those who wanted to hinder his memory. Indeed, Hamilton divided people into two groups: Those who loved him unconditionally and those who saw him as America's answer to Caesar - and those who did see him as the Roman Emperor incarnate had no hesitations about stabbing him metaphorically in the back. Those around him - including his opponents - knew the mass of exuberance Hamilton put into forging the new republic, and many who viewed the treasury secretary as the enemy would likely be envious to know that facets of his achievements remain in place in the twenty-first century: in general, his outline of the economy is followed today to keep America on a capitalistic route, and elements of his discourse in the Federalist Papers is still referred to in judicial proceedings. He was the boy wonder of America, a feat which men like John Adams and Thomas Jefferson, two of his main political foes, could not emulate. While men like Adams, Jefferson, and Burr enjoyed additional decades of life after Hamilton was killed and all succeeded in holding gilded positions in the Executive Office, they refused to let sleeping dogs lie. Adams in particular could not shake the enmity he shared with Hamilton during his lifetime, and the Founders' enduring irks with the late treasury secretary allowed their stars to dim his legacy.

In recent years, however, the rags to riches tale of the gifted orphan from the West Indies has enchanted audiences around the globe. In 2009, actor and playwright Lin Manuel-Miranda appeared at the White House Poetry Jam to perform a new song he was toying with. Speaking to the audience he said, "I'm thrilled the White House called me tonight because I'm actually working on a hip-hop album. It's a concept album about the life of someone who I think embodies hip-hop: Treasury Secretary Alexander Hamilton."[3] Miranda's announcement was met with confused laughter as people, including President Obama, wondered what was inspiring about such a vague figure in American History. Years later, the 44th Commander-in-

Chief introduced a performance by the cast of *Hamilton: An American Musical* cast at the 2016 Tony Awards admitting, "I confess, we all laughed, but who's laughing now?"[4] Since its first opening off-Broadway in February 2015, *Hamilton: An American Musical* has grown to be bigger than even the most complimentary reviewer could have imagined and propelled Miranda, who was already well-known for his musical *In the Heights*, to international stardom. In February 2020, Disney paid $75 million (£64.6 million) for the rights to stream the musical, allowing it to reach fans in every corner of the globe. From its humble origins premiering at the Public Theatre on, fittingly, Lafayette Street in New York to being ranked as the greatest musical ever written, *Hamilton* not only introduced this once-obscure figure back into public memory but catalysed a renewed interest in the American Revolution and the founding of the United States amongst a wave of younger generations, not just in America but around the world. However, *Hamilton* is not the first play about the treasury secretary Broadway had seen. In 1917, the play *Hamilton* written by George Arliss and Mary Hamlin premiered at the Knickerbocker Theatre and Arliss would later go on to play the starring role in the 1931 film adaption. Thus, it is not entirely fair to, as was aforementioned, outrightly declare that Alexander Hamilton was a lost figure for centuries. Yet, it would not be wrong to suggest that he experienced a descent into obscurity over the second half of the twentieth century.

Born in Charlestown on the Caribbean island of St. Kitts and Nevis on January 11 of either 1755 or 1757 (historians tend to lean towards 1757, the year Hamilton himself gave on numerous occasions, but evidence exists for both years), the young Alexander Hamilton was descended from gentrified stock but led an impoverished life. His mother, Rachel Faucette, had inherited a sizeable sum of money and married at sixteen to Johan Michael Lavien, a planter over a decade her senior whom Hamilton would later label as nothing more than a gold digger. The couple had one son, Peter, but in 1750 the marriage crumbled, and Rachel refused to live in the household as man and wife any longer - an offence for which she imprisoned for months on a tiny cell in Christiansted overlooking the bay. After her release, Johan retained their son as Rachel fled the island. During this period, she met James Alexander Hamilton, a young minor aristocrat who had grown up in a castle in the British Isles. James was the son of Hamilton's namesake grandfather, Alexander Hamilton the laird of Grange, whose land was located in Ayrshire on the green, breezy western shore of Scotland. As his father's fourth son, James was not set to inherit his title and thus had carved out a different path for himself. Helped into an apprenticeship in the textile trade by his older brother, James worked through his four-year indentureship but when it expired in 1741 with no real prospects for him to benefit from the enterprise himself, he travelled to the West Indies to pursue the dream of trading sugar cane, rum, rice, and possibly humans in exchange for a Herculean fortune. Alas, this was not in the stars for James, and he died penniless on St. Vincent in 1799. Despite James's pecuniary issues, the blood he passed on to Hamilton makes it easy to see how his son made his economic feats seem effortless. While Hamilton had worked hard during his youth to set himself a course of self-education (due to the fact their parents were not married Alex and James – Alexander and Rachel's firstborn son - were not allowed to partake in the island's educatory system and thus, only received snippets of informal education) by saving to procure books and spending any spare moment during the revolution reading, mathematics was also a skill passed down to him genetically. His fifth great-grandfather was John Napier, 8th Laird of Merchiston, a mathematician who discovered logarithms, invented a form of manual calculator, and popularised the use of the decimal point. Additionally, Napier's father, foreshadowing Hamilton's role as the inaugural treasury secretary, served as the master of the Scottish Mint. While Hamilton was aware of his prestigious ancestry, once declaring, "The trust is that, on the question who my parents were, I have better pretensions than most of those whom in this country plume themselves on ancestry,"[5] the mathematical excellency in his genetics was most likely unknown to him. His illegitimacy, however, would plague him with paranoia his entire life - something John Adams knew and utilised to torture him - and, some historians argue, catalysed his greatness as he worked even harder to prove himself as more than a poor bastard orphan from a disease-ridden sugar island.

In February 1768, both Alexander and Rachel contracted yellow fever. James senior had abandoned the family in 1765 and Rachel had returned with her two young boys to St Croix where she made a living running a shop by the Christiansted seafront. As Chernow outlines in *Alexander Hamilton*, "the sugar islands were visited so regularly by epidemics of biblical proportions,"[6] and living close to the disembarkation port where slaves were unloaded from ships that came in from afar and teemed with mosquitos, it seemed almost inevitable that illness would strike them one day. Sharing their singular bed above the shop, they were administered the entrusted medicinal cures of the period that were believed to aid recovery by purging the body of dangerous miasmas. Rachel and Alexander endured enemas, emetics, and bloodletting. Surely drained of all life, Rachel, aged only thirty-nine (circa), died next to Hamilton on the evening of February 19, leaving her sons orphaned. After escaping death, Alexander and James lived with their cousin Peter Lytton but he was found in his bed swamped in a pool of blood shortly after he took them in. Assumed to have committed suicide, Lytton left all his worldly belongings to his mistress and their newly born son with nothing in his will accommodating his young cousins. Enduring one tragedy after another, Alexander and James were now destitute in St Croix. However, a glimmer of light broke through the clouds in the young Hamiltons' lives, and places were found for both of them. The older James was apprenticed to carpenter Thomas McNobeny, which Chernow suggests possibly proves that Alexander and James's differing dexterities were evident at an early point as, meanwhile, Alexander was taken in by Thomas Stevens, an admired merchant and began clerking for the mercantile house of New York traders, David Beekman and Nicholas Cruger. In regard to Hamilton's lodgings at the Stevenses, the young boy from St. Croix grew close to Thomas's son Edward. The pair shared interests and enjoyed each other's company as they both functioned on the same intellectual level. They had analogous personalities, but more noticeably still was the similar appearance between the two young men. Even as adults their visages were so similar that people audibly announced their belief that Edward and Alexander must have been kin, including General Timothy Pickering who was utterly perplexed about their apparent lack of genetic connection. Yet could it be that Hamilton was not a Hamilton at all, but a Stevens? Some historians have explored the idea that Thomas Stevens was Hamilton's biological father, and it's not an out of the question idea as St. Kitts and St. Croix are close to each other and, as a shop owner, Rachel would have dealt with plenty of merchants, including, possibly, Stevens. Yet, whether Hamilton knew the truth about this saga or not is lost to history.

As the years rolled on, Hamilton worked meticulously. While clerking he perfected his arithmetic, learnt the skills of trading, and read continuously. His life seemed to be continuing along a steady course. Acknowledged to be an adroit master in his role, at the age of fourteen, Cruger left him in charge of the business while travelling. Surely, he was to grow into a learned trader, open his own merchant house, and live out his life on the sunny Caribbean island, profiting on sugar cane and rum. However, on the evening of August 31, 1772, one of the four hurricanes that hit North America and the Caribbean that day made landfall on St. Croix. Having survived the nebulous tempest, and aware of the location of his absent father, Hamilton wrote to James in the following days and captured the ruinous pounding of the storm in vivid prose.

> The roaring of the sea and wind, fiery meteors flying about it in the air, the prodigious glare of almost perpetual lightning, the crash of the falling houses, and the ear-piercing shrieks of the distressed, were sufficient to strike astonishment into angels.[7]

It was this discourse about a meteorological nightmare – assessed by a weather historian to have been at least a Category Three, the same calibre as 2005's Hurricane Katrina - which altered Hamilton's life forever. Hugh Knox, a Presbyterian minister who had arrived on St. Croix the same year and knew Hamilton, sent the letter to the local newspaper *The Royal Danish American Gazette*. The letter was a boom and those who did not already know the gifts of the seventeen-year-old who clerked on the seafront did now. It became clear to the local Christiansted community that Hamilton's obvious talents would be wasted if he remained on St. Croix, even if he became a wealthy and respected merchant, he possessed intellectual prowess which would benefit from the nurturing of a formal education. Soon, a fund was set up to send Hamilton north to the mainland to join one of North America's prestigious institutions of higher learning.

When Hamilton left St. Croix is debatable, for centuries the tale ran with the date of October 1772, yet closer analysis of articles in *The Royal Danish American Gazette* during the winter of 1772 – 1773 led Chernow to believe that Hamilton may have left the island later than first thought, penning additional articles in the interim. Whatever the season, by the time he was heading north on a packet ship to Boston, a historical epoch had begun. Once in New England, Hamilton headed south to New York and began studying at the preparatory school, Elizabethtown Academy, in nearby New Jersey while lodging with tailor and future-spy Hercules Mulligan.

Following his time at Elizabethtown, Hamilton set about searching for a college. He enquired at the College of New Jersey (now known as Princeton) for admission but was refused entry on the terms that the college would not fulfil his wishes for a crammed, accelerated degree – a fact historians refer to as evidence that he was born in 1755 and thus wished to speed up his education. Famously, Hamilton instead turned to King's College in New York (later known as Columbia College). While he was studying, the American Revolution began to heat up and the crescendo of discontent over taxation in the colonies quickly turned bloody when the first shots were fired at Lexington and Concord on April 19, 1775. King's College shut its doors in the summer of 1776, and Hamilton was forced to put his studies on hold, resultingly he was not admitted to the bar until the war had finished. In the early days of the revolution, Hamilton's written adroitness was strengthening, and he penned epistles refuting support for the British. Most notably, in 1775, he quarrelled on parchment with Samuel Seabury, a bishop and Loyalist who had produced several treatises defending the British. Hamilton, with a lust for war and a heart ready to fight for his adopted home country, retorted Seabury's letters with *A Full Vindication of the Measures of Congress*, and the better known, *The Farmer Refuted* – the latter of which receives a full song dedicated to it in Miranda's musical.

During the Revolution, Hamilton went from strength to strength. From at first speaking out against the British at the New York Liberty Pole in 1774 to climbing the military ladder and becoming General Washington's aide-de-camp which saw him engage in action at the Battles of Harlem Heights, White Plains, Trenton, Brandywine, and most importantly, Yorktown, to name only a handful. Not only did Hamilton plant the roots of his future political career during the war, but he also met the woman who was to become synonymous with his name. In 1780, Hamilton first encountered his future spouse Elizabeth Schuyler at the home of her father: soldier, and future New York Senator, Philip Schuyler. With piercing black eyes and hair which - despite the heavy powdering evident in her recognisable 1787 Ralph Earl portrait - was of equal darkness, Elizabeth, known as Eliza or Betsey, was Schuyler's beautiful second child. Her mother, Catherine Van Rensselear - known as Kitty - was pregnant almost continually over a period of twenty-five years with very few non-gestational interludes, having fifteen children in total – which included a set of twins and a set of triplets - only eight of whom survived to adulthood. Kitty was carrying her youngest child, Catherine, at the wedding of Eliza to Alexander in 1780. Despite the connection Alexander and Eliza would share later in life, their first meeting was unnoteworthy. It was only at their second meeting in the winter of the same year when Eliza went with her older sister Angelica to the Continental Army's encampment at Morristown that sparks flew. The young soldier was so enchanted after spending an evening out with the girl from Albany that he forgot the codeword to gain access back to the camp.

Born on August 9, 1757, Eliza was part of a hybrid of some of New York's most prominent families. Both the Schuylers and Van Rensselears were descended from the original Dutch settlers of New Amsterdam. Both her grandfather and great-grandfather from her Schuyler line were the Mayors of Albany. Kitty's great-grandfather was Kiliaen Van Rensselear one of the founders of the Dutch West India Company.

Together Alexander and Eliza had eight children: Philip (b. 1782); Angelica (b. 1784); Alexander Jr (b. 1786); James Alexander (b. 1788); John Church (b. 1792); William Stephen (b. 1797); Eliza (b. 1799); and Philip II (b. 1802). Their marriage, although undoubtedly joyful and intense, was also plagued with America's first sex scandal. In summer 1791, Eliza had taken the Hamilton children upstate to spend the hot months at the Schuyler mansion in Albany. While enjoying the idyllic countryside scenes in her hometown, Alexander was becoming entangled in a liaison he would later describe as an "amorous connection" with a woman called Maria Reynolds. Under the guise of seeking financial support, Maria Reynolds had approached Hamilton claiming that her husband, James, had left her destitute for another woman. Writing in the infamous Reynolds Pamphlet – the mortifyingly honest treatise Hamilton published in 1797 to publicly correct claims that he had been involved in speculation with James Reynolds - he explains how Maria's cries for help briskly became a sexual enterprise.

> The charge against me is a connection with one James
> Reynolds for purposes of improper pecuniary speculation.
> My real crime is an amorous connection with his wife, for
> a considerable time with his privity and connivance, if not

originally brought on by a combination between the husband and wife with the design to extort money from me.

Sometime in the summer of the year 1791 a woman called at my house in the city of Philadelphia and asked to speak with me in private. I attended her into a room apart from the family. With a seeming air of affliction she informed that she was a daughter of a Mr. Lewis, sister to a Mr. G. Livingston of the State of New York, and wife to a Mr. Reynolds whose father was in the Commissary Department during the war with Great Britain, that her husband, who for a long time had treated her very cruelly, had lately left her, to live with another woman, and in so destitute a condition, that though desirous of returning to her friends she had not the means—that knowing I was a citizen of New York, she had taken the liberty to apply to my humanity for assistance.

I replied that her situation was a very interesting one—that I was disposed to afford her assistance to convey her to her friends, but this at the moment not being convenient to me (which was the fact) I must request the place of her residence, to which I should bring or send a small supply of money. She told me the street and the number of the house where she lodged. In the evening I put a bank-bill in my pocket and went to the house. I inquired for Mrs. Reynolds and was shown upstairs, at the head of which she met me and conducted me into a bedroom. I took the bill out of my pocket and gave it to her. Some conversation ensued from which it was quickly apparent that other than pecuniary consolation would be acceptable…After this, I had frequent meetings with her, most of them at my own house; Mrs. Hamilton with her children being absent on a visit to her father.[8]

Hamilton argued in the Reynolds Pamphlet that he had been the victim of blackmail as James Reynolds threatened the expose his liaisons with his wife if he did not provide a regular pecuniary gift. Alexander would also presume that this may have been Maria's intention from the offset.

Eliza burnt the vast majority of her correspondence with Hamilton. Burning letters was not unusual, indeed Martha Washington did the same with the correspondence between herself and her husband to ensure that the man she knew would be revered by history would retain some sort of privacy. But resultingly, historians are at an impasse to know how Eliza reacted to the Reynolds Affair. Certainly, one does not need to have any of their letters to know that the infatuated Eliza was heartbroken. Entirely enveloped in their relationship since she was twenty-two, Eliza had dedicated her entire life to being Hamilton's wife. From supporting the troops alongside Martha Washington by helping at army encampments, to being a sounding board for his ideas and boring him six children - with the sixth arriving only twenty-one days before Hamilton publicly admitted to his affair - Eliza believed he was as obsessed with her as she was with him. Indeed, the letters that have survived do suggest that the couple had mutual idée fixe with each other, with Hamilton writing her passionate sonnets and seemingly longing for her embrace anytime they were apart. While a mystery exists surrounding how Mrs. Hamilton reacted to news of her husband's torrid affair, it is evident that they not only reconciled but did so quickly as they conceived their penultimate child, Eliza, a little over a year after the Reynolds Pamphlet was released.

Eliza dedicated the rest of her life after Hamilton's death fighting to ensure that his legacy was not tarnished by the venom his opponents spouted, insisting that "Justice will be done to the memory of my Hamilton."[9] A common vignette called upon to illustrate Eliza's longing for her husband is how she would regale visitors to her Washington D.C. home with tales about the life she once lived, and the man with whom she lived it. Dressed in dark mourning clothes, in her old age she would show callers Giuseppe

Ceracchi's marble bust of Hamilton and artefacts of a bygone era, including a treasured wine cooler gifted by the Washingtons. Eliza was a young woman during the Revolution and was blessed with longevity. She lived to the grand old age of ninety-seven, but all those she had known during Hamilton's glory days, save for her children, were gone. By the time she died in 1854, it was approaching a century since the ideological frustrations of the American Revolution began, and Eliza felt every minute of it. Evidently ready to leave this world, she would often show a melancholic but macabre excitement about knowing she would soon see Hamilton in death. Ron Chernow's *Alexander Hamilton* opens with a prologue about a fireside game of backgammon with a visitor. After playing, the nonagenarian Eliza "leaned back in her chair a long time with closed eyes, as if lost to all around her. There was a long silence broken by the murmured words, 'I am so tired. It is so long. I want to see Hamilton.'"[10] Upon her death, the necklace she wore eternally around her neck was opened and a sonnet from her long-passed husband tumbled out. It read:

> Before no mortal ever knew
> A love like mine so tender, true
> Completely wretched – you away
> And but half blessed e'en while you stay
> If present love (*unintelligible*) face
> Deny you to my fond embrace
> No joy unmixed my bosom warms
> But when my angel's in my arms[11]

Written early on in their courtship some seventy-four years beforehand, it was so old and had been read so often that she had sewn the crumbling paper back together.

Although Eliza found it in her heart to forgive her husband, the Reynolds Affair deeply tainted Hamilton's career and was gold dust for any anti-Alexander politician who used his lack of moral compass as their prime topic for slander; John Adams, who had somewhat of an obsession with discussing Hamilton's sexual deviancy, was in his element. Certainly, one cannot discuss Hamilton without discussing his political rivalries, and the three main combatant figures in his life feature in this anthology: John Adams, Thomas Jefferson, and Aaron Burr. Undeniably, Hamilton's post-Revolution career saw him become one of America's preeminent Founding Fathers, arguably more involved in building the pragmatic economic basis of the United States than Adams, Jefferson, or Burr combined. While men like Adams and Jefferson applied moral and civic ideals to the U.S., Hamilton applied method and practicality, and his role in the birth of the nation was not lost on the generations of statespeople to come. In 1923, Republican Senator Henry Cabot Lodge said, "Hamilton was the greatest constructive mind in all our history and I should come pretty near saying…in the history of modern statesmen in any country."[12] Hamilton's arguments with Jefferson, Adams, and Burr would spill over into slanging matches in the newspapers, fracture cabinets, and, ultimately, create a party system in America. Yet, it was his friend and foe relationship with the latter which has come to be a defining facet of Hamilton's life. After years of sour back-and-forth between Hamilton and Burr, the ten-dollar-Founding-Father's life met its end with Burr's bullet fired during what has come to be labelled as the 'most famous duel in American history' at the duelling grounds in Weehawken, New Jersey, in 1804.

All three of Hamilton's primary adversaries tarried in London and left an exceptionally detailed path for future historians to trace, especially the journeys of Aaron Burr - whose actions in Weehawken undoubtedly contributed to his reasons for travel - and John Adams, who held an inaugural position in the city for three years. For Americans, adapting to life in eighteenth-century London was an arduous task as the metropolis was vastly dissimilar from the U.S. cities most were living in at least part-time: Philadelphia, New York, and Boston. For one, London was the most populous city in the world; in the late eighteenth century the populations of Philadelphia,

New York, and Boston were still in the tens of thousands meanwhile London was edging ever closer to one million. Architectural differences only exacerbated the claustrophobic feeling on the streets of London compared to its American counterparts. Philadelphia was built on William Penn's brainchild of a refined version of the already-existent grid system with spacious avenues. Conversely, London was, and still is, a labyrinth of alleyways, twisting streets, and confined squares. Despite improvements made following the Great Fire of London in 1666, elements of medieval London still existed and those living in the conurbation experienced a cramped and narrow existence. Those in Hamilton's circle who travelled to the heart of the Old World were apt to note the differences between not only London and a variety of American cities, but also other European cities. Thomas Jefferson provided comparative discourse on the city's architecture with Philadelphia and Paris, meanwhile, finical John Adams could not help but take issue with London's pavements.

Health differences derived from the cramped living spaces also caused issues, and while the States saw its fair share of epidemics, the general health of Londoners was poor. While average life expectancy in both London and America hovered around forty during this period, it was evident that England's miasma did not agree with the constitutions of many Yankee visitors. Abigail Adams – although arguably generally prone to migraines and colds – blamed the London climate for aggravating a seasonal bout of influenza which she says produced a "violent puking"[13]. Meanwhile, within a few months of arriving in London, the usually perky middle-aged Benjamin Franklin was bedbound with a strain of malaria he had contracted from the mosquito-laden fields around Westminster.

Moreover, surviving in London was one thing, but successfully travelling to and from England was another coup entirely. Despite modern humans having traversed the open ocean since before the Common Era, sea travel was still a highly dangerous pursuit. The passage could only truly be afforded by the wealthy and the seafaring conditions were still torturous. Sea travel was not a glamourous affair and motion sickness was rife: Abigail and John Adams write at length about their health at sea and Aaron Burr also discusses being bedbound by the constant rocking of the waves. Benjamin Franklin, however, as eccentric in his physiology as he was in his character was not afflicted by nausea and would often be up on deck carrying out experiments while those below would be suffering their bouts of vomiting and vertigo. There was, of course, not only seasickness to contend with, but the actual object of making it to the final destination. Disappearing during spells of rough weather was common and, during the American Revolution, escaping interception by a hostile vessel was miraculous: Abigail Adams feared both her husband and son dead or captured in 1778 when they made their maiden voyage to France, and in January 1813, Aaron Burr's daughter, Theodosia Alston, disappeared at sea the age of twenty-nine.

Overall, the change from America to London was a weighty alteration both mentally and physically whether that be in the spheres of travel, etiquette, health, business, or society. However, it was a change that many of Hamilton's contemporaries took in their stride as they journeyed around the capital, soaking in the essence of a country of which they were once classed as citizens. For the first time, this anthology dives deeply into Alexander Hamilton's connections to London: This is the story of those who loved or hated him, saw him as the greatest statesman or the most depraved politician. It is the story of those who moved between the Old World and the New, running around the Anglo metropolis while Hamilton remained at home, laying the foundations of the America we know today while yearning to follow in their footsteps. It is the tale of where his killer, Aaron Burr, descended into obscurity; of where John Jay negotiated a treaty which avoided Hamilton commanding an Anglo-American war; where Thomas Jefferson's enslaved concubine first saw European glimmers of freedom; where Benedict Arnold escaped to after he betrayed the Patriots; where Benjamin Franklin was blamed for the Boston Tea Party; where John Adams originated the Special Relationship; and where Angelica Church purchased the duelling pistols which would end both Hamilton and his son's lives. It is the story of how profoundly he was entwined with a city without ever being there. It is the story of Alexander Hamilton's London.

The locations listed in this anthology are by no means exhaustive, and I encourage you to further research the spots mentioned. Nor is this book intended to provide holistic biographies of the figures mentioned, nor of the era. Instead, I would recommend the following forerunners in the biographical category to read alongside *Alexander Hamilton's London*: *Alexander Hamilton* by Ron Chernow; *Eliza Hamilton: The Extraordinary Life and Times of the Wife of Alexander Hamilton* by Tilar J. Mazzeo; *John Adams* by David McCullough; *Abigail Adams: A Life* by Woody Holton; *Thomas Jefferson: The Art of Power* by Jon Meacham; *Benjamin Franklin: An American Life* by Walter Isaacson; *The Notorious Benedict Arnold* by Steven Sheinkin; *John Laurens and the American Revolution* by Gregory D. Massey; *John Jay* by Walter Stahr; *Fallen Founder: The Life of Aaron Burr* by Nancy Isenberg. Interestingly, Angelica Schuyler Church is yet to receive a biography. Nevertheless, biographers such as Chernow and Mazzeo do a wonderful job of weaving snapshots of her life into their publications. Dr. Tom Cutterham at the University of Birmingham in England is also working on researching Angelica's life in full.

———————————

CHAPTER ONE

ANGELICA SCHUYLER CHURCH

Born on February 20, 1756, at her family's mansion in Albany to Philip and Catherine Schuyler, Angelica was Hamilton's dark, coquettish sister-in-law. The eldest of Schuyler's fifteen children, she received a good education and, as an adult, would mix her intellect with charisma to negotiate and charm her way through society. Undoubtedly an alluring woman, she is portrayed in Miranda's musical as a headstrong leader, alluding to indications of the early murmurings of feminism in the colonies. In recent years, as a result of the musical's fun but fallacious storyline, many have come to imagine that Angelica and Hamilton were in the grips of a fervent love affair. This issue divides historians and, arguably, there is evidence both for and against the suggestion. A small number debate that yes, surely there was a sexual aspect to their relationship, while others maintain that their friendship was brimming with purely intense platonic affection. In truth, Angelica seemed to mentally seduce just about any man she met, including some of the most erudite men of the Revolution who she would come to count amongst her closest friends. When Angelica departed from a two-year stay in Paris in 1785, Thomas Jefferson wrote to her, "the morning you left us all was wrong, even the sunshine was provoking, with which I never quarrelled before."[1] The British-Italian artist Maria Cosway, who was also staying in Paris and is said to have had her own love affair with Jefferson, predicted that Angelica would become the "reigning Queen"[2] of his heart. Ron Chernow points out in *Alexander Hamilton* that, while Eliza may have withstood slight philandering from her husband, who was known to have a raging libido, the Schuyler family adored Hamilton until the day he died and long after, making it seem unlikely that they would have pardoned him for having such a virile affair with the unfalteringly faithful Eliza's older sister.

The musical, while undoubtedly sparking a revitalised interest in the American Revolution, took creative liberties with the tale's chronology for dramatic purposes, creating a surfeit of inexactitudes which many now take to be gospel. One of the major inaccuracies is the idea that Angelica met Hamilton on the same night as her sister and that Hamilton, on choosing Eliza as his bride, plunged Angelica into a lifetime of longing for her intellectual equal. In reality, although Angelica may have spent many of her years yearning for her sister and brother-in-law's company, she was already married and had just given birth to her second child when Eliza and Hamilton began their courtship during the Continental Army's tumultuous residence at Morristown in 1780. Furthermore, Alexander Hamilton was, by all accounts, extremely handsome with a charm that made just about anyone swoon. Thus, when the musical describes Angelica's husband – who is not mentioned by name but played a key role in Hamilton's life – as "not a lot of fun"[3], it is unduly harsh as it is hard to imagine anyone who would have seemed as alluring to any of the Schuyler sisters who practically worshipped the ground the aide-de-camp walked on. Added to the mix, the relationship between Hamilton, Eliza, and Angelica was intense amongst all three of them. In a 1789 letter to his sister-in-law, Hamilton tells Angelica that, "Betsey and myself make you the last theme of our conversation at night and the first in the morning. We talk of you; we praise you and we pray for you,"[4] illustrating that, while Angelica and Hamilton did enjoy a close relationship, Eliza was just as much a part of their storge ménage à trois.

Moreover, Alexander Hamilton was definitely not the love of Angelica's life. Labelled a "strange choice"[5] by Chernow, in 1776 Angelica was so beguiled by a young man named John Carter, a businessman visiting her father at the Schuyler mansion, that they eloped after her family designated him as forbidden fruit. The Schuylers were concerned about the young beau's lack of backstory, and they had a right to be. John Carter was actually born John Barker Church in an English coastal town in 1748. He had previously had a business in his native country before his debt swelled and he saw an opportunity to adopt an alias and emigrate to America; some suggested that into the bargain he had also killed a Tory politician in a duel. Despite his rather scandalous exit, John succeeded in escaping his creditors, yet Angelica proceeded to use her husband's alias in the formative years of her marriage, parading as Angelica Schuyler Carter. The "Carters" initially lived in Boston and in 1778 Angelica gave birth to the first of eight children, Philip Schuyler Church, named in honour of her father. Their brood followed in quick succession and the Churches lived in an era of anticipatory excitement as Americans waited with bated breath to see the outcome of the war.

A central figure in Angelica's life was her sister, Eliza. Since Eliza destroyed most of her correspondence, only small beams of her personality have survived. Those around her said that she was vivacious, intelligent, and brought a sprightliness to everything she did. In this sense, although we cannot measure to what extent, she was similar to Angelica and cherished their close bond intensified by their kindred personalities. In 1782, Eliza had just given birth to her and Hamilton's first child. Like her sister and brother-in-law, they had a son named Philip, and she and Hamilton were settling into married life. The War of Independence had come to a close and

Hamilton, her courageous husband, who had miraculously survived the Battle of Yorktown, was forcefully shaping the economic strategy of the new republic and indulging his young family with the unconditional love his own childhood was void of. Yet, an integral facet of their life was about to be ripped away for the best part of two decades and, in its place, a potent longing to follow it.

LONDON

"You and my dear Hamilton will never cross the Atlantic,"[6] Angelica lamented to Eliza in a letter sent from Yarmouth, England. In 1783, John B. Church was named as an envoy to France, and a pregnant Angelica left her beloved America and crossed the ocean with her husband and young family. The Américains à Paris were society darlings in the pre-French Revolution city where the champagne flowed, and no one foresaw the calamity of unrest that would plague the city six years later. Their vivacious social circle included individuals who mirrored their colourful personalities such as polymath Benjamin Franklin who had garnered French support during the Revolutionary War; Hamilton's political foe Thomas Jefferson who was enchanted by Angelica; the artist Maria Cosway, to whom Jefferson wrote the soliloquy between his head and his heart; and the Connecticotian painter John Trumball, who was to become the most prolific artist of the Revolutionary Era. Known wherever she went as being amiable, charming, and intelligent, the lady from Albany was a hit in cosmopolitan Paris. Amongst Angelica's acquaintances, however, were those who were to lose their heads during the Reign of Terror. In the final months of the bloody ruckus, Monsieur Lally-Tollendal wrote to Angelica to tell her of the deaths of her two friends, Madame de Gramont and Madame de Chalet, both of whom had connections with the French Royal Family and illustrate the illustrious company Angelica kept.

Despite Paris's haughty grandeur and a society that possessed a moral looseness paired with refined intelligence which suited Angelica well, the Churches' time in France was to be short-lived. In autumn 1785, after spending two years in Paris, the family relocated in Europe via a trip to New York. In early November, the Hamiltons stood on the Battery on the southern tip of Manhattan Island and watched Angelica's ship sail out of the harbour, once again entering a period of residence an ocean away. Alexander bewailed to his sister-in-law:

> With aching hearts and anxious eyes we saw your vessel, in full sail, swiftly bearing our loved friend from our embraces. Imagine what we felt. We gazed, we sighed, we wept; and casting "many a lingering longing look behind" returned home to give scope to our sorrows, and mingle without restraint our tears and our regrets.[7]

Their destination this time was not France, but the womb-like walls of America's old master: England. On arrival in the British Isles, however, the Churches did not head for John's hometown of Lowestoft in Suffolk, but for London. Ultimately, Europe was a much better fit for Angelica's personality than some elements of America. She was a popular hostess, and her salon was the place to be seen if one wanted to make it in the elite but libertarian strand of London society, but she longed for America: for being in New York state, walking along Broadway, and entertaining in Manhattan. But most of all she longed for the Hamiltons. Angelica was desperate for Alexander and Eliza to join her, especially after he told her that her insinuations of the couple visiting England had caused her sister to grow more intense in her desire to travel. Hamilton yearned to vacation in Europe and often asked Angelica if she would be glad if they visited her. "You and Betsey in England," she reflected in August 1793, "I have no ideas for such happiness, but when will you come and receive the tears of joy and affection?"[8] Of course, as Angelica foretold in her letter to Eliza, Hamilton and her sister never crossed the Atlantic. Yet, she put down roots which inextricably connected Hamilton to London: she dined with future Prime Ministers, entertained the heir to the throne, and ingratiated herself in the society her brother-in-law had fought against, much to his consternation. For Angelica, London was a synonym for hedonism. She watched plays from private boxes, had portraits rendered by an artist who painted redcoats and positively flagellated herself with luxury. But, despite all the pomp and pageantry, she was never quite wholeheartedly there. Moving with ease between the east and the west, she walked the thin line between the Old World and the New: she entertained the Prince of Wales but sailed home for Washington's inauguration. She supported her British husband in the House of Commons but would never betray her American soul. Angelica's time in London was, despite her inner yearning for home which undoubtedly overshadowed the era, a bittersweet highlight in her life but it was far more than an elongated sojourn - it would ultimately change the course of Alexander Hamilton's life, and thus American history, forever.

SACKVILLE STREET, PICCADILLY

The letters that arrived for Angelica from across the world between 1785 and 1797 were addressed 'Mrs. Church, Sackville Street'. Short and wide, akin to a petite avenue in New York's Greenwich Village - albeit with classic Palladian cream-coloured walls and Georgian architecture - Sackville Street became the hub of the Churches' London life. Inhabiting a house aptly named 'The Albany', the family switched on their societal charms and began entertaining frequently. In 1788, John purchased an additional abode: the Verney in Wendover. Located near Windsor, the Wendover home was a literal political investment as John was being encouraged to run for the county seat in British Parliament by his friend Charles James Fox, a Whig politician who despised George III. The Verney also added to their property collection which included a country estate called

Down Place in Berkshire; highlighting her wit, Angelica would make it clear to correspondents which one of her trio of properties she had written from by calling The Albany 'Town Place'.

Charles James Fox, the Churches' stereotypically British friend, was a hugely influential politician with pro-American sympathies. Born in 1749 to a gentrified family, his grandfather had been an administrator at the court of Charles II despite being born to a farmer in the seat of Hampshire. Fox's father was Henry Fox, 1st Baronet Holland - a man with a title but whose modest hereditary background in husbandry could not be hidden by the family's elevation from paupers to courtiers in less than a century. Henry, who served as the Leader of the House of Commons, joined the Whig faction and together with other pro-American thinkers of the day, including William Pitt the Elder, berated the actions of the Tory government against the colonies. Charles James Fox himself was married to a suspected former prostitute and ardently supported the American Patriots during the war. In 1790, John B. Church won the seat of Wendover and was initiated into His Majesty's Government. He held the post until 1796, spending his entire time in government as a member of the opposition party who battled the Tories led by the anti-American William Pitt the Younger. Undeniably, John had come far from the day he covertly fled from England. He now had friends in high places, had created an opulent life for his family, and was an elected lawmaker, however, Angelica couldn't help but compare him to the political and intellectual machine that was her brother-in-law. In October 1787, writing from Sackville Street, Angelica told Hamilton, "Church's head is full of politics, he is so desirous of making once in the British House of Commons, and where I should be happy to see him if he possessed your eloquence."[9]

Bizarrely, the Wendover seat was co-held by Lord Hugh Seymore who had served in the British Navy during the American Revolution and fought in the Great Siege of Gibraltar. This was just one singular facet of the incongruous life that the Churches led in England. Living in the affluent area of West London in such close proximity to the Royal Family's residence at St James's Palace and the hub of British political power in Westminster meant that the Churches would not be able to escape awkward links to the past. Sackville Street itself was teeming with Loyalist figures: John Fane, a Tory MP called the road home, as well as Baron de Wenzel and Dr. Richard Warren, oculist and physician to the king respectively. Molyneux Shuldham, an admiral in the British Navy who had escorted Lord Howe to New York Harbour in 1776 lived at Number 11. Luckily, the family had narrowly avoided calling Thomas Hutchinson, the former Governor of the Province of Massachusetts Bay who migrated to England in 1774, their neighbour as he and his haughty Loyalist beliefs had left the street a few years prior. While individuals such as Shuldham did not receive invites to dine with the Churches, John and Angelica's coterie was peculiar and ironic at the least and most likely treasonous to Patriots. Yet, their London social circle shouldn't be a surprise when one considers that the family frolicked with the upper echelons of society in France, though, of course, there existed a somewhat rose-tinted gaze with which the Americans looked upon the French since the pecuniary and military support of Louis XVI had led to Patriot's victory. Still, the friendships made in England were paradoxical. While figures such as Charles James Fox were aligned with their beliefs and held disdain for the monarch, the Churches also counted a far more peculiar face amongst their clique: George Augustus Frederick, the Prince of Wales, son of George III.

The friendship with the Prince of Wales, on the surface, seems the most inexplicable out of all the connections the Churches made in London. At first glance, entertaining the son of George III would only a few years earlier have been seen as fraternising with the enemy. However, the Prince of Wales, despite being his father's son, counted Whigs - including Charles James Fox - amongst his closest friends. George had also described himself as being "rather too fond of wine and women,"[10] and thus slotted right into the milieu of Foxites and, consequently, Angelica Church's social circle. A ball she threw for the heir to the throne apparently was the talk of London society for weeks and she would remain close with the Prince of Wales beyond her stay in London and into his Regency which came about when George III, an already sickly man, began to experience bouts of 'madness' in the 1780s which plunged his reign into chaos and earned him the enduring nickname 'Mad King George'. His illness often came in spurts and modern experts believe he may have been suffering from symptoms linked to Porphyria, a disease that can be detected in those who have close incestuous relations in their familial line. The results of inbreeding were rife in the houses of European royalty. Charles II of Spain has garnered the unfortunate title of 'the most inbred': he could not speak until he was four; sported a massive underbite lovingly known as the 'Habsburg Jaw'; and, on his death, they said his body did not have a single drop of blood, his heart was the size of a peppercorn and that his head was full of nothing but water. In 1811, the king's advisors reached a turning point: George III could no longer rule in full consciousness. The Regency Act was triggered, and the Prince of Wales ruled in his father's stead without a monarchical title for nine years until the king eventually died in a state of delirium in 1820. Early in the Regency era, Angelica wrote to the Prince Regent thanking him for receiving her son - most likely John Barker Church II – at court and hoped that he would also receive her "eldest and favourite son"[11] Philip. Penning her flattering epistle from New York on fragrantly embossed paper, Angelica serenades her British acquaintance with love and signs off 'Your friend'. Not only does her familiar letter and continued connection with the Prince of Wales illustrate, to at least some extent, a lasting appreciation for London, but her desire to present two of her sons outlines Angelica's enduring enchantment with the Prince of Wales, whom she favoured, despite her Yankee heart. Indeed, her sons were raised with a particular Anglo-American flavour, especially Philip who was educated at Eton and Middle Temple in London before engraining himself in the American cause working as his uncle's aide-de-camp in the late 1790s. It does not take a great stretch of the imagination to assume that Hamilton inwardly disdained, and was possibly slightly embarrassed, at his nephew's haughty Anglo upbringing studded with the attention of a future monarch. It was certainly not a backstory one wanted to flaunt while serving in the U.S. Army.

Sackville Street.

Angelica and John's frolics on Sackville Street could not escape the judgement of prying American eyes. Tales of the Churches' clique reached the ears of U.S. Treasury Secretary and brother-in-law Alexander Hamilton who was, understandably, perplexed. While Hamilton was conceiving the infrastructure of a new republic, hearing tales that his dearest Angelica was throwing parties for the son of the tyrant who had waged war with the Americans was stymieing. Illustrating his confusion at the ironic company she kept, Hamilton wrote to Angelica in October 1790 saying, "You hurt my republican nerves by your intimacy with "amiable" Princes. I cannot endure that you should be giving such folks dinners…."[12] Nonetheless, he continued in his classic Hamiltonian style which has left historians to ponder if their relationship went beyond the platonic. Echoing Angelica's coquettish disposition, Alexander reassures her, "you must be a very naughty girl indeed before you can lose the place you have in my affection."[13] Hamilton wasn't to worry though. In a letter to Eliza, Angelica showed that her heart beat the red, white, and blue of the Stars and Stripes, not the Union Flag, when she rhetorically pondered, "What are Kings and Queens to an American who has seen Washington?"[14]

ST. JAMES'S CHURCH, PICCADILLY

Opposite the end of Sackville Street sits a small redbrick church, obviously decades older than the surrounding Palladian structures which have dwarfed it. Originally constructed in the late seventeenth century by Sir Christopher Wren, the religious site would have once been a centrepiece in the fields of Piccadilly but is now a relic swallowed whole by the shopping district. The Anglican church has been altered several times having been partially destroyed by a number of catastrophic events such as the Blitz. It has also witnessed a profusion of historic events including the baptism of William Blake and the funeral of anatomist William Hunter who had links to Benjamin Franklin (see *Chapter Four*). For Angelica, St James's was not just her local parish, but the scene of pivotal events in her loved ones' lives.

Records kept at New York's Trinity Church in Lower Manhattan show that the Hamiltons were present in the church community. Alexander Hamilton rented pew ninety-two at the church, but records kept by the church's rector, Benjamin Moore, show that the treasury secretary was not an ardent attendee. Eliza, however, was and is recorded in his List of the Communicants of Trinity Church which was started in 1801. While Hamilton does not seem to have attended religious ceremonies every week with his family, he was heartily involved in the bigger picture of the church. Not only did he offer Trinity his law services need they be of assistance, but he was also involved with electing Reverend John Bassett to the post of assistant minister. In October 1788, Alexander and Eliza baptized three of their older children at Trinity over the course of a few days. Angelica, home at the time to attend the inauguration of George Washington the following April, is recorded as the baptismal sponsor for their eldest daughter and her namesake, Angelica Hamilton. While the records from Trinity are not a measure by which to indicate Angelica's general commitment to churchgoing, records from St. James's do show that she was involved in her local parish church in London. They also present the possible extent of Angelica's longing for home while in London, and her yearning to be with Hamilton. On February 16, 1792, Angelica gave birth to the sixth of her eight children, and the only one to be born on British soil: Hamilton's nephew and namesake, Alexander Church. Alexander was baptised at St. James's on April 10. His baptism is listed in the church's records as 'Alexander Church, son of John-barker and Angelica'. Angelica and John already had three sons by the time Alexander was born named Philip, John, and Richard. None carried Alexander's name even as a middle handle, yet their second daughter was christened Elizabeth. Conversely, the Hamiltons had named their first-born daughter Angelica. Could Angelica's choice to name her son Alexander at this time emphasise her longing to be home? Perhaps. Some would say almost certainly. Like his uncle though, young Alexander was not to enjoy longevity. Sadly, the babe that carried Hamilton's monikered link to London was only to survive a decade. He died in New York City in 1803.

The birth of Alexander Church was not the only cradle-to-grave link between Hamilton, Angelica, and St James's. The Churches returned to New York in 1797 and were home for seventeen years when Angelica herself passed away in March 1814, aged fifty-eight. Famously, she is buried in Trinity Church near Alexander and Eliza Hamilton and other Revolutionary figures, such as Hercules Mulligan. Following Angelica's death, John left his adult children in the land of their mother and retreated to his native England where he ended his days, outliving his wife by only four years. On April 27,

St. James's Church, Piccadilly.

1818, he died in Piccadilly and his burial is listed in St. James's records as May 2. His abode is listed as Duke Street which runs adjacent to one of London's most luxurious department stores, Fortnum and Mason, but his age is incorrectly listed as seventy-two when he was, in fact, sixty-nine.

Like many inner-London churches, St. James's lacks an extensive churchyard. With the boom of the population growth in the late eighteenth century further crowding what was already the most populous city in Europe, in 1790, St. James's Church purchased new burial grounds two miles north in Euston as its tiny churchyard could not cope with the numbers it was originally built for. The new grounds, then in the outer pastures of London, were used for nearly sixty years until 1853 when the land was turned into St. James's Gardens. In the process of developing the graveyard into a scenic pleasure garden, the headstones of those interred where removed, leaving an estimated sixty-one thousand people buried in unmarked plots. Despite being listed in the funeral records, Angelica's husband lacks a memorial at the Piccadilly church, pointedly suggesting that he is likely buried in north London amongst a bouquet of people from all walks of life, from London's paupers to esteemed figures, such as Captain Matthew Flinders, the navigator who circumnavigated Australia.

John Barker Church is a lesser-known figure in the life of Alexander Hamilton. In recent years, even as Hamilton's story has had a resurgence, the Englishman's name is still not oft mentioned with the retinue of figures synonymous with the Founding Father. John, however, was a significant presence in Hamilton's life: the two exchanged frequent letters, were close brothers-in-law and Hamilton got Church a job as a director at the Manhattan Company. Additionally, Hamilton entrusted his monetary affairs to Church in the event he died in debt, and the Englishman even accompanied Hamilton to the office of future president James Monroe to discuss issues relating to the Reynolds Affair which Monroe had investigated along with Frederick Muhlenberg and Abraham Venable in 1782. The two head-strong Founders nearly ended their talk in an 'affair of honour' and Church along with Monroe's colleague, Republican David Gelston, reportedly had to pull the two men off of each other. Church, although not necessarily the man fans of the musical think Angelica should have ended up with, was a main character in the life of Alexander Hamilton and a good, loyal friend to the man in question. Thus, the trail he leaves in London is as integral as Angelica's.

Euston is now classed as a relatively central point in London and Euston Station is a major travel hub with links all over Britain. In autumn 2018, archaeologists began to excavate the area where an estimated forty-five thousand people are buried to prepare the land for Britain's new high-speed rail line (known as HS2) to be laid. John Barker Church is likely among them, however, whether efforts will ever be made to identify the bones via DNA analysis remains to be seen.

NUMBER 7 HENRIETTA STREET, COVENT GARDEN

Despite being the most famous American woman in London, like Eliza, Angelica was immortalised in very few paintings. For decades there were thought to be only two artworks depicting Hamilton's favourite sister-in-law: a painting presenting her, her son Philip, and a servant by John Trumball (c.1785) and an engraving by Maria Cosway's spouse, the famed miniaturist Richard Cosway. However, in 2017, historian and writer Susan Holloway Scott came across an image on social media from London's Philip Mould Gallery which piqued her wealth of Hamiltonian knowledge. The post depicted a watercolour-on-ivory miniature portrait of a young woman with dark eyes and fair hair wearing a peach dress with blue accents. On the reverse side of the miniature portrait is the name of the artist, Samuel Shelley, accompanied by his address at 7 Henrietta Street where he was based during his peak years. The sitter's identity, however, was a mystery. Scott, author of *I, Eliza Hamilton*, had spent years researching the family and instantly recognised the long, pointed face Shelley had captured. She immediately contacted the company to share her idea: this unknown sitter was Angelica Schuyler Church. In an article for her website, Scott says, "To my eye, the Trumball and Shelley portraits show the same woman. It's an uncommon face for an 18thc beauty: a long nose (which also turns up in portraits of her father), a small mouth, the dark, slightly close-set eyes. The Shelley miniature also seems to capture both the flirtatious charm and intelligence that Angelica's contemporaries all mention."[15] Scott contacted Philip Mould miniature specialist consultant Emma Rutherford who reviewed the suggestion. While her reply was not promising at first - Rutherford mentions that Shelley never exhibited an Angelica portrait and thus could not say for sure it was her - the gallery agreed that the facial similarity (including eye colour) is so strong that they would amend the cataloguing to say that it is 'possibly' a portrait of her. As of 2021,

Philip Mould's cataloguing has again been updated to say for certain that the sitter is Angelica Schuyler Church.

Angelica Schuyler Church. Samuel Shelley, c. 1784 – 1794.

If Angelica is the beautiful sitter with bouffant hair and a lace-trimmed bodice, she would have been one of the hundreds who sat for Samuel Shelley at his Covent Garden home. The Whitechapel-born Shelley lived on one of the flower market's streets for a decade between 1784 and 1794. These years align with the Churches' time in London, adding to the certainty that the sitter is Angelica Church. Henrietta Street itself was a hub of creative souls during the latter 1700s owing to the fact that the Royal Society of Arts was founded at the street's Rawthmell's Coffee House in 1754. Shelley painted a wealth of profiles including British officers in all their red-coated glory; Sir Ashton Lever, who operated a museum in Leicester Square; and young, flirtatious women, such as Lady Lavinia Bingham who married into Princess Diana's ancestral Spencer family. Indeed, in the Philip Mould Gallery's analysis of Shelley, the experts reveal that refined, conservative gentlemen would seek miniaturists such as John Smart, whereas those fishing for a painter to capture the racy hedonism and glamour of the era would have chosen Shelley who had a knack for capturing swagger and dalliance.

Today, Henrietta Street retains a wealth of original features. Like the majority of Covent Garden's buildings, the street is constituted of mainly eighteenth-century Palladian structures with the trademark light paintwork and beautiful details, and is swelling with restaurants, bars, and the ghostly shadows of history.

THEATRE ROYAL DRURY LANE, COVENT GARDEN

One of Covent Garden's oldest establishments is Theatre Royal Drury Lane. Originally opened in 1663, the theatre has had four reincarnations that have ensured its longevity. The original seventeenth-century theatre was built during the revival of artistic non-religious pass times in England which had been banned during the eleven-year period that Britain was a republic under Oliver Cromwell and, for a period, his son Richard. The theatre was built at the behest of the newly instated Charles II. The king, who had spent nine years in exile following his defeat at the Battle of Worcester in 1651, was a divine gift for non-Puritanical English subjects who had spent over a decade under Cromwell's rule during which time they were subject to the antithesis of Charles II's joyous reign: celebratory aspects of Christmas were banned; women could not wear make-up or bright colours; inns shut; theatres were closed. Oliver Cromwell was a devout Puritan whose New Model Army rose to victory in the English Civil War which led to the execution of Charles I outside the Banqueting House on Whitehall. In the crowd was believed to be Edward Winslow, Mayflower passenger and three-time Governor of Plymouth Colony, who had returned to England and befriended Cromwell. Known as the Lord Protector of the Commonwealth of England, Scotland, and Ireland, Cromwell died in 1658 leaving his son – in a not very republican manner – to inherit his title. However, Richard Cromwell's term as the head of the republic was short-lived and the future Charles II returned from France, sparking a period known as the Restoration. Charles epitomised the return of fun and frivolity to the isles and earned himself the title the 'Merry Monarch'. Widely adored by his subjects, adoration for the monarch grew further when he reopened theatres by commissioning two companies to be established. One was founded by Thomas Killigrew, the playwright son of a courtier. Killigrew's company, aptly named the King's Company, established Theatre Royal and the playhouse opened on May 7, 1663. By the time Angelica and John arrived in London, the theatre was in its second reincarnation, with work underway while they were in the city to rebuild the theatre again.

During the time it was open, the Churches had a private box at the theatre which the couple frequently used to drink up the playhouse's entertainments. Shortly after their marriage, Angelica and John moved to Boston where John had managed numerous business ventures. The Massachusetts city had not yet fully moved away from its Puritanical traditions and public entertainment, including theatres, were still banned. Meaning that, like many Americans arriving on the continent, the first time the couple experienced theatre was in France and England.

The last performance at the first incarnation of the theatre Angelica would have known was on July 4, 1791. She would have been able to again view the stage before she left as the third building opened in 1794. If Angelica was a frequent theatregoer, she most likely saw the actress of the day, Sarah Siddons, perform at Drury Lane multiple times. Abigail Adams, who was in London during the same period as Angelica, mentioned Siddons continually in her letters before she had even seen her perform, indicating the breadth of her fame (see *Chapter 2*). Siddons, born in Wales, had first appeared at Drury Lane ten years before Angelica arrived in England but had initially failed to impress the London crowds. By the time the Churches were watching the stage from the plush confines of their private box, however, she had taken the stage by storm, often appearing as Lady Macbeth, and listing an extensive retinue of other Shakespearean characters amongst her performances.

Drury Lane was more than a theatre; it was a social hub where one would go to see and be seen. The king and queen oft frequented the establishment, and the theatre was the location of one of two attempts made on George III's life on the same day on May 15, 1800. A man named James Hadfield, who was later acquitted of the crime on the grounds of insanity, fired into the royal box during the national anthem, missing the king by mere inches.

For Angelica, despite possessing access to a private box and the most lauded performances of the day, writing to Hamilton on February 4, 1790, she groaned, "I am so unreasonable as to prefer our charming family parties to all the gaieties of London."[16] It seemed no amount of unprecedented exposure to London's frivolities truly reconciled her longing to be home.

NUMBER 7 HAYMARKET, PICCADILLY

Less than half a mile on foot from Sackville Street is a sprawling road with centuries of history where the low afternoon sunlight hits the magnolia walls of the two theatres straddling the pavement. Called Haymarket, the street has existed for over five hundred years and was originally used for selling - as the name would suggest – farm wares. Over time, the street evolved into a wider consumer spot and, by the eighteenth century, had leaped from selling hay to husbandmen to flaunting everything from umbrellas to tobacco to the affluent elite of the city. Every day, residents of Mayfair and other surrounding prosperous neighbourhoods would flock to the street to purchase their desired commodities and window shop at outlets, such as Fribourg and Treyer's snuff shop where George IV was a patron and Angelica knew the owners. Thousands of pounds exchanged hands and Haymarket sellers feature in the memorandum books of some of history's most well-known characters. Amongst all the non-consequential purchases made on the street since its pre-Elizabethan birth, in the late 1700s, Angelica and John made an acquisition at Number 7 Haymarket that would alter the course of American history.

The front of Number 7 Haymarket.

Rebuilt in the early nineteenth century as part of architect John Nash's redevelopment of Theatre Royal Haymarket, Number 7 today operates as a restaurant connected to the neighbouring playhouse. Over the past three centuries, a plethora of businesses have traded on the site, including print-sellers, art dealers, and the headquarters of the United States Line shipping company. Until the early twentieth century, Number 7 also operated as a gunsmith. During Angelica's London residence, the gunsmiths Robert Wogdon and John Barton ran their business from Number 7, and their duelling pistols were the crème de la crème of weaponry used in affairs of honour. Sometime during their residence in London, Angelica and John purchased a set of the famed pistols from the gunsmiths and carried them back across the Atlantic to New York where they were soon used in the 'most famous duel in American history'.

Preceding his father's infamous death at the hands of Vice-President Aaron Burr, Philip Hamilton was killed in a duel defending his father's reputation. On July 4, 1801, New York lawyer George Eacker gave a speech hosted by the Aaron Burr-supported Tammany Society in which he said Alexander Hamilton had used his position in John Adams's administration to bully his opponents and, most controversially, that he was prepared to overthrow Thomas Jefferson's presidency. Four months later, the Hamiltons' eldest son, Philip, confronted his fellow King's College alumnus at the Park Theatre in Manhattan. Philip, along with his friend Stephen Price, got into a fracas with Eacker. In the ensuing argument, both Philip and Stephen challenged Eacker to duels, the first of which took place on November 22 between Price and Eacker. In a coincidental turn of events, Price - who would go on to purchase the Park Theatre - would later manage Angelica's playhouse of choice, Theatre Royal Drury Lane, in the 1830s. Price and Eacker's fought a bloodless duel, shook hands in a gentlemanly fashion, and remained unscathed. The next day though, Philip Hamilton's young life would come to an end when, as instructed by his father, he failed to raise the heavy duelling pistol in the air after he and Eacker counted to ten. Eacker, at first also failing to raise his pistol, did not mirror Hamilton's plan to perform a delope. Instead, he fired at Hamilton shooting through his right hip and lodging the bullet in his left arm. Philip was rowed back across the Hudson River and taken to Angelica's Manhattan home where he later died in the early hours of the following morning with both his parents at his side. Eliza was around two months pregnant at the time with her and Alexander's final child. When the baby arrived the following June, the couple named him in honour of his late brother. 'Little Phil' as he was known, was the only one of Alexander and Eliza's children to have been photographed. A picture taken in 1880 shows a likeness to portraits of his father with a wide forehead, long face, and shapely nose.

The death of Philip Hamilton deeply impacted the entire Hamilton-Schuyler clan, but none more so than Philip's sister and Angelica's goddaughter, Angelica. Two years younger than Philip, Angelica and her brother were so close that, upon his death, her mental health suffered so much so that she was thought to have been trapped in a state of eternal childhood and was cared for by Eliza for the majority of her life.

Less than three years after Philip died in an affair of honour, Alexander Hamilton suffered the same fate. As the early sun played on the Hudson River ripples on the morning of July 11, 1804, Hamilton and Burr crossed the water to Weehawken. The duel was the result of years of political feuding between the two Founders which saw them quarrel continually while also working alongside each other. Notably, they were partners in the courtroom in the case of Levi Weeks and also business partners in the Manhattan Company. However, Hamilton thought Burr a politician with no grounded beliefs or morals, and thus liable to be easily swayed for power and money. Meanwhile, Burr, like his fellow Democratic-Republicans, thought Hamilton an Anglophilic dictator. Already harbouring deep, historical enmity for one another, tensions rose further in the run-up to the 1804 Election as Burr believed, and not inaccurately, that Hamilton was responsible for widespread defamation. One defining episode which Chernow notes "triggered a chain of events that led inexorably to Hamilton's duel with Burr"[17] was a dinner held by Judge John Tayler on State Street in Albany. At the dinner, Hamilton and other guests, including Federalist James Kent, denounced Burr, labelling him as dangerous among other things. Fellow diner Dr. Charles D. Cooper wrote a letter to his friend Andrew Brown in which he described the slanderous dinner table talk. One way or another the letter was intercepted and parts of it were printed in the *New York Evening Post*. Public denials were made about these comments including by Hamilton's father-in-law Philip Schuyler who argued that Hamilton had agreed to stay neutral during the election. As back and forth ensued about whether Hamilton had so brazenly aired his grievances about Burr, it soon became evident that no amount of refuting would alter Burr's mind that enough was enough and, if Hamilton wanted to aloofly slander him in private or spew obloquies in public, it was time for Alexander to put his money where his mouth was. It was time to finish this with an affair of honour. Although illegal in both New York and New Jersey, duels hovered in a grey area in the latter where they were seen as almost outside of the law and dealt with slowly. Resultingly, the Weehawken duelling grounds along the banks of the Hudson River became the unofficially designated spot men would flock to in order to defend their honour.

As Hamilton, Burr and their seconds, Nathaniel Pendleton and William P. Van Ness, made the crossing, packed on the boat were the pistols bought at 7 Haymarket. The brass, walnut, and gold weapons were laying silently, encased in their hard wooden box, and on the precipice of firing an epoch through the pages of American history.

Following the same advice he had given to his son, Hamilton intended to perform a delope to avoid killing Burr. The actual events of the duel are somewhat blurry, some accounts suggest that Hamilton did fire at Burr, while the accepted account declares that he fired into the air and that his shot hit a tree. Indeed, the most certain part of the event is that Hamilton was shot by Burr. The bullet punctured his abdomen and lodged itself in his spine, but Hamilton did not die instantly. As he rested his head on a rock while waiting to be carried back across the river, no one could have guessed that he would have to endure a further thirty or so hours before he finally succumbed to his injury with the ever-faithful Eliza and Angelica at his side. In his final hours, he received friends and family at the house of William Bayard Jr. in Greenwich Village where he had been taken to rest. Benjamin Moore gave the dying Founder his last Holy Communion after initially refusing as duelling was seen as a sin. Hamilton finally slipped away on the afternoon of July 12, 1804.

Following the duel, rumours amounted that the Wogdon and Barton pistols used hairline triggers which gave a dueller an advantage as less pressure was needed to fire the weapon. This created the first wave of hateful rumours surrounding Hamilton post-death as whispers amounted that he had intended to kill Burr using this sneaky tactic. However, hairline triggers were commonplace and in fact, according to Pendleton, Hamilton had not switched his on.

Interestingly, John B. Church had already duelled Burr in 1799 when he became irked by Burr's directing of the Manhattan Company. However, Aaron Burr noted that the pistols used in that instance were his own and not the cursed set from the Haymarket.

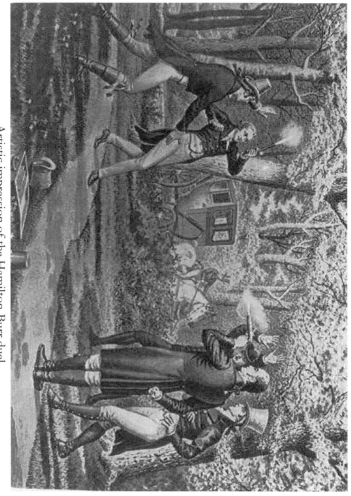

Artistic impression of the Hamilton-Burr duel.

In the spring of 1797, Angelica left Europe for the final time. John B. Church was so wary that they were not lost to the cruel mistress that was the Atlantic that he made his family sail over in two separate voyages: he with their sons and she with their daughters. Arriving in New York in May, Angelica was finally, and permanently, home. Following Hamilton's death, she was instrumental in supporting Eliza in fighting for Hamilton's legacy. However, sadly, according to Eliza biographer Tilar J. Mazzeo, by early 1814 Angelica looked far older than her fifty-eight years. The once vivacious hostess was racked by a cough she just couldn't shake, and Eliza would walk through New York City every day come rain, sleet, and snow to sit by her side. By March, Eliza was once again following a coffin to Trinity Church. As Angelica had stoically sat with Eliza at Alexander's bedside as he slipped away, Eliza now held Angelica as she passed on to the other side. A decade earlier, Eliza had lost her son, husband, and both parents within the space of three years, now the woman who was her rock had gone too.

Angelica Schuyler Church was an American in her heart and her head. Having spent nearly a quarter of her life across the Atlantic, however, Europe - and London specifically - undoubtedly left not only a mark on her soul, but on history. Indisputably, she is the closest character in this anthology to Hamilton to have spent time in London, and the purchase she and John made at Wogdon and Barton's was also the most consequential connection between Hamilton and the city. Of course, London was not responsible for Hamilton's death. Had Hamilton not owned the duelling pistols bought at the Haymarket, others could have been swiftly procured, yet the importance of what was, at the time, a seemingly noneventful purchase during a shopping jaunt to the street cannot be overstated, and marks Number 7 Haymarket as arguably the most important spot to peruse on a tour of Hamilton's London connections.

For Angelica, London was not America, but America in turn was not London. While she bemoaned her elongated stay in the metropolis, she adored certain aspects, revelled in her suave coterie, and left a significant trail of Hamiltonian links to London for historians to explore.

CHAPTER TWO

JOHN ADAMS

A"bastard brat of a Scotch peddler"[1] was John Adams's summary of Alexander Hamilton in an 1806 letter to his friend and fellow Declaration of Independence signatory, Dr. Benjamin Rush. This was not the first nor last insult thrown. Often referencing his womanising or Caribbean roots, the ageing John Adams could not stop attacking his old foe, even after Hamilton had been laid to rest in Trinity Church. Short, balding, erudite, and paranoid, the congressman from Massachusetts was both the only other mainstream Federalist and Hamilton's most vigorous slanderer. Up against the Democratic-Republicans, one would think that Adams and Hamilton would have been united in their efforts to forge Federalism. Alas, their desire for a strong central government, as opposed to state-level organisations, caused Adams and Hamilton to collide in their efforts in the early administrations, and the two politicians engaged in a battle which was not only a meeting of minds but also pride. Both Adams and Hamilton were men known for their vanity, immodesty, and habitual need to uphold their reputations; Hamilton often wrote under pen names in newspapers to repudiate his opponents, and his 1797 Reynolds Pamphlet is one of the best examples to reference to illustrate his incessant need to uphold his pride, and no part of the scandalous essay is more telling of this than the full title: *'Observations on Certain Documents contained in No. V and VI of the History of the United States for the year 1796, in which the charges of speculation against Alexander Hamilton the late Secretary of the Treasury is fully refuted. Written by himself'*.

In the pamphlet "written by himself" he admitted to an extramarital affair to right a distorted story that his big secret was that he had engaged in speculation. It appears that, to Hamilton, the public knowing about his promiscuous antics was less of a smudge on his reputation than having actions he took while in the treasury questioned. Meanwhile, history remembers Adams as extremely umbrageous, reactive, and volatile. Modern historians have suggested that he was a chronic depressive and exhibited symptoms of bipolar disorder. Adams's attacks on Hamilton ventured beyond the musings of Jefferson, who regularly engaged in slanging matches in the papers regarding politics, and moved into a more personal sphere. To be sure, however, Adams gave as good as he got, and Alexander Hamilton was no innocent bystander in a metaphorical pillory ailing while the president flung affronts at him. Legendarily, Hamilton had run about town in the lead up to the 1788 -1789 election persuading delegates to vote for the tall, classically uneducated Virginian from Mount Vernon who had led the Patriots to victory over the other leading name on the ballot: simple John Adams from Braintree. Despite the congressman from Massachusetts being indubitably better suited for the role of executive politician, George Washington's appeal as a uniting figurehead whose key role would be to remind the public why the country had claimed independence was alluring. Comparable to the 'Golden Hour' in trauma treatment, the inaugural years of a young republic are vital to its survival. To Washington's – and thus Hamilton's – credit, the republic survived its initial growing pains, and the U.S. Constitution reigns supreme as the longest-serving constitution in the world. But, also to Hamilton's credit, Adams missed out on the top job, and the Bostonian lawyer knew it.

Not only did Hamilton actively try to inhibit Adams's election in 1789, but when the older statesman did gain his role in the Executive Branch in 1797, Hamilton proved himself to be a thorn in his side. Taking on the new role of Commanding General of the U.S. Army, Hamilton saw a Franco-American war with Napoleon as inevitable and constantly pushed Adams to prepare for such event. Adams convinced such event would not happen at the time, an instinct that proved to be right, found Hamilton's preparation for war - right down to the position of buttons on uniforms - irksome. For the soldier who had made his name in America under General Washington, a man built for nothing but war, Hamilton added Adams's slow diplomatic approach to avoiding combat to his growing list of grievances and, in the months leading up to the 1800 Election, successfully dedicated himself to ensuring Adams was not re-elected. Amongst the measures Hamilton took to inhibit Adams's grasp on power was publishing a coruscating disquisition. One week before the voting opened, Hamilton released a letter titled *"Concerning the Public Conduct and Character of John Adams, Esq. President of the United States"*, which opens with paragraphs dotted with half compliments before launching into an acrid chastisement. At first recognising Adams's role in the achievement of American independence, Hamilton lauds:

> I was one of that numerous class who had conceived a high veneration for Mr. Adams on account of the part he acted in the first stages of our revolution. My imagination had exalted him to a high eminence, as a man of patriotic, bold, profound, and comprehensive mind.[2]

Whatever idea Hamilton initially had of this "patriotic" man with a "comprehensive mind" had been smashed during the war and brought into technicolour during the Confederation Period and beyond. He then continues:

> But in the progress of the war, opinions were ascribed to him, which brought into question, with me, the solidity of his understanding. He was represented to be of the number of those who favoured the enlistment of our troops annually, or for short periods, rather than for the term of the war; a blind and infatuated policy, directly contrary to the urgent recommendation of General Washington, and which had nearly proved the ruin of our cause. He was also said to have advocated the project of appointing yearly a new Commander of the Army; a project which, in any service, is likely to be attended with more evils than benefits; but which, in ours, at the period in question, was chimerical, from the want of persons qualified to succeed, and pernicious, from the peculiar fitness of the officer first appointed, to strengthen, by personal influence, the too feeble cords which bound to the service, an ill-paid, ill-clothed, and undisciplined soldiery…To refrain from a decided opposition to Mr. Adams's re-election has been reluctantly sanctioned by my judgment; which has been not a little perplexed between the unqualified conviction of his unfitness for the station contemplated, and a sense of the great importance of cultivating harmony among the supporters of the Government; on whose firm union hereafter will probably depend the preservation of order, tranquillity, liberty, property; the security of every social and domestic blessing.[3]

Hamilton's letter *Concerning Public Conduct* is scathing obloquy and worth reading in full to comprehensively understand how the feud between the two men was more than just a silly dislike derived from several quarrels, but a pot of hatred which had been simmering at full-heat for years, with the letter being the climactic boiling point propelling steam out of every aperture. Unquestionably, the rivalry between Hamilton and Adams is one of America's greatest episodes of political antagonism. Driven in part by the men's similar characteristics as well as their differences of opinion, it has come to define both of their careers during the 1790s and represents a pivotal aspect of the birth of the party system in the United States - and thus makes Adams's residence in London an integral facet of this anthology.

John Adams was born in Braintree, Massachusetts in late October 1735. The son of a puritanical family, John descended from Henry Adams, a Somersetian farmer who was amongst the earliest settlers in Massachusetts Bay Colony having emigrated from England in around 1632. His mother's side of the family arrived much earlier and marked him early on as being more American than apple pie. Possibly foreshadowing his later actions breaking free of the constraints of England and pioneering independence, his great-great-grandparents arrived in Massachusetts on the Mayflower in November 1620. His ancestral grandfather, John Alden, was procured by Captain Christopher Jones in Southampton to work aboard the Mayflower as a cooper but decided to stay with the colonists when the ship returned to England in April 1621. In Plymouth Colony, he married Priscilla Mullins whose entire family had perished in the first winter. Daughter of William Mullins, Priscilla's family were not part of the Leiden congregation of Separatists, but rather formed part of the Merchant Adventurers who funded the voyage. Together John and Priscilla had ten children and their granddaughter, Hannah, married Joseph Adams in 1688. In the first of several cyclical events that would crop up in Adams's life, John Alden and William Mullins were signatories of the Mayflower Compact. The epochal scroll signed aboard the ship before the colonists disembarked is an enduring symbol in American history as it is the first known document to establish self-governance in the New World and comparisons between the compact and the Declaration of Independence have been made since 1776. Although the English had already founded a colony at Jamestown a decade earlier, the establishment of Plymouth colony, and subsequently Massachusetts, determined the birth of the United States. John Adams was well aware that his family were at the heart of the catalytic landing on Cape Cod, something which he prided himself on following the American Revolution. Reflecting in his diary in 1785, John declared:

> Neither my father or mother, grandfather or grandmother, great-grandfather, or great-grandmother nor any other relation that I know of or care a farthing for have been in England these 150 years. So that you see, I have not one drop of blood in my veins, but what is America.[4]

Not venturing far from where the Pilgrim Fathers had stepped onto Plymouth Rock, the Adams family lived in Braintree, Massachusetts. The teenage John entered nearby Harvard University in 1751 and was expected to become a minister in a patrilineal fashion. However, in a somewhat similar way the educatory expectations of Benjamin Franklin – who, by the time Adams was deciding what to do with his life, had already retired – John broke free of the chains of clergy and moved to the study of law. Adams's chosen occupation as a lawyer chartered a new course for the man who at heart was a New England farmer. Yet, the graduate of the class of 1755 did not pursue formal law education until 1758, resultingly Adams descended into occupational law at the same time as the seeds of discontent in the colonies began to be sown. Five days after John's twenty-fifth birthday, King George II dropped dead at Kensington Palace. His grandson, George William Frederick, was to be his problematic successor. George III and John were only three years apart in age and their lives were to grow in tandem, intersecting each other's story again and again.

John Adams was known to be a stickler for law, tradition, and protocol, something which would become more than evident to his fellow countrymen in 1770. As the French and Indian War, which had been raging in the colonies for nearly a decade, came to a close in 1763, the British began taxing the colonists for expenses derived from keeping British troops stationed in America to protect the land. The first legislation came in the form of the Sugar Act in 1764 followed in close succession by the Currency Act and then the Quartering Act a year later. The 1765 Stamp Act, and the following Townsend Acts in 1767, were the final nails in the coffin and are seen as a turning point in the ideological battles of the American Revolution. Further acts, such as the Intolerable Acts implemented following the Boston Tea Party, only acted to inflame already roaring tensions. Despite his reservations against the British, John Adams wanted to ensure the course of fair trials in the colonies and, as a result, a confusing turn in his career cropped up in November 1770 when he took on the role as the defence for the British soldiers involved in the Boston Massacre - a significant event during the ideological period of the American Revolution which saw five colonists killed in a standoff with British soldiers outside the Old State House in Boston. Not only did he defend them, but he successfully attained their acquittal, with only two of the eight troops found guilty of manslaughter. John's choice to overlook the fact that his clients were redcoats and defend them purely as soldiers doing their job perplexed some colleagues, yet it did not hinder his prospects. As the crescendo of war rose, Adams was elected to serve as a delegate in the Continental Congress, a position which would not only make him a Founding Father but set him on course to hold several puissant positions in the maiden years of the republic. Subsequently, he served as an envoy to France, the Minister to the Netherlands, the Minister Plenipotentiary to Great Britain, and later served two terms as the first vice-president under George Washington but - in part because of Hamilton's meddling - only one term as the second president.

The Adams family's political prowess did not end with John's death in 1826, in fact, a political lineage was established. The most prominent member of the line after John Adams was his eldest son,

John Quincy Adams, who followed in his father's footsteps in several respects, including as the Minister to Britain after the War of 1812, and, in 1825, becoming the sixth President of the United States. Like his father, he was only to serve one term. Despite becoming the first person to hold the office who was not directly involved in the Revolution, or Confederation Period, JQA often corresponded with Hamilton towards the end of the treasury secretary's life just as Adams junior's political career was beginning to heat up. Unsurprisingly, John Quincy held the same contempt for Hamilton as his father, and those who had supported Hamilton looked down their noses at him as his father's son.

Importantly, beyond being a central cog in the dawn of the United States, John Adams is also oft remembered as part of one of the Revolution's most famous duos. In 1764, he married a woman who was to become as famous as he: Abigail Smith. The couple had six children: Abigail (b. 1765 and referred to from this point by her family nickname of Nabby), John Quincy (b. 1767), Grace Susanna (b. 1768 and died two years later), Charles (b. 1770), Thomas Boylston (b. 1772) and Elizabeth who stillborn in 1777. Yet, Abigail was far more than a colonial housewife. Born in Weymouth in 1744 to a Congregational minister, Abigail Adams represents an early form of feminism in the colonies. She was good friends with Mercy Otis Warren, a headstrong political pamphleteer, and was an ardent advocate for women's rights in the spheres of property and education. She is best remembered for being her husband's closest advisor and inciting John and his colleagues to "Remember the ladies"[5] while creating their new nation. You cannot have John without Abigail and vice-versa. Consequently, although this chapter's cynosure is John since his relationship with Hamilton defined an era of American political history, Abigail played as crucial a role in the tale of the Adamses in London as her husband.

LONDON

On February 24, 1785, John Adams was appointed by congress to serve as the first United States Minister Plenipotentiary to Great Britain. Adams was working in France at the time alongside Ben Franklin and Thomas Jefferson when he was given the poisoned chalice of forging a productive relationship with the country – and the man – that he and his colleagues had divorced. On the eve of his departure from Paris, Adams recalled in his diary two conversations he had with contemporaries in France. In receiving well wishes for his mission from the Comte de Vergennes at Versailles, Adams commented that his appointment "merited compassion more than felicitation."[6] Moreover, the Duke of Dorset offered his support to Adams. In a conversation with him, the American aired his concerns about how he was to be received in England, "He [the Duke of Dorset] said I should be stared at a good deal. I told him I trembled at the thoughts of going there, I was afraid they would gaze with evil eyes."[7] Despite these remarks, Adams was seemingly keen to undertake the role. David McCullough, historian and author of the Pulitzer Prize-winning biography *John Adams*, writes that Adams rejoiced when it was confirmed that Jefferson would succeed Franklin as the Minister to France as this left the door open to him to take on an ambassadorial role in Britain. Even if he was not necessarily excited at the possibility of being posted to England, he was keen to represent the U.S. in diplomatic relations and illustrate the legitimacy of his country. Abigail Adams on the other hand was less than thrilled at the prospect. Although London itself did not bother her, as she commented on her 1784 tour (more about anon):

> I am better pleased with this city than I expected. It is a large magnificent, and beautiful city, most of the streets 40 feet wide built strait, the houses all uniform, no [*unintelligible*]

small tenements, many fine open squares where the nobility reside, and where most of the public buildings are erected.

Nonetheless, writing to Cotton Tufts the month before arrival, she made it clear that she had forthright reservations about her husband's appointment:

> The exchange of climate must be for the worse…I fear he will appointed to England he will not have a less thorny road to tread than those which he has already past. There are many difficulties and perplexities to adjust in order to bring England and America yet together even in a commercial intercourse.[9]

In terms of tracing the Adams family's time in London, John Adams's diary is sporadic and - although it does contain some descriptions of his social sphere – is mainly orientated towards his business and career. Conversely, Abigail Adams's letters from London are saturated with information and her domestic reports paint a vivid picture of the future First Family's time in London. From her thoroughly American discourse on polite London society to her constant complaining about the British press where she becomes almost Trumpian in her obsession with defamatory stories, Abigail's eyes are the best with which to view, and plot, the course of the family's time in the city.

The stint in London during John's tenure as minister plenipotentiary was not a virgin visit for any of the Adams family. John, along with John Quincy, had briefly stayed in London in 1783 after the Treaty of Paris had been negotiated. The two men vacationed at the suggestion of James Jay, the brother of fellow Founding Father and Treaty of Paris negotiator, John Jay.

Additionally, in 1784, Abigail and Nabby had tarried in London on their way to France. When it became clear to John that his work in France would not be over soon and there was talk of making him the minister to Britain, he begged his wife and daughter to join him. At this point, Abigail and Nabby had not seen their beloved patriarch since he left Boston with John Quincy five years beforehand. The two women, who had never even left Massachusetts before, set sail for London on the packet ship the *Active* on July 21, 1784. Vomiting profusely before they had even left Massachusetts Bay, the two Adams ladies would have had no idea they were not to return to their home country for another four years, but in that time they, and their patriarch, would plant the seeds of what was to become the strongest relationship in the western world. At the time, however, Abigail and Nabby would have sneered at the thought of an Anglo-American 'Special Relationship' and had no qualms about being proud republicans while in London. Nevertheless, they lapped up the delights of the city and closely followed a list of must-see places John had sent to Nabby, "The British Museum, Sir Ashton Lever's Museum, Wedgwood's Manufactory of Earthen Ware, Parker's Manufactory of Glass, I saw with great pleasure. You cannot see Mrs. Siddons, as she is absent. Westminster Abbey, and St. Paul's Church you should see."[10] Aware that London was a world away from the life they led in Massachusetts, John also included in his letter a profound observation – possibly a veiled warning - on the city, "In London you see one of those enormous masses of human nature, which exhibit to view its utmost extremes of grandeur and littleness, of virtues and vices, of wisdom and folly."[11]

THE BATH HOTEL, PICCADILLY

John, accompanied by Abigail and Nabby, left France in mid-May and reached London on the afternoon of Thursday 26. They immediately waded their way through the horse-filled streets towards the Strand with plans to take up lodgings at Osbourne's Hotel – a hospitality outlet in the Adelphi building complex where all three had previously boarded during their respective stays in the metropolis. Not only was Osbourne's their hotel of choice, but it seemed written in the stars as the architect was a Mr. John Adam, something John had become enchanted with two years prior when he first arrived in the city and asked a post-boy to take him to the best inn in London:

> Whether it was the boy's cunning, or whether it was mere chance, I know not; but I found myself in a street which was marked John's-street,' the postilion turned a corner, and I was in 'Adams-street.' He turned another corner, and I was in 'John Adams-street.' I thought surely we are arrived in fairy land. How can all this be?[12]

Yet, the family's best-laid plans for obtaining comforting and familiar rooms were scotched when, on arrival, they found the hotel, and most others in the city, full. Abigail Adams explained in letters to her nearest and dearest that the swelling of London's hotels was due to the perfect storm of the king's birthday celebrations, a performance of George Frideric Handel's music at Westminster Abbey - which she was to attend - and the sitting of parliament. Instead, a relation of the family, Charles Storer, arranged rooms for them at the Bath Hotel in the thriving shopping district of Piccadilly.

Overlooking Green Park at the intersection of Piccadilly and Arlington where The Ritz Hotel now sits, the hotel was not to the vanilla taste of the Adamses. Luxury in the middle of a dirty London, the family would not have been for want of comfort, but the Bath sat on one of the city's busiest thoroughfares. "This being the Court end of the city," Abigail told her sister Mary Smith Cranch in June, "it is the resort of a vast concourse of carriages."[13] The family, who led a quiet existence in America at their homely Braintree farm, found the constant bustle of the who's-who of elite London society gallivanting in their coaches up and down the street "too public and noisy for pleasure"[14]. John and Abigail were known for their agricultural amore and, in a perfect world, would have preferred to spend their days turning manure and pruning the bushes. Indeed, in later years John was berated by his colleagues in

America for his lackadaisical approach to being physically present at the humming seat of power in Philadelphia, and later in Washington. During one diplomatic session, President Washington pronounced, "Presuming that the vice president will have left the seat of government for Boston, I have not requested that his opinion be taken."[15] Adams spent nearly three-quarters of the year in Boston. One could have excused his persistent absenteeism while serving as vice-president since his role was somewhat titular – a fact which Hamilton likely revelled in - however, his approach to governing in absentia did not stop when he became president. During his time in the Executive Branch, he was still spending nearly half an annum outside of the federal district succouring his need for tranquillity but equally dimming his legacy. A sense of puritanical simplicity and morals was hereditary, and John had already been perturbed by the extravagances of Paris and those who delighted in its infidelities. French splendour and bawdy exploits - the enduring legacy of the Sun King, Louis XIV - was relished by his contemporaries, such as Jefferson who had a penchant for spending. The lewder side of France was enjoyed by Benjamin Franklin. The septuagenarian had once engaged in a game of chess with Claude-Guillaume Le Veillard in Madame de Brillon's bathroom while she watched the match from her bathtub. Not something one could imagine happened all too often in eighteenth-century Boston where censorship was rife and men with Mayflower blood still lived in the moral shadows of their ancestors. While John enjoyed some of the more naturalistic aspects of London, such as his common walks along the Edgeware Road, which runs from Westminster to Barnet, where he would observe and compare British farming methods to American ones – "This may be good manure, but is not equal to mine,"[16] he once smugly observed - the Bath Hotel was just another cog in the extravagance of Old World cities which was not appreciated by the agrarian family.

Abigail and Nabby too preferred their walks through Kensington Gardens and Ranelagh Gardens. Writing to Thomas Jefferson shortly after her arrival, Abigail notes that, out of choice, the hotel would not have been opted for, but necessity caused their residence.

Comparing their new lodgings to the idyllic tranquillity of their less expensive but grander French home in Auteuil, she told Jefferson that "the noise and bustle of this proud city almost turned my brain for the first two or three days."[17]

London, in general, was not to John's liking. After just a fortnight in the city he was already longing for the environment he had grown fond of at Auteuil, and the dissimilarities between the American neighbourhood grid systems and the claustrophobic nature of British architecture was evident. "I miss my fine walks and pure air at Auteuil," he grieved to Jefferson, "The smoke and damp of this city is ominous to me. London boasts of its trottois [pavements] but there is a space between it and the houses through which all the air from kitchens, cellars stables and servants appartements ascends into the street and pours directly on the passenger on foot. Such whiffs and puffs assault you every few steps as are enough to breed the plague if they do not suffocate you on the spot."[18]

Despite complaining about the nauseating miasma of London, John, unlike Abigail, left us nothing of significant note on his feelings about the Bath Hotel. He did, however, spark an aeon of Anglo-American relations from their rooms. No sooner had the foreign party settled into their new surroundings that Adams wrote immediately to Francis Osborne, Marquess of Carmarthen informing him of his arrival and requesting an audience. Osborne was the Tory son of the 4th Duke of Leeds who was serving as the Secretary of State for Foreign Affairs (from here referred to as the Foreign Secretary). He left a mark in the mind of Adams's colleague Thomas Jefferson as undoubtedly disobliging and unwilling to forge a positive relationship. Writing in his autobiography, the Virginian recalled Carmarthen's apparently obvious distaste for the Americans, "The distance and disinclination which he betrayed in his conversation, the vagueness & evasions of his answers to us, confirmed me in the belief of their aversion to have anything to do with us."[19] Not only was Osborne a Tory, but he was also serving in the government of the virulently anti-American William Pitt the Younger.

The Adamses' stay was bookended by residences at the Bath. In March 1788, with John on a diplomatic visit to The Hague in Holland, Abigail packed up and moved out of the quiet townhouse that they were to procure (more about anon) and back into the Piccadilly residence for a fortnight prior to their departure from England, surely ending her stay as she had started it - complaining about the Londonian noise.

ST. JAMES'S PALACE, WESTMINSTER

The gentleman from Boston had been in London for less than a week when he was required to undertake the most taxing job of all: being officially received by King George III. Once seen as Anglophilic in his native country for serving as the Counsel for the British in the Boston Massacre, his metamorphosis into one of the most vocal proponents in the Continental Congress for independence ensured his place on the Committee of Five: a quintuple team of delegates who worked in tandem to write, draft, and edit the Declaration of Independence. By 1785 Adams's loyalty could not be questioned. However, as Federalists, he and Hamilton were still looked upon as holding British sympathies in comparison to their fellow countrymen because, amongst other reasons, their desire to install a central government resembled, to Democratic-Republicans, the British system. Adams himself was seen as an Anglophile for several reasons, including his indifference towards France compared to men like Jefferson whose soul was, in part, Parisian, and his seemingly conceited demeanour and hoity tendencies which led some to label him with the royal title the 'Duke of Braintree'. Undoubtedly, Adams was excited at the prospect of being made minister to Britain, but in no way did he see himself as anything other than an American, something which he would spell out in no uncertain terms to George III himself.

On June 1, Adams endured his baptism of fire at St. James's Palace. Set off the Mall, the sixteenth-century dark-bricked palace sits on the site of a former hospital dedicated to St. James the Less (identified in Christianity as the possible brother of Jesus) which was used for treating those suffering from the bouts of leprosy which ravaged London. The palace was witness to several significant events in British history, including the birth of Charles II and the marriage of Queen Victoria to Prince Albert in 1840. By the reign of George III, the palace was still the official residence of the Royal Family and was used primarily for staging the monarch's engagements, including meeting foreign dignitaries sent to serve in his kingdom. Following the audience, Adams swiftly put pen to paper and delineated the day at length in a letter to John Jay, who was now serving as the U.S. Secretary of Foreign Affairs. Adams, at pains to illustrate the conduct of the British to his American colleague, forewent a concise but precise description of his tête-à-tête with the king, for a chronological account of the entire afternoon, starting at the doorway of the Bath Hotel. "At one on Wednesday the first of June, the Master of Ceremonies called at my house, and went with me to the Secretary of State's Office in Cleveland Row, where the Marquis of Carmarthen received me."[20] A short carriage journey from Cleveland Row to the gates of St. James's led the American into a scene of, as he had prophesised to the Duke of Dorset, illicit staring by courtiers and other representatives, who, after nearly three decades of struggle, were seeing a representative from an independent America set foot inside the court of George III. John notes he was only relieved from such a display by the ministers from Sweden and Holland – both of whom represented countries who had shown sympathy for the American cause - who wandered over to engage with the Yankee diplomat.

After lingering too long for comfort in the palace's reception rooms, the foreign secretary fetched Adams for his moment of reckoning. On entering the king's chamber, Adams recalls the ridiculous monarchical ritual which amplified the disparities between British and American societies from the offset. "I made the three reverences, one at the door, another about halfway and the third before the presence, according to the usage established at this and all the northern courts of Europe."[21] Adams's three bows have epitomised his meeting with the king in historical memory and were presented facetiously in the 2008 HBO miniseries *John Adams*.

The scene which unfolded next is one every American historian would sell a piece of their soul to have witnessed. John Adams, the lawyer from a quiet colonial town, stood in front of the man who ruled half the world but could no longer count his visitor as a subject. The two men had been part of the same story playing out on opposite sides of the Atlantic and, undisputedly, Adams was most definitely included amongst the "dangerous and ill designing men"[22] the king had referenced in his Proclamation of Rebellion of 1775, in which he declared America to be under the influence of dark revolutionary powers. Now with the Treaty of Paris officially signed, Adams embarked on a solicitous soliloquy he had memorised which, in attempts to achieve amicable relations with Britain, was overly laudative and eulogising:

> Sir, the United States of America, have appointed me their Minister Plenipotentiary to your Majesty, and have directed me to deliver to your Majesty, this letter, which contains the evidence of it. It is in obedience to their express commands that I have the honour to assure your Majesty of their unanimous disposition and desire, to cultivate the most friendly and liberal intercourse, between your Majesty's subjects and their citizens, and of their best wishes for your Majesty's health and happiness, and for that of your Royal Family.
>
> The appointment of a minister from the United States to your Majesty's court, will form an epocha, in the history of

England and of America. I think myself more fortunate, than all my fellow citizens, in having the distinguished honour, to be the first to stand in your Majesty's royal presence, in a diplomatic character: and I shall esteem myself the happiest of men, if I can be instrumental in recommending my country, more and more to your Majesty's royal benevolence and of restoring an entire esteem, confidence and affection, or in better words, "the old good nature and the old good humour" between people who, though separated by an ocean and under different governments have the same language, a similar religion and kindred blood. I beg your Majesty's permission to add, that although I have sometimes before, been entrusted by my country it was never in my whole life in a manner so agreeable to myself.[23]

The king, seemingly surprised by the affable nature of the American, was induced to deliver an emotional reply:

Sir, the circumstances of this audience are so extraordinary, the language you have now held is so extremely proper, and the feelings you have discovered, so justly adapted to the occasion, that I must say, that I not only receive with pleasure, the assurances of the friendly dispositions of the United States, but that I am very glad the choice has fallen upon you to be their minister. I wish you, sir to believe, and that it may be understood in America, that I have done nothing in the late contest, but what I thought myself indispensably bound to do by the duty which I owed to my people. I will be very frank with you. I was the last to consent to the separation: but the separation having been made, and having become inevitable, I have always said as I say now, that I would be the first to meet the friendship of the United States as an independent power. The moment I see such sentiments and language as yours prevail, and a disposition to give to this country the preference, that moment I shall say let the circumstances of language, religion and blood, have their natural and full effect.[24]

The stunned minister plenipotentiary continued to Jay:

The king then asked me, whether I came last from France, and upon my answering in the affirmative, he put on an Air of familiarity, and smiling or rather laughing said "There is an opinion, among some people, that you are not the most attached of all your countrymen, to the manners of France." I was surprised at this, because I thought it, an indiscretion and a descent from his dignity. I was a little embarrassed, but determined not to deny the truth on one hand, nor leave him to infer from it, any attachment to England on the other, I threw off as much gravity as I could and assumed an air of gaiety and a tone of decision, as far as was decent, and said "That opinion sir, is not mistaken, I must avow to your Majesty, I have no attachments but to my own country.[25]

The king, as quick as lightning, replied, "An honest man will never have any other."[26]

Despite the gauche reception John had received on arrival at St. James's, he believed that he had sparked an amicable relationship with the king. Concluding his letter to Jay, the minister remarked that he hoped for a more congenial welcome than the flavour of hostilities he had experienced yet was keen to point out that a cordial relationship that had sparked between George III and himself should not be taken as a confirmation that the inaugural minister plenipotentiary had succeeded in his mission. "I may possibly expect from it a residence here less painful, than I once expected, because so marked an attention from the king will silence many grumblers but we can infer nothing from all this concerning the success of my mission."[27]

St. James's Palace was to become a regular haunt for the Adams family during their time in the city. Not only did John meet the king there on June 1, but the entire family returned frequently to appear at the king and queen's levées. Several days after meeting the king, John introduced himself to George's consort, Queen Charlotte. In a letter to friends and family, Abigail describes the queen's levées: from what she wore to how long it took. Writing to John Quincy Adams, Abigail notes that during their first presentation, she and Nabby stood for four hours while the king and queen made small talk with everyone. Unlike her husband, who endeavoured to apply himself to the rituals of British diplomacy with an ineffable seriousness, the steadfast republican couldn't resist satirising the event and the monarchy, remarking, "I could not help reflecting with myself during the ceremony, what a fool do I look like to be thus accoutred and stand here for four hours together, only for to be spoken too, by "royalty.""[28] Exhibiting thoroughly modern humour littered with sarcasm and bluntness, in a letter to her sister Mary Smith Cranch, she opens with the mocking line, "Congratulate me dear sister it [her first levée] is over."[29] Over the next three years, Abigail would often mention the levées, providing vignettes of Queen Charlotte, some of the princesses, and British polite society in general - and not always in a particularly flattering light. Of English women, she said that they were not as beautiful as their American counterparts and that the court of George III was "like the rest of mankind, mere men and women, and not of the most personable kind neither."[30]

Nabby Adams also shared her mother's attitude towards the court. Writing to John Quincy in the summer of 1785, she aired her thoughts that Queen Charlotte may think that she and her mother were offended by the events of their first elongated and monarchical levées. She left this reflection on her experience at the audiences:

It is not in the power of the smiles or frowns of Her Majesty to affect me, either by conferring pleasure or giving pain. I was wholly incapable of taking the place she seemed to assign me when I was presented to her. I suppose she assented to the assertion made by some persons in this country that there were no people who had so much *impudence* as the Americans, for there was not any people bred *even at courts* who had so much confidence as the Americans. This was because they did not tremble, cringe, and fear, in the presence of Majesty.[31]

An official servant of his country to the kingdom of George III meant that John and the entire Adams family were invited to attend the king's annual birthday celebrations. One cannot truly fathom the likelihood that a key signatory of the Declaration of Independence attended George III's annual birthday gala - indeed it borders on the ridiculous - yet that was the bizarre world of John Adams in London. The celebrations were nationwide and were even marked in pre-Revolutionary America with parades, speeches, and bonfires. In his biography of Thomas Jefferson, Jon Meacham notes how every year grand festivities would be held in the colonial capital of Williamsburg.

On Saturday, June 4, 1785, the annual celebration was held at St. James's, only this year it had the added lustre of an American presence. George's forty-seventh birthday would be the first of several attended by the family and Adams's inaugural attendance at the bash did not go unnoticed by the British press. The Tory journalists milked every story they could out of Adams's appointment and Abigail had already complained at length to family and friends at home about the slander of her husband and wider family in the press. "The Tory venom has begun to spit itself forth in the public papers as I expected, bursting with envy that an American minister should be received here with the same marks of attention politeness and civility which is shown to the ministers of any other power."[32] Amongst the stories she said had been published in an attempt to bring forth a response from her husband were rumours that John could not hold a public dinner since the Continental Congress could not afford it; that William Stephens Smith [the Secretary of Legation] was illiterate and received a mediocre education unbecoming of an assistant to a foreign minister; and that Abigail's own carriage "was a little better than going in an old chaise to market with a little fresh butter."[33] The newspaper the *Public Advertiser* reported on the king's birthday celebrations. Their tale of the party did not stop at a satirical roundup of John Adams's presence, but also attacked one of the leading Tories themselves:

> Amongst the various personages who drew the attention of the drawing-room on Saturday last, Mr. Adams, Minister Plenipotentiary from the States of America was not the least noticed. From this gentleman the eye of Majesty and the court glanced on Lord—; to whose united labours this country stands indebted for the loss of a large territory and a divided and interrupted commerce.[34]

The unfortunate Lord the newspaper took a swipe at is Lord North. A man who, as we will see, became somewhat of a constant figure in the domestic London life of the Adamses. He was Prime Minister from 1770 to 1782 and was largely looked upon as responsible for losing the colonies. In a rarity for the diary and letters of John Adams, he provides a small sketch of the party in a report to Thomas Jefferson:

> The king and queen speak to everybody. I stood next to the Spanish minister, with whom his Majesty conversed, in good French, for half a quarter of an hour, and I did not lose any part of the discourse and he said several, clever things enough. One was 'Je suis convaincu que le plus grand Ennemy du Bien, est le mieux.' [*I am convinced that the greatest enemy of the good is the best*] You would have applied it as I did,

to the crowd of gentlemen present who had advised his Majesty, to renounce the 'Bien for the Mieux' [*Good for the better*] in America. And I believe he too had that instance in his mind.[35]

Although a seasoned statesman, it seems that Adams was, much like Abigail, not fond of the tedious and elongated nature of the ceremonies at St. James's Palace, which saw the monarch and consort make tiresome and irrelevant small talk. A place to be seen more than anything constructive and to play the game of wealth and status, the levées were nothing but a waste of time for republican persons who were concerned with building a country. Writing to Jefferson in early June 1785, Adams told the minister to France that "You would die of ennui here, for these ceremonies are more numerous and continue much longer here than at Versailles."[36]

LONDON'S PALACES

Buckingham Palace | The Tower of London

Now the centrepiece of most Americans' summer vacations when in London, Buckingham Palace - known in the eighteenth century as Buckingham House - was a standout spot for John Adams and his son John Quincy Adams in 1783. The father and son future presidential duo – the only pair to hold this title until George H. W. Bush and George W. Bush both held Executive Office – were working in France on the Treaty of Paris when it was officially signed on September 3, 1783, after a year and a half of negotiations. The following month, John and John Quincy - who had been serving his father as a secretary during the negotiations - sailed north to London. Attempting to cram the curiosities of the Old World into their short trip, John wrote in an autobiographical piece for the *Boston Patriot* in 1812, that, "Curiosity prompted me to trot about London as fast as good horses in a decent carriage could carry me."[37] The pair had lodged first at Osborne's Hotel and then at private lodgings owned by John Stockdale, a bookseller on Piccadilly where Henry Laurens – father of Hamilton's friend John Laurens – had stayed the year earlier.

The roots of Buckingham Palace can be traced back to the man who was on the throne when Adams's ancestors boarded the Mayflower: James I. The Scottish king, who was later crowned King of England upon the death of Elizabeth I, began to grow mulberries on the land in the early seventeenth century to cultivate silkworms. The property then passed to Charles I who bestowed it to Lord Aston of Forfar. After Aston's ownership, it was passed along several titles until, in 1698, the house was given to the Duke of Buckingham who curated the metamorphosis from former mulberry plantation into the landmark house and gardens we know today. While the main house was most definitely worthy of figures in high society, it wasn't until George III acquired the property in 1762 that the palace became associated with the Royal Family. While the official family residence remained at St. James's Palace, George bestowed Buckingham House to Queen Charlotte, thus earning it the moniker the 'Queen's House'. It was not the official royal household until 1837 when it became Queen Victoria's main London residence.

By the time he was a young man, John Quincy Adams was better travelled than most of us in the twenty-first century. He had first accompanied his father to Europe in 1778 when the pair travelled through France and Holland while John senior was attempting to procure support for the American Revolution. In France, John Quincy had grown up around Benjamin Franklin while his father and the sage wooed the French to join the war. In 1781, his father sent him to Russia where he served as a French-language interpreter for fellow Massachusettsan and former leader of the Sons of Liberty, Francis Dana, who was serving as the U.S. envoy to the court of Catherine the Great. John Quincy Adams's letter to his cousin Elizabeth Cranch in April 1784 offers an insight into some of the worldly wonders the Adams men got to see during their first visit to the capital. A highlight for both father and son was Buckingham Palace. "By particular favour," John Quincy explains, "we got sight of the Queen's Palace, called Buckingham House…There we saw the apartments, of the King, of the Queen, and, of the rest of the family, as also a great number of beautiful paintings, by the greatest masters, at the head of which are the cartoons of Raphael, looked upon as the masterpieces of the art. But besides this we also saw there the models in miniature of every fortress, and of every man of war in the service of the government."[38] Meanwhile John senior, again for the *Boston Patriot,* writes of the day:

> Accordingly, in the absence of the Royal Family at Windsor, we had an opportunity at leisure, to see all the apartments, even to the queen's bedchamber, with all its furniture, even to her Majesty's German bible, which attracted my attention as much as anything else. The king's library struck me with admiration; I wished for a week's time but had but a few hours. The books were in perfect order, elegant in their editions, paper, binding, etc. but gaudy and extravagant in nothing. They were chosen with perfect taste and judgment; every book that a king ought to have always at hand, and as far as I could examine, and could be supposed capable of judging, none other. Maps, charts, etc. of all his dominions in the four quarters of the world, and models of every fortress in his empire.[39]

When John was to return as the minister plenipotentiary two years later, George III granted him access to freely use the library.

Another remarkable sight which the Americans visited was the Tower of London which had once acted as the residence of the Royal Family in antiquity, but now served as both a prison and tourist attraction. Given the fortification nature of the castle, it was – and still is – used to guard the nation's most prized possessions:

the Crown Jewels. Wowed by the ancient structure with its moat, array of gems, and some remaining exotic animals – originally introduced to the Tower as far back as 1210 when King John kept lions at the castle – John Quincy remarked:

> The Tower is remarkable for the admirable disposition of the small arms, which are all placed in a most beautiful order: there are also some wild beasts there, but no great number. They show still many old things, and among others, the axe with which the famous Earl of Essex (they say,) was beheaded…The royal treasure, or regalia, is also kept there. It consists of a number of crowns, sceptres, rtc. The crown which the kings wear at their coronation is said to be worth a million.[40]

However, in true American fashion, John notes that he thought "The money might I think have been better employed."[41] For his father, the object on display that left a lasting impression was the holy oil used to anoint the kings and queens of England upon their crowning.

The Tower of London held another significant meaning in the life of John junior. Fourteen years later in 1797, the castle looked on as he married one of only two foreign-born First Ladies at the opposite church, All Hallows by the Tower. JQA had met his bride, London-born Louisa Catherine Johnson, while serving as a diplomat overseeing the ratifications of the Jay Treaty, negotiated by Founding Father and Federalist Papers author, John Jay (see *Chapter Six*). During his mission, he was invited to dinner at the home of American merchant Joshua Johnson on Coopers Row near Tower Hill. The Adams and Johnson families were already acquainted with each other as John Adams had visited the merchant during their 1783 visit when they also used the Johnson's home as their London mailing address. At the dinner, he met his future wife, the twenty-year-old Louisa, eight years his junior. Interestingly, Louisa, a beautiful young woman who suffered from a weak constitution and would for the rest of her life, was illegitimate. For years, Louisa's mother remained an unknown figure, however, her Anglo-American heritage was confirmed when her mother was discovered to be Catherine Newth (sometimes spelled Nuth), a woman living near her father in the City of London. Oddly, and still without explanation of the delay, Catherine and Joshua did eventually marry in August 1785 at St. Anne's Church in Soho, some ten years after Louisa Catherine Adams was born.

Cyclically, All Hallows by the Tower's links with America had started the century beforehand when William Penn, the founder of Pennsylvania, was baptized there in 1644. Today, the wedding ledger for the Adamses, as well as the baptism record of William Penn, can be viewed in the church's crypt museum.

NUMBER 9 GROSVENOR SQUARE, MAYFAIR

Clearly not impressed by the bright lights of Piccadilly, at a levée with Queen Charlotte on June 9, Adams told her majesty that he had ensured himself a house that very morning: Number 9 Grosvenor Square. Built in 1735 by bricklayer William Barlow, the house was part of the project to further develop the already prestigious area which had begun in the previous decade. During the eighteenth century, the square was one of the largest in London, second only to Lincoln's Inn Fields.

Abigail had discussed that other legations had their residences paid for them by their native country but that the young republic had not offered this service. Forced to procure the first American Legation themselves, over the week leading up to June 9, Abigail had been delighting her friends and family back home with the news that her intellect had led her to Grosvenor Square and that, in doing so, she had found, "one of the most reputable and prettiest squares in London"[42] to live on. Eager to escape the Bath Hotel, John had signed the lease on the house before venturing off to meet the queen. The red-bricked Georgian townhouse was a far cry from Braintree,

Number 9 Grosvenor Square

but Abigail seemed to be pleased with it nonetheless, especially in comparison to their current lodgings. The location was ideal, close enough to Westminster for John's work but quiet and discreet enough in Mayfair for two Americans who enjoyed their republican ideals and their luxuries. The ledger for the house shows that the Adamses purchased it from Vice-Admiral John Byron, the grandfather of the Romantic poet Lord Byron. Describing the square to her sister, Mary Smith Cranch, Abigail provides the sense of gentrification which the square perspired:

> We are agreeably enough situated here in a fine open square, in the middle of which is a circle enclosed with a neat, grated fence; around which are lighted every night about sixty lamps. The border next the fence is grass, the circle is divided into five grass plots. One in the middle is a square upon which is a statue of George II on horseback. Between

each of the plots are gravel walks and the plots are filled with clumps of low trees thick together which is called shrubbery, and these are surrounded with a low hedge, all together a pretty effect.[43]

Although Abigail supplies us with ample information about their whereabouts, it is Nabby Adams – who married her father's Secretary of Legation, William Stephens Smith, at the house in 1786 – who truly brings to life how the Adamses set up their home through letters to her brother John Quincy in the July of 1785.

> Our house stands at the corner of Duke Street. The situation is much in its favour. It is a descent house, a little out of repairs, but such a one as you would not blush to see, any of the foreign ministers in. The front door is a little in the corner. At the entrance there is a large hall, with a large staircase, all of stone. On the left hand, is the dining room, which will hold fifteen persons with ease, and, next to it is a little room, more retired in which we usually dine, when we have no company, and from this you go into a long room of which Pappa has, made an office, for doing public business. The kitchen is below stairs. Above, over the dining room is the drawing room, as large as the room below and from it a little room of which Mamma has made a common setting parlour, to breakfast and drink tea if we choose and out of it is another long room in which Pappa has put his library, and in which he writes usually himself. This is a very descent suit of rooms, and we have another very small one which serves to breakfast and set in at this season. Our chambers are upon the third floor, of which there are four besides a dressing room. Mamma took one of the front chambers to herself, the other she has appropriated for to stand empty for a spare bed, to which you will be perfectly well come if you will come and spend the night with us. I have a chamber over the small setting room. It looks only

into a little piece of a yard with which we are favoured. It's so situated that the sun does not approach it any part of the year, and I have a most extensive prospect from it, of the tops of all the houses which surround us, and I can count a hundred chimneys from it—and see North's.[44]

"North" being Lord North, the man whom all eyes had been on at the king's forty-seventh birthday party. The proximity of the Adamses to those whom they once opposed did not slip the notice of Abigail who, writing to Thomas Welsh, declared, "If I could feel myself elated by my vicinity to nobility I might boast the greatest share of it, of my square in London, but I am too much of a republican to be charmed with titles alone."[45] The "nobility" who graced Grosvenor Square during the late eighteenth century included the Foreign Secretary who lived at Number 2; Viscount Sydney - the Home Secretary and namesake of Sydney, Australia - and Earl Percy who resided at Number 3; The 4th Earl Fitzwilliam at Number 4; and, at Number 50, on the south side of the square, lived Lord North, the former politician dubbed 'The Prime Minister Who Lost America'. Now his most embarrassing defeat was literally thrown in his face and was living on his doorstep - indeed, if one wanted to evaluate the success of the American cause through the lens of the Adamses' neighbours, one only had to knock on the door at 50.

Nonetheless, despite the almost comedic value of living in the vicinity of Lord North, Abigail raged about it in her letters. To Mary Smith Cranch she wrote, "We are in the same row if not in the same box of most of the great people in this country, opposite however to Lord North."[46] And to Thomas Welsh, "[Omitted from final letter: *We are, however, still opposite to Lord North.*] We have not taken a side with Lord North but are still opposite to him."[47]

By this time, Lord North was ailing and falling deeper into the lap of senility. Having been forced out of the premiership in a vote of no-confidence as a result of General Charles Cornwallis's surrender at Yorktown, early on in the Adamses' stay the fifty-four-year-old began to lose his sight. Now an ageing and shunned politician, Lord North was more of an unwanted presence than anything that would truly jeopardise Adams's role. Yet, while most anti-Americans did not pose an active threat to John Adams's position, it didn't mean that there was a total lack of those who truly wished to see Adams come to harm. Harrison Gray, the former treasurer of Massachusetts who, like so many loyal to the crown, went into exile in England during the Revolution, declared that he would hang Adams had it been within his power. The news of Gray's murderous wishes reached the ears of Abigail who described him as, "No Tory so bitter that I hear of"[48]. Interestingly, in a turn of events that illustrates how interconnected prominent figures within the American Revolution were, Gray's son-in-law was Samuel Allyne Otis, brother of Abigail's friend and staunch Revolutionary pamphleteer, Mercy Otis Warren.

Lord North was not the only predominant figure in the American Revolution to have a connection with the square highlighting the cyclical, fateful events in Adams's life. For example, Number 9's previous tenant, Byron, had fought during the War of Independence at the Battle of Grenada. Most notably though, on the last day of 1738, Charles Edward Cornwallis was born at a townhouse on the north side. A mere stone's throw from the Adamses' abode, today the townhouse is non-existent and, in its place, stands the building from which General Eisenhower commanded American troops in Europe during the Second World War. Evidently, American links existed on Grosvenor Square prior to the Adamses' arrival, however, it was the family's residence at Number 9 which commenced the association of the square with the U.S.A. Today, the square is the physical embodiment of the Special Relationship and has been bestowed the nickname 'Little America'. Number 9 still stands, although, while it is one of only four buildings on the square which has retained its original 1730's shell, the interior has been renovated.

During the Adamses' stay at Number 9 they did their best to entertain members of both the London elite and American sympathisers. A surviving list from John Adams's diary titled '*Visits*

Paid and Returned in London' from summer 1785 gives a small flavour of the social circle of at least John, if not the whole family. Meeting with figures such as Le Comte de Lusi, the Prussian minister; Richard Penn, the grandson of William Penn; and politician and future member of the American Philosophical Society, Lord Mahon at Downing Street. Flitting across the city and going door-to-door, it is clear that John quickly got to work with his role as a statesman in Britain. The diplomat was so immersed in introducing himself to every politician, courtier, and MP he could find that Abigail remarked she was hesitant to bother him with domestic matters.

Number 9 Grosvenor Square as seen from Duke Street.

One of the most historically noteworthy guests at Number 9 was not a politician, or courtier, or businessman, but a teenage girl. Not only did the house serve as the first American Legation, but also as the stage for the start of one of the most controversial affairs of the Antebellum period - an affair which is still causing arguments over two hundred years later. In June 1787, Thomas Jefferson's third daughter, Mary, arrived at the Adamses'. Accompanying her was a young, enslaved woman called Sarah 'Sally' Hemings. Three years earlier in 1784, Jefferson's youngest child, Lucy Elizabeth, had died in Virginia, leaving the future president with only two remaining children: Martha 'Patsy', aged fifteen, who was to serve as First Lady during Jefferson's premiership, and Mary, aged nine. Given her young age, Mary could not join a ship full of sailors to cross the Atlantic alone. The Eppes family, close friends of Jefferson with whom Mary had been staying, chose an enslaved woman to accompany her. However, she fell pregnant before leaving and could not make the passage. In her stead, another enslaved person from Monticello was chosen: fifteen-year-old Sally Hemings. Known to be extremely beautiful with long, dark hair cascading down her back, Sally was not only Jefferson's property, but his sister-in-law and Mary's aunt. Sally was born as the result of rape between Elizabeth Hemings - an enslaved woman whose mother had been brought to America from Africa and had been impregnated by a white Captain Hemings - and John Wayles, Jefferson's father-in-law whose property, including the Hemingses, were inherited by TJ upon his death. She stayed in France with Jefferson, his family members, and her brother, James, who had been taken to learn French cooking. In September 1789, when the American party returned to Virginia, Sally was heavily pregnant, as the vast number of historians have now accepted, by her master. She would go on to have at least eight more children. Over a decade later, on September 1, 1802, scandalous journalist James Callender - the same man who publicly revealed the Reynolds Affair in his pamphlet *The History of the United States for 1796* - alluded to amorous goings-on on the mountaintop with a 'Dusky Sally' in the *Richmond Recorder*. Following Callender's revelations, the newspapers started to satirise the fact that the quiet politician had taken a concubine. Cartoons with phallic imagery began appearing, including one of Jefferson as a chicken titled 'A Philosophic Cock' and even offensive stanzas:

Of all the Damsels on the green

On mountain or in valley
A lass so luscious ne'er was seen
As Monticellan Sally[49]

Despite Callendar's attempts to hurt Jefferson's premiership with salacious gossip, the president never commented on the subject. Although, it reared its head again in 1873 when an elderly Madison Hemings gave an interview to the *Pike County Republican* in which he stated that his father was the third president of the United States. Callendar's article had been one of scandal, but Madison's was autobiographical and described in shocking detail his mother and father's relationship which features excerpts worth quoting in full:

> During that time [in France] my mother became Mr. Jefferson's concubine, and when he was called home, she was *enceinte* by him. He desired to bring my mother back to Virginia with him, but she demurred. She was just beginning to understand the French language well, and in France she was free, while if she returned to Virginia, she would be re-enslaved. So, she refused to return with him to induce her to do so he promised her extraordinary privileges and made a solemn pledge that her children should be freed at the age of 21 years inconsequence of his promises on which she implicitly relied she returned with him to Virginia soon after their arrival she gave birth to a child of whom Thomas Jefferson was the father. It lived but a short time. She gave birth to four others and Jefferson was the father of all of them their names were Beverly, Harriet, Madison (myself) and Eston - three sons and one daughter. We all became free agreeably to the treaty ended in to by our parents before we were born.[50]

Madison Hemings stated he was named so as Dolley Madison, wife of Democratic-Republican and future fourth president, James Madison, was present at his birth and requested to name him.

Arguably a strange turn of events if Sally was just another of Jefferson's six-hundred or so slaves. Yet, for years so-called 'Jefferson Defenders' have refused to acknowledge the president's relationship with Hemings, writing it off as nothing more than a conspiracy, and insisting that Sally's children were fathered by either Peter or Samuel Carr, Jefferson's nephews. However, in 1997, Annette Gordon-Reed, Professor of History at Harvard Law School, wrote the ground-breaking book *Thomas Jefferson and Sally Hemings: An American Controversy* which persuasively argued that Jefferson was the father of Sally's children. Referencing evidence such as the fact that the only slaves Jefferson ever freed or let leave Monticello were Sally's children; that Sally never conceived while Jefferson was away from the mountaintop; and that she worked entirely in the house while her children were allowed to spend the day with her, Gordon-Reed's book once again set the cat among the pigeons and her undisputable argument was later proven correct when DNA analysis the following year confirmed that at least one of Sally's children was fathered by Jefferson, leading to the conclusion that he is responsible for the paternity of all of them. Despite this, there are still those who choose to fight the scientifically proven reality and the subject even divides descendants, with some refusing to let the Hemings line be buried at Monticello.

The nature of Thomas and Sally's relationship also splits people into numerous factions. While not forgetting the fact that Sally was Jefferson's property, some believe that the pair did harbour loving feelings for one another. This, although an uncomfortable reality to face, was not unheard-of in the south. Sally's own sister, Mary Hemings Bell, lived as the 'wife' of a white man, Thomas Bell. They had two children and lived together in a de-facto marriage. Yet, due to anti-miscegenation laws in the south, she had to live in the house under the guise of a slave after Jefferson agreed to sell her to Bell. Sally also kept items of Jefferson's which she gave to their children as sort of mementos and family heirlooms.

Furthermore, Jefferson kept his word about freeing their children. He helped his two eldest surviving children with Sally escape the plantation: Beverly was allowed to leave, and he supposedly personally organised for his daughter, Harriet, to be put in a coach with some money and sent north. Upon Jefferson's death, as stated in his will, their remaining children, who were under twenty-one, were freed. Meanwhile, Patsy Jefferson did not officially free Sally, yet she let her leave Monticello to 'have her time' - insinuating that she likely knew the truth about her aunt and father despite refutations she would make on the subject.

For all intents and purposes, at seven-eighths Caucasian, under Virginia law, the Jefferson-Hemings children were classed as white. Although it was not unusual to see the offspring of slaves and masters at plantations around the south, apparently the pure number of white children raised suspicion and the community around Monticello was more than aware of the Jefferson-Hemings relationship. Sally Hemings was so fair that, in later life when she was allowed to leave the plantation, she - as did all but one of her children with the president - noted their race as white on U.S. Censuses. However, despite the fact that Sally was largely Caucasian, the legal doctrine partus sequitur ventrem (Latin for 'that which is born follows the womb') passed in Virginia in 1662 meant that the children fathered by slaveholders followed in the condition of their enslaved mother. Thus, Sally's familial position would not have been recognised even before she and Jefferson had children, and it is why their children in turn were never formally acknowledged.

From Grosvenor Square, Abigail wrote several letters to Jefferson regarding his daughter. At first lambasting him for not coming to pick her up in person - she suggests that Mary did not even remember him – her letters quickly focus in on Sally. Writing to Jefferson on June 27, Abigail states:

> The girl who is with her is quite a child, and Captain Ramsey [captain of the ship which brought Mary and Sally to England] is of opinion [she] will be of so little service that

he had better carry her back with him, but of this you will be a judge. She seems fond of the child and appears good natured.[51]

By July 7, Abigail's opinions grew more forthright, "The girl she has with her, wants more care than the child, and is wholly incapable of looking properly after her, without some superior to direct her."[52] Gordon-Reed suggests that, while eighteenth-century figures were undoubtedly influenced by ignorant racial thinking - even those who were ardent abolitionists were affected by unconscious bias - Abigail may have been unamused by Sally for several other reasons as well. One being that Sally did not live up to the serious and prude Abigail's expectations of what a young woman should be in terms of maturity. And two, possibly most importantly, that Hemings, for whom no portrait exists but who was known for being exceptionally beautiful, may have been tempting for the widowed Jefferson who was known to enjoy the company of women, and who was devastated by his wife's death - Sally, with the same paternity as Martha, could remind Jefferson of the love of his life. Yet, despite her hesitancy about sending Sally on to France, she bought her clothes from the Strand alongside other more ostentatious outfits for Mary, as she felt both women were only dressed appropriately for sea travel, not polite company, "As both Miss Jefferson & the maid had clothes only proper for the sea, I have purchased & made up for them such things as I should have done had they been my own to the amount of about eleven or twelve guineys. The particulars I will send by petit."[53]

In fascinating invoices Abigail sent to Jefferson for her expenses in taking care of Mary and Sally - who she never refers to as a slave only as her maid - she bills TJ for the clothes. While expectedly spending more on Mary and purchasing finer clothing becoming of the daughter of a U.S. diplomat, Abigail bought Sally twelve yards of calico "for two short gowns and coats"[54], four yards of Irish linen for aprons, three pairs of stockings, two yards of lining and one shawl handkerchief. It seems, although she was less than complimentary about Sally's childminding skills, in providing clothing for Sally she was venturing beyond what was expected of her, in keeping with Abigail's own abolitionist mindset and her quite modern maternal nature.

Over the years, as Jefferson and Hamilton's haranguing raged on, Hamilton alluded to knowledge of the Jefferson-Hemings affair. No evidence for this is as strong as an article written for the *Gazette of the United States* in October 1796. Penning the polemic under the name Phocian, Hamilton admonished Jefferson's contradictions on race, especially his stance that, when slaves were emancipated, they should be transported for resettlement in Africa to inhibit miscegenation, by subtly – or not so subtly – invoking his affair with Hemings.

> At one moment he is anxious to emancipate the blacks to vindicate the liberty of the human race. At another he discovers that the blacks are of a different race from the human race and therefore, when emancipated, they must be instantly removed beyond the reach of mixture lest he (or she) should stay in the blood of his (or her) master, not recollecting what from his situation and other circumstances he ought to have recollected - that this *mixture* may take place where other negro remains in slavery. He must have seen all around him sufficient marks of this *staining of blood* to have been convinced that retaining them in slavery would not prevent it.[55]

Ron Chernow supposes that Hamilton most likely had knowledge of the Jefferson-Hemings affair prior to Callendar's article via Angelica Church who had kept in contact with Jefferson, moved within the same circle of friends, and made a trip to Paris in December 1787, a few months after Mary and Sally had arrived.

The raging tides of debate and argument that swirl around the Jefferson-Hemings Affair could not have been foretold when Sally Hemings crossed the threshold of Number 9 Grosvenor Square in the summer of 1787. Her short-lived presence at the residence, however, should not be lost to history or just slotted in somewhere between the rest of the visitors who called on Adamses during their three-year stint. Sally Hemings's stay in Mayfair is as much a part of the tapestry of Little America as any other element in its history, and possibly even holds a more pertinent importance as it sparked an aeon in American history which caused decades of scholars to re-examine the relationship between Thomas Jefferson and race.

WESTMINSTER ABBEY, WESTMINSTER

During the last week of May 1785, Abigail Adams attended one of the events she had noted as a reason the Adamses were not able to stay in their hotel of choice: The Commemoration of Handel. The celebration ran for a week between May 26 and June 5 at both Westminster Abbey and the Pantheon on Oxford Street. Adams attended a show at Westminster Abbey and later elucidated to Jefferson how the music may have made her feel as if she was part of a higher order of beings had she not been sat in front of rowdy attendee:

> I went last week to hear the music in Westminster Abbey. The Messiah was performed, it was sublime beyond description. I most sincerely wished for your presence as your favourite passion would have received the highest gratification. I should have sometimes fancied myself amongst a higher order of beings; if it had not been for a very troublesome female, who was unfortunately seated behind me; and whose volubility not all the powers of music could still.[56]

This was not her first visit to the abbey, having toured the ancient site during her stopover in 1784. In 1783, John and John Quincy had also visited Westminster Abbey during their whistle-stop tour of London. "We saw a great collection of tombs of kings, heroes, statesmen, and poets," an enthralled John Quincy described, "There are some very ancient monuments: a number of figures in wax and the chairs in which the kings and queens of England are crowned: they are said to be more than 1400 years old."[57] Yet, John senior, in a characteristic manner, had to find fault with the magnificent millennium-old church. Thirty-two years after first visiting the abbey, he unloaded some opinions about the landmark when writing to his grandson, Charles Francis Adams, complaining sourly, "I wish, they would call it Westminster Temple, or Palace, or Castle, or Edifice or anything rather than Abbey."[58]

THEATRES

Haymarket | Sadler's Wells | Theatre Royal Drury Lane

Abigail Adams seemed to be somewhat enchanted by the actress of the day, Sarah Siddons. Early in the family's residence in London, she wrote several letters to her friends declaring that while she had not yet visited the city's theatres, when she does, she is sure that they will not envelop her as much as their Parisian counterparts. Making such avowals as, "We all went last week to accompany Mr. Short [William Short, an American diplomat] to the Hay Market, but who can relish the English after having been accustomed to the French stage? A Siddons may reconcile me to it, but I believe nothing else will,"[59] and, "After having been accustomed to those of France, one can have little relish for the cold, heavy action, and uncouth appearance of the English stage. This would be considered as treason of a very black dye, but I speak as an American. I know not how a Siddons may reconcile me to English action, but as yet I have seen nothing that equals Parisian ease, and grace."[60]

When Abigail finally saw Sarah Siddons at Theatre Royal Drury Lane in September 1785, she was mesmerised. Evoking poet John Milton's poem *Paradise Lost*, Abigail told William Stephens Smith, "I was last evening however at Drury Lane and saw for the first time Mrs. Siddons. Grace was in all her steps, heaven in her eye, and every gesture dignity and love."[61]

Born in 1755, Siddons would often appear on stage pregnant, and Abigail saw one of her gestational performances. Writing to her sister Elizabeth Smith Shaw, Abigail recounts:

> [In broken text] I think in one of my letters to you last fall I promised to give you some account of the celebrated actress Mrs Siddons, who I was then going to see; you may well suppose my expectations were very high, but her circumstances were such then as prevented her from exerting that force of passion, and that energy of action, which have rendered her so justly celebrated. [The following sentence was crossed through and features missing words] *She was [...] in the [...] of her pregnancy. You [...] suppose that she ought not to have appeared [...][. . .] upon appeared at all upon the stage; I [...] have thought so too if I had not [...] her. [. . .] contrived her dress in such a manner as wholly to [...] her situation and [...] only those tragedies where little exertion was necessary.* The first piece I saw her in was Shakespeare's Othello. She was interesting beyond any actress I had ever seen.[62]

While exuding the excitement of a woman who had read plays but never seen them (The Adamses' native colony of Boston had banned theatre performance in 1642. Fellow Founding Fathers Samuel Adams, John's second cousin and fellow delegate to the Continental Congress, and John Hancock, President of the Continental Congress, were both supporters of the ban. Meaning that, like Angelica and John Church, the first time the Adamses saw performance was in Europe), Abigail's description of Siddons in

Othello also presents some of the most derogatory words she ever wrote about Black people.

> She [Siddons] was interesting beyond any actress I had ever seen: but I lost much of the pleasure of the play, from the sooty appearance of the moor. Perhaps it may be early prejudice, but I could not separate the African colour from the man, nor prevent that disgust and horror which filled my mind every time I saw him touch the gentle Desdemona, nor did I wonder that Brabantio thought some love portion, or some witchcraft had been practiced, to make his daughter fall in love with what she scarcely dared to look upon.[63]

Adams was a staunch anti-slavery proponent - one of the only things she and Hamilton would see eye-to-eye on if they had ever met – and rarely spoke about Black people in such a bluntly defamatory way. Resultingly, her aforementioned expressions of shock at Drury Lane's entertainment are often analysed by historians as a fascinating caveat when discussing Abigail's relationship with race and slavery.

On April 24, 1786, John Adams and Colonel Smith attended a performance of Richard Brinsley Sheridan's *The School for Scandal* at Theatre Royal Drury Lane. Theatres had also been on the radar for John and John Quincy in 1783. Both men saw Sarah Siddons perform as Isabelle in David Garrick's *The Fatal Marriage,* and JQA described her as that "wonderful, wonderful, wonder of wonders, Mrs. Siddons. The most capital performer upon the stage; not only of Europe, at present, but that ever was seen."[64] However, he did not fall in love as generally with the English stage as his mother had. Noting of a performance of *Hamlet* and Arthur Murphy's *The Citizen* at Drury Lane in late October that, "I must confess; I do not think they act tragedy so well here as in Paris."[65] John Adams himself, although not making any notable comment while in London, regularly referenced Sarah Siddons and Garrick's plays in letters during his retirement, even recounting a conversation he had with

Queen Charlotte during his stay, "As the Queen of England once said to me "Mrs. Siddons acted Jane Shore last night horribly well.""[66]

THE BRITISH MUSEUM, BLOOMSBURY

On April 24, 1786, the Adamses, along with Jefferson and Colonel Smith, visited the British Museum. The visit was arranged by Benjamin Vaughan, a member of the American Philosophical Society who knew Adams through his work as a commissioner during the negotiations for the Treaty of Paris. The museum was a very different sight from what one envisages when discussing the institution today. The formative version was based at Montagu House on the site of today's ginormous establishment and operated on an 'invite only' basis, with those invitations only going to distinguished individuals visiting the city. The American party received a tour of the museum by botanist and curator, Edward Whitaker Grey.

The British Museum at Montague House in Bloomsbury.

While the group would have seen such treasures as Queen Elizabeth I's letters and the Magna Carta (See *Chapter Three: Thomas Jefferson* for discourse on the Magna Carta and the Declaration of

Independence), John Adams's diary entry on the topic was more concerned with Grey's opinion on two of the day's preeminent scientists: Georges-Louis Leclerc, Comte de Buffon, a French naturalist, and Carl Linnaeus, a Swedish botanist whose work influenced Grey's reorganisation of the museum. In his diary, John recorded:

> Viewed the British Museum. Dr. Grey who attended us spoke very slightly of Buffon. Said he was full of mauvais Fois. No dependence upon him. Three out of four of his quotations not to be found. That he had been obliged to make it his business to examine the quotations. That he had not found a quarter of them. That Linnaeus was quoted from early editions long after the last edition was public of 1766 the 12th, which was inexcusable. He did not think Buffon superior to Dr. Hill. Both had imagination etc. This is partly national prejudice and malignity, no doubt.[67]

This was not John's (nor Abigail and Nabby's) first visit to the museum, however, which explains why he may have been so preoccupied with Dr. Grey's personal opinions on the day's philosophers as opposed to the displayed artefacts.

————————————

HACKNEY

The Adamses often ventured north of the city to see friends in what would have then been classed as small villages on the outskirts of London. Abigail and Nabby, for example, would often spend the day in the leafy suburb of Hampstead. They would also travel to Hackney to visit a key friend of theirs while in London: Dr. Richard Price, the Welsh-born Nonconformist minister of the Newington Green Unitarian Church. Among Dr. Price's many feats, he was an ardent supporter of the American Revolution and, knowing his friendly disposition and pro-American stance, the Adamses would make the effort to attend his Sunday sermons. Informing their son of their new London routine, Abigail told John Quincy in mid-June 1785:

> This is the third Sunday we have attended his meeting, and I would willingly go much further to hear a man so liberal so sensible so good as he is. He has a charity which embraces all mankind and a benevolence which would do good to all of them. His subjects are instructive and edifying."[68]

The minister was a constant source of comfort and friendship for the Adamses in London and both John and Abigail frequently mentioned him in letters home. Abigail lauded his character and, in comparing the treatment he received in England for his views she noted how, if in her home country, he would be "revered and caressed, as his merits deserves."[69] On leaving England, she bemoaned how deeply she regretted the loss of Dr. Price's sermons in her life.

However, Dr. Price was not just a friendly supportive face in a once-enemy country, for John Adams, he was also a key facet in the creation of the Jean-Antoine Houdon statue of George Washington which stands in the Virginia State Capitol Building in Richmond, VA. Houdon, a prolific sculptor in eighteenth century France, came at the recommendation of Benjamin Franklin who thought a bust Houdon had made of him was the best representation of himself he had ever seen. Franklin did not sit for Houdon's bust; instead, the sculptor had created it from memory having seen the old doctor around Passy a number of times. When the Virginia Assembly tasked Thomas Jefferson with procuring an artist to enshrine the hero of the Continental Army in marble, Franklin could think of no one better. However, there was just one problem: an ocean divided the two men. There was no way that the war hero was going to make his first cross-Atlantic journey just to have his statue made when more pressing matters were at hand in the young republic. Thus, the

Frenchman would have to make the arduous journey to America. Sitting in his study at Grosvenor Square, Adams would have mulled over this post-script on a letter from Jefferson in July 1785:

> P.S. Monsieur Houdon has agreed to go to America to take the figure of General Washington. In the case of his death, between his departure from Paris and his return to it, we may lose 20,000 livres [about $150,000]. I ask the favour of you to inquire what it will cost to ensure that sum on his life, in London, and to give me as early an answer as possible, that I may order the insurance, if I think the terms easy enough. He is, I believe, between 30 and 35 years of age, healthy enough, and will be absent about 6 months. T.J.[70]

Dr. Price undertook enquiries for Adams and pointed him towards an insurer in his local Hackney. However, Adams failed to procure the insurance or inform Jefferson. Confusion ensued, and TJ was left in an anxious state when word did not quickly reach Paris of Houdon's safe arrival in America, leaving him to wonder whether Virginia would have to fork out thousands in order to pay for the Frenchman's life. Luckily for Jefferson, Adams's rather careless approach to procuring insurance in London was no bother and Houdon had reached the eastern seaboard in one piece. Despite this faux pas, Hamilton's father figure was immortalised in Carrera marble and stands erect, watching over the lawmakers in his home state.

In 1910, a series of replicas were made by the Gorham Manufacturing Company in Rhode Island and sent as gifts both around the United States and the world from the Commonwealth of Virginia. One copy was sent to the people of Great Britain and Ireland in 1921 and can be found today in Trafalgar Square on the right-hand side of the entrance to the National Gallery. Comparatively small when sized up next to London's other monuments, many walk by the bronze cast without noticing the American general. Dressed in military garb leaning against thirteen fasces which represent the original thirteen colonies, legend has it that when the statue was sent to London, along with it came a delivery of Virginian soil. In an attempt to stay true to Washington's wishes that he would never step foot in England, the American dirt was placed underneath the statue so that the general does not have to stand for eternity upon such a treasonous country.

Four miles to the west of Hackney was the Foundling Church, more generally referred to as the Foundling Hospital (today known as the Foundling Museum), which had been a common spot visited by Benjamin Franklin during his stay in London the decade earlier. The Adams family, in particular Abigail and Nabby, also marked out time in their London schedule to journey to the church. Had the Hamiltons ever travelled to London it is likely that they too would have visited the establishment as foundlings would have been a cause close to their hearts; not only was Alexander orphaned, but later in life, Eliza would serve as the co-founder of New York City's first private orphanage (now known as Graham Windham).

THE HOUSES OF PARLIAMENT, WESTMINSTER

Prior to his role as the minister plenipotentiary, John Adams had already seen the Unites States' relationship with Britain hesitantly flourish from sworn enemies to slowly warming acquaintances. Not only had he negotiated the Treaty of Paris but, during his 1783 visit, his role as a prominent American in Britain became known when he attended the State Opening of Parliament as a guest of William Murray, 1st Earl of Mansfield, then the Lord Speaker in the House of Lords. The visit was arranged by John Singleton Copley, the Anglo-American painter who is responsible for some of the most recognisable images of figures in the American Revolution - both

British and American - including John Hancock, Paul Revere, Thomas Gage, and Mercy Otis Warren.

While in London in 1783, Adams had a portrait painted by his friend Copley, with whom he had been corresponding for years. Abigail and Nabby later saw the finished piece, which was full of symbolic imagery surrounding Adams's role in Europe as a peacemaker, on display in 1784 and Abigail commented:

> I have been to see a very elegant picture of Mr. Adams which belongs to Mr. Copley, and was taken by him, it is a large full-length picture. He is drawn with a globe before him, the map of Europe in his hand and at a distance two female figures representing Innocence, and Peace. It is said to be an admirable likeness.[71]

Writing in his 1812 piece for the *Boston Patriot*, Adams recounted his visit to the Houses of Parliament on November 11, which saw him witness George III officially open parliament and the Prince of Wales being formally introduced after his twenty-first birthday:

> Mr. Copley, another of my countrymen, with whom I had been much longer acquainted, and who had obtained without so much royal protection, a reputation not less glorious; and that by studies and labours not less masterly in his art, procured me, and that from the great Lord Mansfield, a place in the House of Lords, to hear the king's speech at the opening of parliament, and to witness the introduction of the Prince of Wales, then arrived at the age of twenty-one. One circumstance, a striking example of the vicissitudes of life, and the whimsical antithesis of politics, is too precious for its moral, to be forgotten. Standing in the lobby of the House of Lords, surrounded by a hundred of the first people of the kingdom, Sir Francis Molineux, the

John Adams painted by John Singleton Copley in London, 1783.
Abigail Adams describes the painting incorrectly. There is only one
figure in the background.

gentlemen usher of the black rod, appeared suddenly in the room with his long staff, and roared out with a very loud voice—'Where is Mr. Adams, Lord Mansfield's friend!' I frankly avowed myself Lord Mansfield's friend and was politely conducted by Sir Francis to my place. A gentleman said to me the next day, 'how short a time has passed, since I heard that same Lord Mansfield say in that same house of lords, "My Lords, if you do not kill him, he will kill you."' Mr. West said to me, that this was one of the finest finishings in the picture of American Independence."[72]

Unknown to Mr. West – Benjamin West, the painter responsible for works such as *Benjamin Franklin Drawing Electricity from the Sky* (1816), that is – the picture of American Independence was far from finished, and Mr. Adams's duty to ensure that independence was seen as legitimate in England had not even truly begun.

John Adams's final letters in England are ones of thanks and apology. Two separate letters written to George III and Queen Charlotte are full of gracious thanks for the felicities he had received at court, and once again hammered home his continued mission on "behalf of the United States of America, their assurances of their friendly dispositions and of their continued desire of a liberal intercourse of commerce and good offices, with your Majesty's subjects and states."[73] He also penned letters to various aristocrats apologising for not saying farewell before departing England.

Overall, John Adams had at least somewhat enjoyed his time in London, his wife, however, had not. While waiting for the weather to change at Portsmouth to carry them home, she reflected "Indeed I have seen enough of the world, small as [it] has been, and shall be content to learn what is further to be known from the page of history. I do not think the four years I have passed abroad the pleasantest part of my life. 'Tis domestic happiness and rural felicity in the bosom of my native land, that has charms for me. Yet I do not regret that I made this excursion since it has only more attached me to America."[74]

Like many figures in this anthology, John Adams made his excursion to London before he met Alexander Hamilton. While Hamilton's physical links to London (i.e., letters), did not land on John's London desk, and Abigail did not purchase some form of paraphernalia which Hamilton would later use as Angelica had done, during Adams's time in London he was sat right on the precipice of his divisive feud with Hamilton. Those holistically aware of Hamilton's story know how deeply engrained Adams was in its pages. Arguably, in the same way that you cannot have John without Abigail, one also cannot have Hamilton with Adams. And, more undeniably so, the triangle of hostility between Adams, Jefferson, and Hamilton (see *Chapter Three* for more on Jefferson) and its responsibility for creating the enduring party system in America ranks spots such as Number 9 Grosvenor Square amongst the top locations for those on the hunt for Hamilton's London.

CHAPTER THREE

———————

THOMAS JEFFERSON

With a love of botany and cultivation - and owning a cohort of six hundred and seven slaves over his lifetime - Thomas Jefferson was a true son of the south. Standing at six feet two-and-a-half inches (half an inch taller than the man renowned for his height, George Washington, and a whopping five-and-a-half inches taller than Hamilton), with powdered hair which concealed his auburn locks and eyes of which colour no historian can quite agree, he exists in public memory almost solely in the spheres of France and Virginia. Although he is known to have travelled through central Europe during his diplomatic postings in the mid-to-late 1780s, his six-week sojourn to England remains somewhat a well-kept secret.

In 1871, Jefferson's great-granddaughter Sarah Nicholas Randolph edited a compilation of her ancestor's papers in a publication called *The Domestic Life of Thomas Jefferson,* in which she suggests that her family were amongst the earliest settlers to America. Randolph asserted that the Jeffersons listed on the legislature at the first

English colony of Jamestown in 1619 were the president's forefathers, making the family's ties to the land – in a similar fashion to John Adams's – rich, ethereal, and forever marked in history. Yet, researchers at Monticello have struggled to provide concrete evidence linking Jamestown to Jefferson, marking it more probable folklore than fact. On the other hand, Thomas's maternal line is far easier to pinpoint and features a particular London flavour. While his mother's paternal family had first emigrated in 1642, she herself had been born in London, on the now non-existent Shakespeare Walk in an area called Shadwell. Her father, Isham Randolph, was a Virginian planter who had recently sold his property in the southern colony and moved to London to trade tobacco grown along the James River. He soon became a glorified merchant and remained in the capital for around fifteen years. He married Jefferson's grandmother, Jane Rogers, at St Paul's Church in Shadwell – where Jefferson's mother was also to be baptised - before returning home with his young family to Virginia sometime prior to 1725. Jane married Jefferson's father, Peter - a skilled planter, surveyor, and a member of the Virginia House of Burgesses in the mid-1750s – in 1739. The Founder said of him that, "My father's education had been quite neglected, but being of a strong mind, sound judgment and eager after information, he read much and improved himself."[1] Despite his lack of formal education, in 1751, Peter's talents for surveying and cartography - skills which he would pass onto his son – were made public when, along with Joshua Fry, a professor at Thomas's future alma matter of the College of William and Mary, he travelled along the Blue Ridge Mountains creating the first truly accurate map of the Allegheny Mountains and Virginia's border with North Carolina. Evidently, the Virginian terrain played a central role in young Peter Jefferson's life, and he had already set to work making his mark on the landscape in the decades proceeding the Allegheny mission. In 1731, he inherited part of his deceased father's property in Albemarle County and began making it his own. When developing the area, he named part of it Shadwell in homage to his wife, and it was there on April 13, 1743, that Thomas Jefferson was born on land named after a London hamlet.

The third president was an extremely learned and successful man; however, he is probably best remembered for one thing above all others. Following the Lee Resolution on June 7, 1776, Jefferson was selected to serve alongside John Adams, Benjamin Franklin, Roger Sherman, and Robert Livingston on the Committee of Five to generate a document declaring independence and scuppering any hope of rapprochement with Britain. While his four colleagues were involved with the drafting and editing process, it is Jefferson, a skilled essayist commended amongst his contemporaries for his eloquence in producing written dictums, who is credited as the main author of the Declaration of Independence. After writing the independence document, the already-experienced politician climbed the political ladder serving as a minister in France and later Washington's Secretary of State before ingratiating himself in the Executive Branch as the second vice-president and then serving two terms as President of the United States between 1801 and 1809.

When Thomas Jefferson met Alexander Hamilton, a trigger was pulled which would ultimately create a party system and alter the path of American politics forever. Assumed to have met in Philadelphia between Jefferson's return from France and the Compromise of 1790 - the pivotal meeting between the two men and James Madison to decide the fate of the bank and the capitol - both men initially enjoyed a cordial but not particularly close relationship, yet the façade of kinship soon crumbled. Jefferson was twelve - or fourteen – years Hamilton's senior and had invited the young glittering politician to social events a handful of times alongside his Federalist Papers co-author Madison, but Hamilton's drive and determination to forge a Federalised governmental system and influence Washington's cabinet ground against Jefferson's republican values to build an America based an agrarian economy. As a result, Washington led a fractured cabinet and even had to intervene several times and encourage the two men to work out their differences. Despite the efforts of the president, the two men rarely ever saw eye-to-eye, to put it mildly, and their feud has been the subject of several academic papers and books, such as John Ferling's *Jefferson and Hamilton: The Rivalry That Forged a Nation*, given in most part to the fact that, as the title of Ferling's book suggests, their enmity was the biggest contributor to the development of the current political party system in the U.S. in the years following Washington's resignation and death.

In recent years, Hamilton has been misquoted in a widely circulated contumely. According to the humorous but false statement, Hamilton told Jefferson, "There are approximately 1,010,300 words in the English language, but I could never string enough words together to properly express how much I want to hit you with a chair."[2] There is no evidence to suggest that Hamilton ever said this, and the provenance is altogether uncertain. That being said, it does not unfairly misrepresent the quarrelling between Hamilton and Jefferson. Yet, in a surprising turn on Hamilton's part, he endorsed Jefferson for the presidency during the election of 1800. Viewing Jefferson as the lesser of two evils when up against another name on the ballot, Aaron Burr, Hamilton's actions in the first election of the nineteenth century were assuredly added to the list of atrocities Burr felt the politician had put him through. In publicly announcing his support for Jefferson, Hamilton guided other Federalists – who knew a Federalist candidate was not going to be elected after John Adams's calamitous term - to throw their support behind TJ. However, the path to the presidency was not a smooth one. When the votes were counted in February 1801, Jefferson and Burr initially drew with seventy-three votes each. The ballots had to be retallied thirty-six times before Federalist James A. Bayard of Delaware and a handful of other representatives cast blank votes, thus ending the impasse and electing Jefferson as president, and Burr as his disgruntled vice-president. Undeniably, while Jefferson saw Hamilton as his archival, he was also the man who, in large part, propelled him to the presidency.

Often voted as one of the best U.S. presidents of all time – more so because of Americans' nostalgia for the Founding era as opposed to his actual politics or sense of morality – Thomas Jefferson is an integral facet in this anthology. Like John Adams, he came to represent a pivotal era in the life of Alexander Hamilton and American history. Arguably, whether or not they would have liked to admit it, the trio of men would not have necessarily been able to inject themselves so deeply into the fabric of the American story without each other, and that is why, although TJ only spent a fleeting six-weeks in England in a period before he even knew Hamilton personally, the tale of Jefferson in London is still a fascinating story to follow for any fan of Hamilton and the Founding Fathers more widely.

LONDON

Prior to his role as Secretary of State in Washington's cabinet, Jefferson had served as the U.S. minister to France. Arriving in Paris in August 1784 to receive the baton of diplomacy from Benjamin Franklin, Jefferson soon established himself as the sophisticated American: a man of the world and yet still a true republican. The Virginian saw first-hand the early murmurings of the French Revolution and was only a few months shy of leaving his post when the Bastille was stormed on July 14, 1789. The following month, he aided the Marquis de Lafayette in writing the epochal French document heavily influenced by his own work called the Declaration of the Rights of Man, and of the Citizen, and subsequently suffered tremendous embarrassment and anger when George Washington issued the Proclamation of Neutrality in April 1793. Jefferson's time in Paris has been the subject of films, many of a romantic nature as it was in Paris that the widowed Jefferson became entranced with Maria Cosway and his affair with enslaved woman, and his late wife's half-sister, Sally Hemings began. In Paris, he also propelled himself further into the debt that would plague his life and result in the sale of his beloved Monticello.

In February 1786, John Adams sent his Secretary of Legation, Colonel William Stephens Smith, to Paris with a request that Jefferson urgently attend to him in London. The minister plenipotentiary required the assistance of the seasoned stateman in his negotiations with the Barbary States of North Africa. Writing anxiously in mid-February, Adams had told of his fruitless meetings at the London home of the Tripolitanian Ambassador. Sitting in front of a roaring fire, drinking strong coffee, and inhaling tobacco through a pipe Adams said was so long it reached the floor, the Tripolitanian representative had requested an official peace treaty akin to the U.S.'s similar agreement with England. Adams, understandably perplexed, questioned why a treaty was needed when the two nations were not engaged in hostilities. Dancing around the issue, it seemed the ambassador desired it more as a nicety than as anything concrete but warned that, without a treaty, Americans were not necessarily free to navigate around the Mediterranean. With this threat, the ambassador set about collecting papers for Adams to peruse and incited him to return in the next few days to negotiate and sign the unnecessary pact. Baffled, Adams understood the threat the ambassador laid out could have consequences but wailed to Jefferson, "How can we preserve our dignity in negotiating with such nations?"[3] Confirming with congress whether he could engage in a treaty with Tripoli would take months and, into the bargain, Adams would also have to negotiate with the minister from nearby Portugal who also had trade interests in the region. Traversing treaties with interested parties in England was not something Adams could handle alone, thus Jefferson's support was vital.

Departing from Paris on March 1, Thomas Jefferson set off for England. Despite having visited the country before on his way to France in 1784, Jefferson had never visited the city which, at the time, was viewed as the capital of the world. On his way home to Virginia in 1789, although being stationed at Cowes waiting for the Atlantic winds to perfect, he did not return to London. Though this is unsurprising as, save for his appreciation of horticultural and scientific prowess, he was apathetic towards the city. Despite the haste with which Adams requested Jefferson's assistance, negotiations were slow and an actual treaty with Tripoli was not signed until 1796. However, the forty-eight days Jefferson spent in England between March 11 and April 26 - exploring the sovereign land, purchasing thousands of pounds worth of goods, and drinking in London's entertainment - are a goldmine for Hamilton's links to London.

NUMBER 14 GOLDEN SQUARE, SOHO

Arriving in London on March 11, Jefferson took up lodgings at Number 14 Golden Square in Soho. A short walk to both John Adams's townhouse and the soon-to-be home of Angelica Church, the square – which had formerly served as a plague pit during the 1665 outbreak of the Black Death – would have appealed to Jefferson's cosmopolitan tastes. A lover of the arts, beautiful women, and other luxuries that were worlds away from his life as an agriculturalist in Virginia, one can see why Jefferson chose Golden Square over the more grandiose neighbourhoods developing to the west of Piccadilly.

In the seventeenth century, the square had been a magnet for the gentry. Supposedly designed by Sir Christopher Wren, Golden Square had once housed individuals moving in the upper echelons of society, such as Barbara Villiers, the Duchess of Cleveland, who was mistress to Charles II and bore him five of his nineteen illegitimate children. By the end of the eighteenth century, however, the gentry were being seduced by homes in Mayfair, and the square lost the gilded sheen that the Adamses were experiencing less than a mile away in Grosvenor Square. In their places, a party of libertines moved in in the form of artists, performers, and foreign dignitaries; indeed, in Charles Dickens's 1839 novel *Nicholas Nickleby*, the square is described as "a great resort of foreigners"[4]. In the decade or so leading up to Jefferson's arrival, Golden Square had witnessed the arrival of a cosmopolitan milieu, including the Swiss painter Angelica Kauffman and the Italian soprano Caterina Gabrielli.

Jefferson left no opinion on the square, just noting in his memorandum book that he paid "Mrs. Conner, Golden Square No. 14. for lodgings etc. £11–18,"[5] (£913/$1,265). Unfortunately, along with most of the square's original houses, the Number 14 that Jefferson had spent his nights at was demolished in 1912 to make way for more modern structures.

Golden Square today. Along this row of buildings sat the lodging house where Jefferson stayed.

ST. JAMES'S PALACE, WESTMINSTER

A week after leaving Calais, Jefferson was subjected to the same torturous endeavour that his friend John Adams had endured a year earlier: meeting King George III. Although not an official presentation as Jefferson was not serving as a foreign dignitary to Britain, the meeting was arranged by John Adams who thought it sensible that Mr. Jefferson meet the monarch given his status as a prominent diplomat. Proceeding from Mayfair to St. James's Palace with Adams as his escort, Jefferson could not have expected much from meeting the man about whom he had once written such a scathing ad hominem. Understandably, while Adams had received a tepid reception from some at court, he was tolerated and, in fact, had amiable words to say about George III the person, if not his position. One must note, Adams was thought to be a raging Anglophile, while Jefferson was most definitely recognised for his Francophilian, pro-Américain Anglophobia. Resultingly, the visitor felt the glare of English eyes upon him, which is not surprising when one remembers that the following words - which are imbued in the souls of Americans - came from his pen:

> The history of the present King of Great Britain is a history of repeated injuries and usurpations, all having in direct object the establishment of an absolute tyranny over these States…A prince whose character is thus marked by every act which may define a tyrant, is unfit to be the ruler of a free people.[6]

Adams had of course debated and edited the declaration, but the words had come from Jefferson's mind. As the ink ran onto the parchment in early July 1776, and the red-haired Virginian had stood against the cool walls of the Pennsylvania State House listening to Colonel John Nixon reading aloud the hallowed document, the thought of one day meeting the tyrannical prince was far from a likely scenario. While the two countries had come far since 1776, the monarch's reception of Jefferson was ostensibly far from cordial according to the Virginian's account of the day in his 1821 autobiography:

> On my presentation as usual to the king and queen, at their levées, it was impossible for anything to be more ungracious than their notice of Mr. Adams & myself. I saw at once that the ulcerations in the narrow mind of that mulish being left nothing to be expected on the subject of my attendance; and on the first conference with the Marquis of Carmarthen, his minister for foreign affairs, the distance and disinclination which he betrayed in his conversation, the vagueness & evasions of his answers to us, confirmed me in the belief of their aversion to have anything to do with us.[7]

Interestingly, John Adams did not record the meeting in any capacity, leaving Jefferson's autobiography as the only known eyewitness account. In the nineteenth century, Adams's grandson, Charles Francis Adams, edited his grandfather's papers, adding his own insertions and embellishments. The Massachusetts Historical Society is at pains to illustrate how heavily edited Charles's works are; he altered swathes of his family's correspondence, even transforming his aunt's loving family nickname of Nabby to Abby to seem more formal and, in doing so, lost a lot of essence and truth. One example of a new story which Charles included in his publication claims that when meeting Jefferson, the king had "turned his back upon the American commissioners, a hint which, of course, was not lost upon the circle of his subjects in attendance."[8] The historian Charles R. Ritcheson suggests that Charles's story was nothing more than an embellishment. Noting how John Adams was a stickler for diplomatic protocol nor was he phlegmatic, Ritcheson says that had the king intentionally snubbed he and Jefferson, that "John Adams' carriage wheels would have scorched the paving stones from St. James's Palace to Grosvenor Square and his dispatch desk,"[9] but John he stayed silent on the matter, not even a sardonic dictum to Abigail or a slanderous entry in his diary.

Moreover, the levées of the British king were less formal than the respect and attentiveness that had to be shown to Louis XVI at Versailles, thus it was common for the king to seem to turn around when making his way around the drawing room; people were even allowed to leave after George had finished talking to them. Additionally, while Jefferson records meeting the king on March 17, newspapers from the time and Monticello concur that he most likely met him two days earlier on March 15, a Wednesday, when the monarch held his mid-week levées. Several historians, including Ritcheson, have suggested that the thirty-five-year gap between meeting the king and writing his autobiography served to warp Jefferson's memory of his day at the palace and cause him to imagine that he must have also met Queen Charlotte when no evidence, aside from his memoirs, suggests this be the case. Indeed, John Adams would have recorded this, and his memorandum books lack records of tipping doormen and courtiers at the Queen's bi-weekly levées.

LONDON'S GRANDEST MUSUEMS

Sir Ashton Lever's Museum | The British Museum | The Tower of London | Buckingham House | Albion Mills

Educated at the College of William and Mary in Virginia, Thomas Jefferson was a polymath who revelled in invention: he developed the swivel chair and, purportedly, the Lazy Susan for his daughter who was always served last and never received a full meal. He also popularised exotic delicacies which one would now think of as American staples, such as French fries, ice cream, and macaroni cheese. In fact, he had such a penchant for pasta that he had a macaroni-making machine shipped to him in 1790, which perpetuated a popular myth that he invented the glutinous comfort.

Far more comfortable with pen, parchment, and books than oratory – Hamilton possessed adroitness in both dexterities – out of all the other Founders, Jefferson was most like Benjamin Franklin in the sense that he was an erudite man of few public words but was enthralled by learning, inventing, and the progression of knowledge; the author George Goodwin notes in his book, *Benjamin Franklin in London*, that both Jefferson and Franklin were clever men, but they were no Demontheses. In his autobiography, Jefferson's colleague Adams wrote of him:

> Mr. Jefferson had been now about a year a Member of Congress but had attended his duty in the house but a very small part of the time and when there had never spoken in public: and during the whole time I sat with him in congress, I never heard him utter three sentences together. The most of a speech he ever made in my hearing was a gross insult on religion, in one or two sentences, for which I gave him immediately the reprehension, which he richly merited.[10]

In line with his sagacious character, Jefferson dedicated a fair portion of his tarry in London habituating the city's grandest museums and historical sites. During his stay, he paid a visit to Sir Ashton Lever's Museum in Leicester Square, the British Museum in Bloomsbury, and the Tower of London. Jefferson's visits to these institutions were far more than touristic pursuits; as he soaked up the collections of Sir Ashton Lever's Museum and explored the nooks of the Tower, his mind was imbibing inspiration to take home to Monticello. He understood the importance of preservation, writing to historian and cartographer Hugh P. Taylor in October 1823 he said, "I agree with you that it is the duty of every good citizen to use all the opportunities, which occur to him, for preserving documents relating to the history of our country."[11] In this respect, he put his sentiments into practice. If one were to visit Monticello, they would be greeted in the entrance hall by a small museum the householder had curated, complete with paintings, maps, and Native American artefacts procured during the Lewis and Clarke Expedition which led Jefferson to eventually call his front reception room the 'Indian Hall'. The room also kept alive the memory of the defining political relationship of Jefferson's career. Visitors to the mountaintop would not be able to get a foot inside the door before they were quite literally faced with their host's enduring enmity with the deceased treasury secretary. Not only did Jefferson exhibit sculptures of philosophers such as Voltaire, but he also displayed busts of himself and Hamilton facing each other. Jefferson, who, in a gesture that would make Sigmund Freud smirk, ensured that his bust was bigger than Alexander's and satirically noted that they would be "opposed in death as in life."[12]

Visiting Sir Ashton Lever's Museum on April 18, Jefferson would have been enthralled by the Leverian collection which included the ephemera of Captain James Cook who had only very recently made the European discovery of Australia in April 1770. Lever's museum also featured a room of clothing taken from Indigenous Australians; some items were made entirely out of feathers. Moreover, the museum had a very American feel as it displayed the natural collection of Edward Arnold who had curated an anthology of birds, insects, and fossils in Norwalk, Connecticut. The collection had made its way to London after Arnold sold it to Loyalist William Tryon, one of New York's last colonial governors.

Jefferson also found time to visit Albion Mills. The institution was situated on Blackfriars Bridge in the City of London close to the bustling printing hub of Fleet Street. While not falling into the category of museum or historical site, Albion Mills - a steam-powered mill owned by the manufacturer and Lunar Society member, Matthew Boulton - would have been a dream visit for Jefferson the Inventor. Given the fact that he had invented the spinning chair and Lazy Susan, the mills were an obvious stop as he seemed to be particularly taken with rotating machinery.

Thomas Jefferson took great inspiration from the English Magna Carta when writing the Declaration of Independence, with some historians even suggesting that it was modelled on it. Both documents - written over half a millennium apart - epochally lay out the terms of men attempting to break free of a tyrannical government. In 1215, following an uprising derived from discontent with King John, the Magna Carta was signed in Runnymede along the River Thames. It saw the king and a number of barons agree to sixty-three clauses that introduced modern principles of liberty. While the charter was written to largely protect those surrounding the king, not the general public, it outlined that no man is above another – in other words, all men are created equal: "No free man shall be seized, imprisoned, dispossessed, outlawed, exiled or ruined in any way, nor in any way proceeded against, except by the lawful judgement of his peers and the law of the land."[13]

Numerous copies of the Magna Carta were made, although only three survive. Jefferson viewed one of the exemplifications held by the British Museum when he joined the Adamses on Edward Whitaker Grey's tour on April 24. The copy was one possibly discovered in a tailor's shop in the seventeenth century and presented to Sir Robert Cotton. Cotton founded the original library upon which the British Library in St. Pancras was based - the copy viewed by Jefferson is now on display there.

On April 13, Jefferson paid eight shillings and six pennies for entry to the grandest attraction of its day: the Tower of London. Having already seen the Tower in all its splendour, it is likely that John Adams did not join Jefferson on his tour of the fortress. Built at the behest of William I, who had invaded England from Normandy in 1066, parts of the medieval castle had been built over seven hundred years beforehand, obviously outdating any European-built structure in North America. At the time of Jefferson's visit, the Tower of London was still a fully functioning prison. Imprisonment in the Tower had a long and gory history. Since the first prisoner, Bishop Ranulf Flambard, arrived at - and subsequently escaped from - the

Tower in 1100, the fortress has witnessed the imprisonment and executions of reams of puissant figures who had displeased the crown with seemingly treasonous acts. The most famous of these is Queen Anne Boleyn - beheaded in 1536, her ghost is still said to haunt the area near St Peter ad Vincula church where she was hastily buried after being thrown in a chest.

For Jefferson, the Tower of London had held a soul much closer to home. In 1780, the British ship *Vestal* was traversing the waters around Newfoundland when it intercepted an America-bound ship carrying the minister to Holland. Despite attempting to evade capture, the diplomat was arrested. He had disposed of confidential documents he had been carrying by throwing them overboard when the British were spotted approaching. However, they were fished out of the watery depths and analysed. The seized papers suggested that the Americans and Dutch were entering into an alliance, proving that - despite Dutch neutrality - they had been supporting the colonies as France had done before it officially recognised the United States as independent in 1778. Resultingly, the British forged the Fourth Anglo-Dutch War. The captured diplomat in question was Henry Laurens: former president of the Continental Congress, and father of Hamilton's close friend, John Laurens. Henry, a slave trader from Charleston, South Carolina, was the only American ever to be imprisoned at the Tower of London and had been released only five years before Jefferson's visit. During his imprisonment at the ancient castle, the guards would taunt Laurens by playing the American folk song 'Yankee Doodle'. Recalling this incident, Laurens reflected "The tune of Yankee Doodle, played, I suppose, in derision of me, filled my mind with a sublime contempt and rather made me cheerful."[14] Laurens remained at the Tower until a prisoner exchange in late 1781 saw the former congressman freed in exchange for General Charles Cornwallis – the British general who had surrendered to George Washington by proxy at the Battle of Yorktown. While in the fortress, Laurens had one of his most recognisable portraits painted with a castle in the background to symbolise his incarceration. Despite his imprisonment, Laurens would later be instrumental in pursuing peace when he was chosen to serve as a member of the American committee that negotiated the Treaty of Paris in 1783, formally ending the American Revolution.

Henry Laurens by Lemuel Francis Abbott, 1781.

THEATRELAND

Theatre Royal Drury Lane | King's Theatre Haymarket | Covent Garden | Sadler's Wells | Pantheon, Oxford Street

Jefferson was in London for no more than forty-eight hours before he was seated at Theatre Royal Drury Lane watching the actress of the day, and the object by which Abigail Adams measured the standard of British theatre, Sarah Siddons, perform as Malvina in John Delap's tragedy *The Captives*. In Paris, Thomas was an ardent attendee of the opera. Arguably a rather bourgeoise exploit for the man who lived in fear of Hamilton installing an American king, thus, however, was Jefferson's character: a man of republicanism and gentrified luxuries. He was, as many historians will tell you, a walking contradiction. His sentiments advocating for the inhibition of slavery while owning over six hundred human beings himself are the most cited in this respect. Jefferson once told his grandson, Thomas Jefferson Randolph, that, "One of the rules which above all others made Doctor Franklin the most amiable of men in society, 'never to contradict anybody.'"[15] It was a rule that the quiet TJ attempted to follow, however, contradicting himself seemed to be another matter entirely. That is not to say that visiting the theatre or opera in London was an activity purely for the rich. In fact, the impoverished thronged to playhouses, however, Jefferson did not stand shoulder to shoulder with the city's poor masses as they watched the entertainment.

In London, Jefferson attended the theatre, opera, or a concert eight times during his six-week visit. On the week beginning April 16, he attended some sort of performance nearly every single night, including seeing Sarah Siddons perform again twice at Theatre Royal Drury Lane in her two most famous Shakespearian roles: Portia in the *Merchant of Venice* and Lady Macbeth in *Macbeth*.

He also attended two operas in London: one on March 18 at the King's Theatre Haymarket where he saw Antonia Salieri's comedic opera *La Scuola de Gelosi*. The theatre sits directly opposite 7 Haymarket where Angelica and John Barker Church were to purchase the Wogdon and Barton duelling pistols. *La Scuola de Gelosi*, which translates to 'The School of the Jealous', was sure to remind the American of glimpses of the sitcom-esque in-fighting of the early republic, and possibly foreshadow the rivalry, if not jealousy, that was to come with the advent of Washington's cabinet and the Hamilton-Jefferson showdowns.

A month later, Jefferson took the short journey from Golden Square to Covent Garden Theatre situated on the site of the present Royal Opera House. There he watched the operatic play from which the vengeful line, "Hell hath no fury like a woman scorned," derives: *The Mourning Bride* by William Congreve. On April 21, he travelled to the second of the duo of theatres that were created by Charles II's Letter Patent: Sadler's Wells Theatre in Islington. There he watched the pantomime, *The Restoration of Hymen.*

As well as the theatre, Jefferson also drank up the city's other entertainments. The American could not resist paying to see the Learned Pig in Charing Cross. The swine had been drawing in the crowds all over the country before being brought to London in 1784 where he delighted the city folk with apparently being able to answer questions using cards. In 1799, the Learned Pig was taken to America and introduced to President John Adams.

On April 18, Jefferson visited, but did not comment on, the Amphitheatre Riding House of equestrian Philip Astley. Newcastle-born Astley, an equestrian who had served in the Seven Years' War, had been operating his entertainment venue in St. George's Fields since the late 1760s. However, in the late 1770s, he relocated his establishment closer to Westminster Bridge, a short walk south-east from Jefferson's lodgings. This pegged the riding house up a notch, and the circus ring soon featured horse shows, jugglers, and tightrope walkers. Considered the father of the circus, according to

Limbird's Handbook Guide to London, Astley re-opened his renovated riding house in 1780 to compete with the nearby Royal Circus which was under construction.

However, while the Learned Pig was definitely one of London's in-demand novelties and gallivanting horses are always entertaining, more likely to have been to Jefferson's tastes was his March 23 visit to the vast and decadent Pantheon on Oxford Street. Built in 1772 by James Wyatt, the high-ceilinged venue with a vertiginous glass dome ceiling was designed as a seasonal alternative to the outdoor Ranelagh Gardens in Chelsea, but it quickly became one of London's premier venues for a vast concoction of entertainment. While Jefferson saw a concert here, it is likely that he was also drawn to the place by the exhibition of a hot air balloon, operated by a man known only to us as 'Mr. Uncles'. Counting natural scientist among his many titles, Jefferson had already shown interest in the new art of ballooning in America and attended lectures discussing the lofty new technology. In April 1784, he had written to his cousin, Philip Turpin, about his new fascination, enlightening his kin with a table of the balloon experiments of the past year and including a list of innovative uses he imagined for the balloons. As well as envisaging the new form of travel as beneficial for trade, he also suggested that, with the aid of balloons, mankind may finally traverse the North Pole by air and be able to safely cross enemy land or areas rife with disease. His love for ballooning was enduring and one he carried with him across the Atlantic. Luckily for him, Jefferson arrived in Paris at the height of balloonomania. It is oft incorrectly reported that Jefferson witnessed the ascension of the first manned hot air balloon in November 1783 along with Benjamin Franklin and John and Abigail Adams. However, he was travelling to the temporary U.S. capitol of Annapolis, Maryland, on this date where he was serving as the Virginian delegate to the Congress of the Confederation. Yet, he did watch the ascension of the Roberts Brothers and Colin Hullin in Paris 1784. He later avidly followed ballooning in America, witnessing the first successful flight take-off with JP Blanchard at the helm in Philadelphia in 1793. Annette

Gordon-Reed suggests that Jefferson's avidity for ballooning was so intense that he may have passed the love on to his son with Sally Hemings, Beverly. Isaac Jefferson, an enslaved man at Monticello with no relation to TJ, had his memoirs recorded in 1847 - in them he said that Madison Hemings once visited Petersburg in Virginia to see his brother Beverly send off, or ascend in, a balloon: 'Sally had a son named Madison, who learned to be a great fiddler. He has been in Petersburg twice: was here when the balloon went up - the balloon that Beverly sent off."[16]

Two years earlier at the Pantheon, the aeronaut Vincent Lunardi had also exhibited his balloon in the venue's central dome, but a skylight hanging from the ceiling had punctured the balloon material. Mr. Uncles's balloon luckily did not get damaged during its exhibit, but Jefferson sadly missed the flight which took place in June at Ranelagh Gardens. If you want to visit the Pantheon today, bitter disappointment awaits as the theatre was destroyed in 1937 to make way for the flagship store of British brand, Marks and Spencer.

RETAIL

For a man who was determined to build an America self-reliant on agriculture as opposed to big-time merchants, bankers, and Federalism, Jefferson had an ostentatious spending habit. By the time of his death on July 4, 1826, (both he and Adams died on the same day, on the fiftieth anniversary of the Declaration of Independence. Legendarily, Adams, unaware that Jefferson had passed hours earlier at Monticello, uttered, "Thomas Jefferson still survives,"[17] on his deathbed) he was $107,000 in debt, nearly $3 million in today's tender. Throughout his life, his debt would plague him. Although evidently harbouring bigoted opinions as is evidenced in his *Notes on the State of Virginia*, he advocated for emancipation and called slavery 'moral depravity'. However, he believed that widespread emancipation would never be seen in his lifetime, and, more specifically, at Monticello.   Indeed,   one contributing reason as to why Jefferson did not emancipate his slaves was his debt. Not only did he spend heavily, but he also inherited debts of $4000 ($134,170/£96, 280 in today's money) from his father-in-law upon his death in 1773. Paired with the less than financially advantageous métier of farming, Jefferson carried the burden of debt for most of his adult life. Upon his death, the executor of his estate was forced to sell his beloved Monticello to cover costs. While the pecuniary rewards his land and crops reaped was never enough to fully clear his account, it seemed it was better than nothing. Thus, to Jefferson, it seemed that he couldn't afford to emancipate his own enslaved people. However, he did do a fair bit of selling in order to advance his financial position; he sold and gifted one hundred and sixty-one - but purchased less than twenty - people in his lifetime.

Jefferson never helped his financial situation. He spent heavily in France, and his predilection for Old World wonders would not cease in London. Starting from his first day in the city, he bought a hat and a watch chain. Then a pair of gloves. Then a map. A walking stick; cotton stockings; knives; a thermometer; a protractor; a globe; a telescope; a solar microscope; boots; books; pocket pistols; boot garters; sealing candles; spurs; a calico gown; shoes; slippers; the list goes on and on. Added on top of his spends for carriage hire, lodgings, restaurants, and general tipping, it was an eye-wateringly expensive trip. Most of Jefferson's shopping was done in the Piccadilly area where he visited some of the most exquisite shops of the day. While Jefferson's memorandum book from the period does not note the merchant of every single shop, and thus we are unable to decipher the location of his every purchase, in some cases he does precede the acquisition with the name of the trader. Some of the most notable purchases include maps from William Fadden, who owned a shop on St. Martin's Lane in Charing Cross, and who TJ later proclaimed to be one of the best map engravers around. Moreover, he shopped at Jesse Ramsden's instrument and ocular outlet the Golden Spectacles, which was opposite Sackville Street where Angelica was soon to live. He bought from there the aforementioned thermometer, protractor, and pocket globe. Ramsden had an excellent reputation and had already been of service to an American statesman three years earlier when he made spectacles for John Adams.

Following in the footsteps of his father, Jefferson had served as the Albemarle County surveyor between 1773 - 1774 and had a prowess for inventing and experimentation. Satisfying his persistent thirst to procure mathematical and scientific instruments, he quickly set about spending an exorbitant amount of money on adding to his already expansive collection. For example, he purchased telescopes from John and Peter Dolland at one of their outlets in Haymarket or St. Paul's Churchyard. Given the proximity of Jefferson's lodgings and the patterns of his other purchases, Haymarket is the most likely location. The purchases made here equal to around £1,250 ($1,721) in today's tender and can be found at Monticello. He also bought a theodolite from John Troughton, an instrument maker from the Troughton Family, from his store at Number 136 Fleet Street; a pantographer from Henry Shuttleworth at Number 23 Ludgate Street; and a microscope from William Jones at 135 Holborn. Jefferson would later order more instruments from Jones during his presidency.

Two pocket pistols in the possession of Monticello are assumed to have been purchased from Thomas Dealtry at 85 Cornhill near the Royal Exchange in the City of London. Dealtry was obviously a skilled and well-known sword-cutler and metal worker as advertising cards for his business are kept secure at the British Museum.

At Number 58 on the Strand, Jefferson purchased from Thomas Roe red and white speckled calico. He later bought additional material, possibly from Mr Roe's Strand outlet again, and a bridle and stirrups from Mackintosh Saddlers at Number 10 Haymarket for a grand total of £379. He later made another purchase for riding gear from Pierce Saddlery up the road at Number 36 and flitted about for some shoes from Duke's Court on St. Martin's Lane.

Jefferson was an ardent bibliophile and utilised the services of two booksellers during his time in London: John Lackington, who was situated on Chiswell Street in the City of London, and John Stockdale, whose shop Stockdale's on Piccadilly was a well-known haunt for the who's-who of London Whig society. As well as a bookshop, it served as the de facto headquarters for the meetings of William Pitt the Elder's supporters. Jefferson had already been corresponding with Stockdale before visiting London and stayed in contact with both Stockdale and Lackington long after he left the city. At Stockdale's, he spent £3,110 in today's money ($4,323) and, the more modest £1,253 ($1,741) at Lackington's.

Always a man for keeping up personal grooming standards, Jefferson also purchased toothbrushes in London. Unlike Washington and Adams, who were plagued with dental ailments, Jefferson had excellent teeth for the period - apparently only losing one adult tooth in his entire life. While Washington's teeth have retrospectively garnered attention as his dentures were made of a mix of ivory and the teeth of animals and enslaved people, not much is known about Hamilton's dental hygiene. However, it does not take one to imagine that they were possibly worse than Jefferson's. The treasury secretary had a love of coffee and a sweet tooth. At the Compromise of 1790 dinner - where Jefferson and Madison agreed to Hamilton's plan to have the national government pay off the state debts in exchange for the national capitol moving from Philadelphia to the banks of the Potomac River - Hamilton, according to historian Charles A. Cerami, "positively exulted"[18] at the dessert of vanilla ice cream in warm pastry. The Hamilton family also seemed to be familiar with the sweet as Eliza had introduced the Washington family to the joys of the creamy indulgence when she served it at a dinner party in June 1789. Yet, since Jefferson was responsible for both the dessert, and popularising ice cream, one would think that he too would be afflicted with dental decay. Alas, he regularly visited the dentist and, as his London trip illustrates, took great care to procure the latest dental devices.

NUMBER 1 WELLS STREET, WESTMINSTER

Jefferson paid £10 (£1,605/$2,232 today) to be painted by Mather Brown at his studio at Number 1 Wells Street in Westminster. He received the final piece in 1788. Sadly, the painting has been lost, however, Brown - a Boston-born artist who had also painted Nabby Adams and Colonel Smith - made a copy of the original and it exists as one of the most enduring images of Jefferson during the Confederation Period. Only forty-three when the masterpiece was created, it exudes a youthful flare compared to others painted later during his presidency, particularly Rembrandt Peale's 1800 creation. It presents Jefferson in an extremely European light, wearing colourful, embellished clothes associated with a dandy as opposed to the darker materials worn in later portraits. Unfortunately, for those historians who are keen to know what Jefferson truly looked like, his secretary William Short commented in 1788 that, "It has no feature like him."[19]

RESTAURANTS

Dolly's Chop House | London Tavern

On March 21, Jefferson's memorandum book shows he paid for dinner at 'Dolly's'. Dolly's Chop House on Paternoster Row in the City of London was more than a mere tavern in 1780s London, it was an inn frequented by some of the most recognisable names in late eighteenth-century society. The famous pub had allegedly been founded by Dorothy Burrow; the former favourite cook of Queen Ann who had the property bestowed upon her by the monarch. The chophouse was known for its steak and ivy-tasting gill-ale, and was simply known, as Jefferson shows us, as 'Dolly's'. The steakhouse,

Thomas Jefferson by Mather Brown, 1786.

with its sign painted by regular patron Thomas Gainsborough, and warm, projecting fireplaces had been popular years beforehand with Benjamin Franklin during his time in the city. In 1786, the restaurant was the scene of an unfortunate turn of events for the stiff John Adams. Jefferson, Colonel William Stephens Smith, and another American, Richard Peters - an official also travelling in Europe at the time - had an engagement to dine with Adams, however, they missed it all thanks to Dolly's gill-ale. Stopping by the famed inn in the afternoon, the three Americans soon spiralled into a classically

British state of intoxication and forgot all about their date with the Bostonian, who was probably left tapping his feet and pacing Grosvenor Square's hallway. At half-past two in the afternoon, they penned a round-robin in poetic prose for Adams in the hopes that the serious statesmen - who wasn't a stranger to heavy drinking himself, starting every morning with a glass of cider - would forgive them:

> One among our many follies
> Was calling in for steaks at Dolly's
> Whereby we've lost—& feel like sinners
> That we have miss'd much better dinners
> Nor do we think that us 'tis hard on
> Most humbly thus to beg your pardon
> And promise that another time
> We'll give our reason not our rhyme
> So we've agreed—Our Nem: Con: Vote is
> That we thus, jointly—give you notice
> For as our rule is to be clever
> We hold it better late than never[20]

The three men wrote their signatures in a circle and off went the apology to Mayfair. We don't know if John Adams ever forgave his colleagues for their absentmindedness, yet, being a stickler for timekeeping and protocol, it isn't too hard to imagine an evening of complaining to Abigail.

Dolly's Chophouse closed its doors in 1881 and, like numerous other streets near the River Thames in the City of London, Paternoster Row was bombed during the Blitz, destroying most of the street. The closest one can get to the drunken exploits of Jefferson is a visit to Paternoster Square: a bank-laden area on the site of the original street. Dolly's exists now only in the writing of some of the most preeminent figures in early modern London, including America's Founding Fathers.

A week after Jefferson's exploits at Dolly's, on March 27 he paid fourteen shillings and six pennies for dinner at the London Tavern. Not only was Jefferson likely to be fed well at the London Tavern, with its menu listing delicacies including turtle, but the atmosphere was likely to succour his intellectual curiosity. Originally called the White Lion, the London Tavern re-opened in 1768 after a fire at the opposite peruke makers burnt the building and surrounding structures to the ground. Although it survived the next century, the London Tavern, like Dolly's, is no longer there and historians rely on the fabled tales of patrons to grasp the importance of the watering hole. Yet, the London Tavern was far more than the local alehouse. Located on Bishopsgate Street in the heart of the City of London near the Royal Exchange - where TJ had purchased his pocket pistols from Dealtry - the tavern was a thriving, well-known destination for society meetings. In the years after Jefferson dined there, a profusion of Anglo-American and revolutionary issues were debated within its walls. The debates may have even seen an appearance from the diplomat had he been in London, especially the audiences held by the Revolution Society. Formed in 1788 to commemorate the centenary of the Glorious Revolution which saw William and Mary of Orange - the namesakes of Jefferson's alma matter - return to England, the Revolutionary Society was a who's-who of radicals and members of the Enlightenment period. Characters, such as the Adamses' friend Richard Price, and Benjamin Franklin's friend Joseph Priestly, sat among its ranks, and met to discuss a cause close to the Virginian's head and heart: the French Revolution. In their founding year, the first meeting at the tavern is recorded. In 1791 the society met again, this time with Thomas Paine, writer of the pamphlet *Common Sense* which further ignited the calls for independence in the colonies. The dinner celebrated Anglo-French ties and the rooms were decorated with tricolour cockades. Jérôme Pétion de Villeneuve, the Mayor of Paris, who would later kill himself to evade capture during the French Revolution, was the guest of honour.

The tavern had elongated Anglo-American ties as well. In 1847, Frederick Douglas, a man born into slavery in Maryland who escaped, received an education, and dedicated his life to social reform and abolitionism, delivered his farewell speech at the tavern after spending nineteen months touring the country delivering lectures against slavery. The tavern was demolished ninety years after Jefferson dined there in 1876.

The London Tavern at Bishopsgate, 1809.

LONDON'S MANSIONS AND GARDENS

Enfield Chase | Moor Park

Thomas Jefferson was, first and foremost, a farmer with vegetal prowess. During his time in London, negotiations with foreign ambassadors stalled and the statesman had time to explore the gardens he had read about in Thomas Whatley's *Observations on Modern Gardening.* Clutching his botanical bible, he travelled extensively, visiting some of the Home Counties' most manicured mansions and gardens. Between April 4 and 10, Jefferson and Adams took an elongated tour of the English countryside, visiting places such as Blenheim Palace, Birmingham, and Shakespeare's birthplace in Stratford-upon-Avon where they cut off a chunk of the Bard's chair as a keepsake. They also visited the University of Oxford, which had educated many of the figures involved with establishing the first English colonies in America, such as Sir Walter Raleigh. Jefferson was also keen to explore the lavish houses and accompanying horticultural lawns dotted around London's suburbia. The culmination of these visits resulted in Jefferson gaining incite and ideas for reviving his mountaintop home at Monticello.

In 1768, Jefferson began developing the land on the mountaintop. Far from the Monticello we are familiar with today, it was a simple two-story, eight-room house which would be easily outsized by the present three-story, twenty-one-room mansion. It did feature elements of the neoclassical Palladian style seen today on the house, specifically the double porticos, but it is impossible not to see the inspiration drawn from the various homes he visited around London embedded into Monticello's second resurrection – and none more so than the now non-existent South Lodge in Enfield Chase and Moor Park, both in north London.

Leaving Golden Square on the morning of March 31, Jefferson and Adams's son-in-law Colonel Smith travelled north to the first stop out of London, Barnet, where he purchased a postillion to guide them to Enfield in the east and Moor Park in the west. Enfield, now a London borough, is mentioned in William the Conqueror's 1086 survey of England and selected parts of Wales: the *Doomsday Book*. Six hundred and eighty-four years later, South Lodge at Enfield Chase – one of three illustrious houses on a sprawling royal hunting ground - featured in Whatley's *Observations*, ensuring a visit from the Founding Father. However, after perusing the grounds, Jefferson was not impressed with the infrastructure, writing in his *Notes on a Tour of English Gardens*, that Enfield Chase was, "Not in good repair. The water very fine. Would admit of great improvement by extending walks etc, to the principal water at the bottom of the lawn."[21] After learning what *not* to do with Monticello, Jefferson and Colonel Smith crossed to the northwest of the city to the grand Moor Park estate. Built in 1720 by the Italian architect Giacomo Leoni, the influence Moor Park had on Jefferson's later designs for the main house at Monticello is evident in his annotations: "The principal front a Corinthian portico of four columns. In front of the wings a colonnade, ionic, subordinate. Back front a terras, four Corinthian pilasters. Pulling down wings of building. Removing deer. Wants water."[22] Moor Park seemed to have left quite an impression on Jefferson. Elements of the house are more than evident in the architecture at Monticello, which Jefferson fiddled with until his death. Moreover, the estate's gardens left an imprint on the Virginian's memory. Five years after visiting, he ordered a strain of apricot plant called 'Moor Park' which had been cultivated on the grounds. The trees can still be seen at Monticello today.

————————

Thomas Jefferson left London on April 26, never to return. In the space of six weeks, he had gone on a whirlwind tour of England; crammed in over seven centuries of British history; viewed the most beautiful botanical feats in the land; and spent thousands of pounds buying up some of the country's most expensive goods. And, after all that, he came away unimpressed. In his autobiography, he used the pages dedicated to his account of this period to slam the monarchy, briefly explain his reason for visiting, and mention his tour of English gardens. In a similar fashion, his *Notes on a Tour of English Gardens,* for the most part, lacks any opinion on his London life or vignettes on city society. Most tellingly, in the summer of 1788, Jefferson was reflecting on a trip he had recently undertaken through central Europe when he sat to write a guide to travelling for U.S. citizens called *Jefferson's Hints on Americans Visiting Europe.* Unlike the other sophisticated destinations listed, such as Venice, Genoa, Nice, or Monaco – London, or anywhere in Britain for that matter, does not receive its own dedicated section. The only hint the Jefferson had set foot in Britain is his reference to the animals kept as amusements at the Tower of London. Indeed, the whole document is very much *sans Britannia.* Not surprising, however, for the man who said, "both town and country fell short of my expectations."[23] This quote is taken from a longer letter to John Page, a fellow Virginian politician. Written shortly after his return to Paris from London on May 4, 1786, Jefferson's brief account of his trip is so telling of his distaste for England that is worth quoting in full:

> I returned but three or four days ago from a two months trip to England. I traversed that country much, and own both town and country fell short of my expectations. Comparing it with this, I found a much greater proportion of barrens, a soil in other parts not naturally so good as this, not better cultivated, but better manured, and therefore more productive. This proceeds from the practice of long leases there, and short ones here. The labouring people here are poorer than in England. They pay about one half their produce in rent, the English in general about a third. The gardening in that country is the article in which it surpasses all the earth. I mean their pleasure gardening. This indeed went far beyond my ideas. The city of London, though' handsomer than Paris, is not so handsome as Philadelphia.

Their architecture is in the most wretched style I ever saw, not meaning to except America where it is bad, nor even Virginia where it is worse than in any other part of America, which I have seen. The mechanical arts in London are carried to a wonderful perfection. But of these I need not speak, because of them my countrymen have unfortunately too many samples before their eyes.[24]

Jefferson's account walks the fine line between a love-hate relationship with London, and England more generally. It is hard not to argue that some of Jefferson's aversions to the country came from a habitual need to dislike England. This is obvious in his declaration that the architecture is the most wretched style he ever saw, yet later drew inspiration for Monticello. Whether he liked or disliked London, however, is redundant in terms of his links to Hamilton. While Jefferson did not correspond with the young general while in London, or Paris for that matter – indeed they were not to meet for another four years – and his travels did not directly impact Hamilton's life like Angelica Church's did, for those keen to immerse themselves in the journeys of the main the characters in Hamilton's story, or those on the trail of the Founding Father's in London more generally, Jefferson leaves a potent and detailed line of breadcrumbs.

CHAPTER FOUR

BENJAMIN FRANKLIN

enjamin Franklin was in the winter of his life during the Confederation Period when Hamilton was blossoming into a political machine. The polymath barely lived to see Hamilton's true rise to greatness as he died less than a year into George Washington's first presidential term. However, he did come into contact with Hamilton at a defining moment early in the young upstart's career at the Constitutional Convention in 1787. Aged and suffering from gout, the eighty-one-year-old Franklin was supposedly carried into the Pennsylvania State House on a sedan supported by four convicts from the nearby Walnut Street jail. Senility was starting to truly take its toll on the man who many remember for his longevity and swashbuckling virility, yet he attended every session and encouraged his fellow statesmen - whom he described as the "most august and respectable assembly"[1] - to support the new document even though he had his own misgivings about it. Most notably, he witnessed Hamilton's pièce de résistance at the convention: his six-hour long soliloquy on his plan for a new governmental system based on the British one, which, predictably, no one else supported.

Born in 1706 on Boston's Milk Street to Josiah and Abiah Franklin, Ben was the fifteenth of seventeen children born to his father and the eighth of ten children born to his mother. Josiah, a silk-dyer-turned-tallow-chandler, had emigrated to the colony from Banbury in Northampton, England, with his first wife Anne Child. Josiah and Anne expanded their family in Boston for seven years before she died in 1689 shortly after delivering Franklin's brother, Joseph II, who too perished within a fortnight. The future Founding Father, who is often perceived to be the most learned of his colleagues in the Continental Congress and is regularly referred to in historical narratives as a 'sage', never received the formal education bestowed upon Hamilton, Adams, or Jefferson. While his father once had plans for his son to attend Harvard, it soon became clear that there were pecuniary obstacles. Like Hamilton, however, Franklin had an insatiable thirst for knowledge which he satisfied by embarking on a course of self-education. At the age of twelve, he was indentured to his printer brother, James, at James's newspaper *The New England Courant,* where he would later anonymously flex his civic wings with the Silence Dogood letters. Unable to afford a vast amount of literature, Franklin coordinated with other apprentices who were indentured to booksellers to sneak freshly printed books home, read them overnight, and return them the next day in mint condition. Amongst his favourite essayists was the London-born pamphleteer Daniel Defoe, best known for penning *Robinson Crusoe.* In a foretelling sense, he also enjoyed John Bunyan's *Pilgrim's Progress*, which explores the trope of sea travel.

James and Ben grated on each other. In 1723, the younger Franklin broke free of the chains of apprenticeship and ran away, initially to New York, and then further south to the city we associate most vividly with the statesman: Philadelphia. In Philadelphia, Ben earned his keep by working at a handful of printers, going from strength to strength and eventually becoming more successful than James, something he went back to Boston to rub his nose in.

In 1730, Franklin married Deborah Read, his landlord's daughter whom he had first laid eyes on after stepping off the ship from New York. She apparently watched him judgementally while he carried and scoffed on bread rolls. Deborah had already married a man called John Rogers in 1725, however, in the same year, Rogers had disappeared from Philadelphia. With no knowledge of whether her husband was dead or alive, Deborah could not enter into official marriage with Franklin in case Rogers returned and she was arrested for bigamy. Thus, the Franklin's began living together in an arrangement called a common-law marriage which saw them as, for all intents and purposes, married. Common-law marriage was accepted in eighteenth-century America where the fates of people often went unknown, and women could not afford to wait for a possibly dead husband to reappear. Ben and Debbie had two children together: Francis, born in 1732 (he later died from smallpox aged four) and Sarah in 1743.

If there is such a thing as being divinely gifted, Benjamin Franklin was blessed in bucketloads. In 1727, he set up the Enlightenment thinking group the Junto - through which the American Philosophical Society was formed - and, in 1728, at just twenty-two years old, he opened his own printing shop. In his thirties and forties, he became even more of a success story: he founded the colony's first library service and fire department; established what would become the University of Pennsylvania; and, in 1753, was named Deputy Postmaster General. Outside of civics, he was also a noted scientist, most often remembered for his work with electricity. Famously, he became an international name for his experiments, especially his Kite and Key experiment in 1752. In 1751, Franklin became involved in the Pennsylvania Assembly. Having already served as a Justice of the Peace, he quickly rose through the political ranks until, in 1757, he was given a role that would alter both his life and the world's politics, forever.

LONDON

When Alexander Hamilton was just an infant, Benjamin Franklin was already fighting for the rights of the American colonies. The Bostonian had amassed a sizeable fortune from his prolific printing company in Pennsylvania and subsequently retired at the early age of forty-two, unbeknownst to him only halfway through his life and the chapters that have been imbued in history had only just begun. He dedicated his retirement to philanthropy, science, and civics as began his metamorphosis into the giant of history that we know. In 1757, the Pennsylvania Assembly named Benjamin Franklin as the latest person to take on the role of Colonial Agent. The French and Indian War was in full flow in the colonies and the people of Pennsylvania were carrying a burden of tax to defend their land. The London-based proprietors of the colony, the Penn family, with their large swathes of colonial land, refused to pay the right tax along with their fellow colonists. The Pennsylvania Assembly could think of no better man for the job of negotiation than the one and only born diplomat Benjamin Franklin.

Setting out for London in the summer of 1757, his mission was intended to last a mere five months, but this hopeful outlook on a speedy turnaround quickly turned sour. The initial delays in proceedings derived from the Penn family's refusal to meet such demands from the assembly. Catching malaria from the fields around Westminster also put the fifty-one-year-old out of action for a season. As Franklin ran about town fruitlessly arguing with the Penns, meanwhile attending meetings at coffee houses and ingratiating himself into the London science scene, the seeds of dissent in the colonies snowballed into the American Revolution. Yet, this did not happen quickly, far from it. Many imagine the

American Revolution to have started when the first shots were fired at Lexington and Concord, when, in fact, the ideological fight for independence from the first signs of disaffection makes the war more than a twenty-year affair. This timeline can be seen clearly in changes in Franklin's ideology during his time in England: he had arrived in London as a proud British subject with intentions to make Pennsylvania a royal colony directly under the command of the monarch but left as one of the staunchest American revolutionaries and labelled one of Britain's most "mischievous enemies"[2].

During his time in the city, he befriended Enlightenment figures; wined and dined with affluent London society and got drawn into admitting his involvement in one of the most consequential scandals in the colonies at the time: the Hutchinson Letters Affair. After initially only planning to stay for less than six months, Franklin's term in London turned into sixteen years. He only ventured home once in that period, for eighteen months between 1762 and 1764. However, Franklin's 1757-1775 stay was not his first rodeo. The sage had first arrived in London on Christmas Eve 1724 as a fresh-faced eighteen-year-old hoping to nurture networks and procure printing supplies. His passage had been arranged for him by Governor William Keith, lieutenant-governor of Pennsylvania and Delaware, however, Keith did not produce the letters of introduction he had promised the young Franklin. Thankfully he took the advice of some learned merchants he had travelled with. Recovering his pride and starting to feel hopeful again, he began seeking work for himself at London's premier printing companies. The sprightly Bostonian was successful in his quest and spent two years working for big names in the industry before returning home to Philadelphia in 1726. As he walked through the streets of the City of London on that frosty December night in 1724, with people flocking to church and preparing for the next day's festivities, he could never have imagined that he would later return as the figurehead for independence in a new nation.

36 CRAVEN STREET, CHARING CROSS

After narrowly avoiding being impounded on rocks on the southern English coast following a chase by hostile vessels swirling in British waters (a regular occurrence in the eighteenth century), Benjamin Franklin, his son William, and two slaves, Peter and King, arrived at Falmouth on July 17. Their safe arrival after a near-death experience so close to land following successful traversal of the Atlantic caused Ben to write immediately to Deborah in Philadelphia:

> The bell ringing for church, we went thither immediately, and with hearts full of gratitude, returned sincere thanks to God for the mercies we had received: were I a Roman Catholic, perhaps I should on this occasion vow to build a chapel to some saint; but as I am not, if I were to vow at all, it should be to build a *lighthouse*.[3]

So far, his second visit to England was not off to a fantastic start, however, conditions were to improve. Travelling to London via Stonehenge and Wilton House, the estate of Lord Pembroke whose antique collection Franklin lauded, the party arrived in the city on July 27. They spent their first night at either the north London home of Peter Collinson, a botanist with whom Franklin had been corresponding for many years, or a small lodging house called the Bear Inn in Southwark; Franklin's papers are hazy in the respect that he notes having stayed with Collinson but bills for lodgings at the Bear Inn also exist.

Within three days, Franklin had permanent lodgings arranged for him by Robert Charles, a fellow Pennsylvania agent who had already been carrying out the assembly's work in London for several years, including organising the casting of the original Liberty Bell at the Whitechapel Bell Foundry. Charles had found the sage rooms at Number 7 – the house's original number - Craven Street in Charing Cross with a Mrs. Margaret Stevenson. A widow who had been left a healthy sum of money, Stevenson rented out rooms in her five-story townhouse which, excitedly for Franklin, sat equidistant from the seat of power in Westminster and the hub of London's Enlightenment period in the coffee shops of Covent Garden. His plush new lodgings were a far cry from the simple board he had procured as a young man in Sardinia Street (then known as Duke Street) in the City of London and it did not take long for Franklin to move into the house; his memorandum books show him dining with Margaret on the night of July 30, most likely the day he moved in, when he paid eleven shillings and five pennies for dinner. Craven Street itself was a fairly young avenue, the grand houses towering along it had only been built in 1730. The land's owners, the Cravens, headed by patriarch William Craven, 3rd Baron Craven, descended from a distinguished aristocratic family who inherited the land in 1637 but subsequently lost it during the republic as punishment for their loyalty to the crown. Following Charles II's restoration, the land was returned to the family, however, the area was not the most congenial of assets. While close to the hub of power in Westminster and walking distance to affluent neighbourhoods, Craven Street still erred close to the red-light district of seedy Covent Garden. Formerly known as Spur Alley, the street was rife with disease and crime, and, by 1720, very few houses were advertised for anything more than a small number of shillings. The Cravens' solution to this abhorrence was to flatten the houses and get to work building a shiny new street. Wanting to attract a new calibre of people to the area, the family built classically Georgian dark-bricked homes, tall but narrow with perfect symmetry in house after house after house. The pretty new street fulfilled its job, and soon a crop of haughty personas arrived to take up residence.

Number 36 had previously been leased to a gentleman named John Hodson in 1730 before Margaret Stevenson began her lease in 1748. Very few details are known about Margaret. She was married to a Lincolnshire-born man named Addinell Stevenson in August 1737. Their marriage was conducted at Fleet Prison in Clerkenwell and is listed in the records as an 'irregular or clandestine' marriage. This could be because Margaret possibly gave birth to twins, John and Thomas, outside of wedlock in the preceding April and wanted the marriage to take place under the shroud of secrecy. Addinell was dead by the time Franklin arrived, but the American became exceptionally close to Margaret, her daughter Mary - known to everyone as Polly - and Polly's husband, the preeminent anatomist William Hewson. They quickly became a surrogate family to Franklin, and Margaret often accompanied him to dinners around town.

Number 36 Craven Street.

William Hewson, whom Polly married while Franklin was in London in July 1770, mapped the lymphatic system and ran an anatomy school from the house. Hewson had fallen out with his partner, the arguably better-known physician William Hunter, over claims to discoveries and subsequently left the business at Great Windmill Street in Soho. Franklin, probably keen to see anatomical experiments in person and feel the ebb and flow of scientific minds growing in his own home, suggested that Hewson branch out and set up an anatomy school on his own terms at Craven Street. Hewson took up the idea and began operating out of his mother-in-law's garden. Anatomy schools, while necessary for the advancement of science, involved the frowned-upon process of grave robbing. The cadavers used at Hewson's anatomy school were not returned to their graves but were re-buried in a mass pit in the house's garden and covered with lime to aid decomposition. Tragically, Hewson died young at only thirty-four after contracting sepsis while working on a corpse the year before Franklin departed from England. Writing home to Deborah, Franklin lamented:

> Our family here is in great distress. Poor Mrs. Hewson has lost her husband, and Mrs. Stevenson her son-in-law. He died last Sunday morning of a fever which baffled the skill of our best physicians. He was an excellent young man, ingenious, industrious, useful, and beloved by all who knew him. She is left with two young children, and a third soon expected. He was just established in a profitable growing business, with the best prospects of bringing up his young family advantageously.[4]

While Margaret and Franklin enjoyed a platonic friendship, the nature of Polly and Franklin's relationship has caused some controversy and divided historians. The Bostonian's reputation as a bawdy older gentleman with enduring concupiscence seemed to transcend oceans and Franklin did indeed fraternise with a host of ladies. Immortalised in artworks such as Norman Rockwell's *Ben*

Franklin's Belles, the sage's love for the ladies and coital affairs was well-known. Before his common-law marriage to Deborah, Franklin had already sired his eldest child, William, with an unknown woman thought most likely to be a prostitute, although some have suggested it was Ben's housemaid, Barbara. Franklin's fraternising was so frequent and obvious that John Adams drew comparisons between the Bostonian and Hamilton, saying of Hamilton's womanising that he had, "As debauched morals as old Franklin, who is more his model than anyone I know."[5] Historian of American Sexuality at Howard University, Professor Thomas A. Foster, has considered whether Franklin fathered up to fourteen other illegitimate children in addition to the acknowledged William.

There is also evidence to suggest that, while in London, he was involved with the coarse Hellfire Club. The head of the club, Francis Dashwood, was a politician and served as the Chancellor of the Exchequer early in Franklin's residence. Known for his promiscuity as well as his politics, Dashwood was a magnet for other amorous, and often adulterous, men in high society and set up the club for other self-confessed 'rakes' of the period - a rake being a man with depraved moral values, especially in terms of sexual activities and numerous conquests. Franklin and Dashwood, who sat in the House of Lords and is referenced in most of Ben's letters as '(Lord) Le Despencer', became good friends. Ben spent time at Dashwood's home and was his guest at the ceremony for the installation of Lord North as the Chancellor of the University of Oxford. Moreover, as part of his association with the Royal Society in London, Franklin joined the Monday Club founded by John Ellicott. The club met at the George and Vulture tavern in Covent Garden. Coincidentally, the George and Vulture was the rumoured meeting spot for the Hellfire Club and involved many of the same faces. In the 1750s, Dashwood moved the meetings to Medmenham Abbey in Buckinghamshire, and then to a set of caves in West Wycombe Hill which were painted with phallic symbols and images of sadistic sexual activity. Franklin visited the rakish caves with Dashwood, further cultivating rumours that he was a member of the Hellfire Club, at the time known as the Monks of Medmenham.

However, while Franklin may have indeed been a monk in Dashwood's club, the folly around Polly and Franklin's relationship derives from a story told by Charles Willson Peale, an artist known for painting some of the most memorable images of Revolutionary figures, notably George Washington. During his time in London in the late 1760s, a young Peale, seeking a fellow American in the city, entered the house to find a woman sitting on Franklin's lap, apparently with their clothes dishevelled. He sketched an image of the scene in charcoal and concluded that this was Polly, yet there is no evidence that it was apart from the fact that she was the young lady of the house. Of course, it could have been one of the hundreds of London girls who were entranced by the charms of the suave American. Or, it could have been an attempt by Peale to scotch Franklin's reputation, thus whether the event even happened is open to interpretation. Indeed, Franklin biographer Walter Isaacson has questioned the context surrounding the scene: "The lady in question was probably Polly, though the sketch Peale later made of the scene is ambiguous."[6] While the debate of whether Polly and Franklin went beyond the filial ensues, theirs is the most beautiful story to come out of Franklin's nearly two-decade-long residence at Craven Street. While Franklin's actions with ladies did, at times, tend to venture beyond the realms of friendship, he also took many women under his wing in a paternalistic fashion. Franklin was an early advocate for women's education and was entranced by Polly who had received good schooling but was yearning to learn further. Franklin, possibly the best person Polly could ever have wished for to turn up at her mother's house, spent years corresponding with her over any scientific questions she may have had. Following the deaths of close family members and the close of the War of Independence, Polly and her children moved to Philadelphia in 1786 to be near her favourite American. Loyal to her friend to the end, Polly was at Franklin's bedside when he died on April 17, 1790.

Ben's closeness with the Stevensons allowed him to use the house as his own. Although his official rooms sprawled across the first floor, he would frequently welcome a milieu of London society and entertain them in Margaret Stevenson's ground floor parlour. Amongst these guests were Joseph Priestly, one of the men credited with the discovery of oxygen and several other noble gases, who was also a Fellow of the Royal Society. Additionally, the pro-American politician William Pitt the Elder, who had served as prime minister between 1766 and 1769, visited 36 Craven Street. The two men could have bonded in later life over the Loyalist beliefs of their two sons – William Pitt the Younger was a vehement Tory and William Franklin would remain loyal to George III - had Pitt not died in 1778. The bouquet of notable individuals who walked through the door earned the house the nickname the 'first de-facto U.S. Embassy', years before John Adams even set foot inside Number 9 Grosvenor Square. Meanwhile, Franklin's neighbours included the same Molyneaux Shuldham who was neighbours with Angelica Church, yet Franklin luckily did not have to stand his presence for too long as he only moved into Number 33 in 1775. Living next door to Franklin for a period was Dr. John Leake, a man-midwife who founded the Westminster Lying-in Hospital. Although the subject of gestation was not Franklin's forte, being so close to a scientist who was breaking into the world of pregnancy and childbirth, a subject which, for centuries, was closeted and almost mythical to men, must have been exciting for Franklin.

Following Margaret Stevenson's passing on January 1, 1783, and Polly's immigration to the U.S., the house continued to be used as a lodging house until the creation of close-by Charing Cross Railway Station in the nineteenth century turned the house into a hotel. Serendipitously, the house escaped rampant bombing during the Blitz which destroyed much of the surrounding infrastructure, including several homes along Craven Street. In 2006, the house was reopened as a museum dedicated to Franklin's time in London. It is Franklin's only remaining residence in the world as his homes in both Boston and Philadelphia have been destroyed, meaning that Craven Street is the most potent link between Hamilton, Franklin, and London.

Benjamin Franklin House at 36 Craven Street.

ST. BRIDE'S CHURCH, FLEET STREET

When Franklin arrived in London in 1757, he was the most famous American in the world. Despite the remarks of Pennsylvania proprietor Thomas Penn that, "Mr. Franklin's popularity is nothing here and he will be looked very coldly upon by great people. There are very few of great consequence that have heard of his electrical experiments those matters being attended to by a particular sort of people,"[7] Franklin's prowess in the natural sciences, especially his experiments with electricity, were renowned. Earlier in the decade, Franklin had proved that lightning was electricity and not the wrath of God as had been assumed for centuries. While not something we necessarily consider as commonly destructive in the twenty-first century, prior to the invention of the lightning rod, the electrical surges from the sky had the ability to cause vast damage which was deemed as divine punishment. The initial Kite and Key experiment was carried out by Thomas-François Dalibard in France in May 1752, with Franklin supposedly performing the experiment in Philadelphia a month later.

The experiment proved Franklin's theory but was far from safe by today's standards. It killed Russian physicist Georg Wilhelm Richmann and caused Franklin a fair amount of injury too. This was not a new phenomenon to him, however, as he had often been sparked getting to the process, most humorously of all are the instances when he would show off his party trick of roasting a turkey with electricity, which ended badly for Franklin, as well as the bird, more than once. Despite the dangers that came with electricity, Franklin's theories catalysed an interest in lightning. Ben become an oracle about the antiquatedly feared sparks and, consequently, people sought his advice about their lightning-related problems, including George III.

In the humid heat of summer, on June 18, 1764, a violent storm hit the south of England which resulted in the usual destruction of buildings but also a number of casualties. Included amongst the carnage was St. Bride's Church Fleet Street. A Wren design with Anglo-American connections, the parents of Virginia Dare – Ananias Dare and Eleanor White, members of the lost colony of Roanoke – had been married in the church, as had the parents of Mayflower passenger and Governor of Plymouth Colony, Edward Winslow. The church is believed to be one of the oldest religious sites in London, with a divine institution having been situated on the land for several centuries. Furthermore, it is also responsible for the root of the road's association with the printing trade ever since printer Wynkyn de Worde set up England's first printing press with moveable type on the church's grounds in 1501.

St. Bride's Church, Fleet Street.

By late June, Franklin's name was being thrown into the mix of potential scientists and inventors who could contribute their knowledge towards protecting St. Bride's. In a letter between two Fellows of the Royal Society, Edward Delaval and Benjamin Wilson, titled *An Account of the Effects of Lightning in St Bride's Church, Fleet-street,*

Delaval discusses Franklin's observations on lightning and lightning rods. Soon, George III was seeking advice from the most famous electrician in the world to aid the future protection of St. Bride's. Franklin suggested using of a variation of lightning rod he had created aptly named the Franklin Rod. The king wanted to use a purely British blunt-ended rod even though Franklin's invention was evidently an evolved option with the power to prevent future damage. George's refusal meant that the Fleet Street press capitalised on the fracas by labelling the monarch as 'Good, blunt, honest George,' and Franklin as the 'sharp-witted colonist.'

THE PRIORY CHURCH OF ST. BARTHOLEMEW THE GREAT, BARBICAN

Benjamin Franklin's grave in Christ Church Burial Ground, Philadelphia, is not adorned with the profound epitaphs that cover the graves of other Founders. Indeed, Hamilton's grave reads:

> To the memory of Alexander Hamilton. The corporation of Trinity Church has erected this monument in the testimony of their respect for the patriot of incorruptible integrity. The soldier of approved valour. The statesman of consummate wisdom; whose talents and virtues will be admired by grateful posterity long after this marble shall have mouldered into dust.

Meanwhile, Jefferson's is inscribed with, 'Author of the Declaration of Independence (and) of the Statute of Virginia for religious freedom & Father of the University of Virginia.' John Adams wanted his epitaph to read, 'Here lies John Adams who took upon himself the responsibility of peace with France in the year 1800'[8] – his desire was never fulfilled, something which would have assuredly delighted Hamilton to no avail. While Jefferson's is a little less ostentatious than Hamilton's, by comparison to both of them, Franklin's was unduly humble. Buried with Deborah, who died at Christmastime 1774 while he was in London, as per his wishes his epitaph simply states his first profession, 'Printer', followed by a witty elegy:

> Like the Cover of an old Book, Its Contents torn out, And stript of its Lettering and Gilding, Lies here, Food for Worms. But the Work shall not be wholly lost; For it will, as he believ'd, appear once more, In a new & more perfect Edition, Corrected and amended By the Author.

Recognising his now-deceased earthly form as 'food for worms', Franklin exhibited a humour not seen on Hamilton or Jefferson's tombs. To be fair, while Hamilton did not dictate his own epitaph, the Bostonian's is typically self-effacing, and facetiousness was, arguably, one of Franklin's defining characteristics; famously, after signing the Declaration of Independence, Franklin apparently said, "We must all hang together, or, most assuredly, we shall all hang separately."[9] At a time when most of the congressmen were agonising over whether their actions would result in liberty or death, Franklin was making execution jokes.

As illustrated by his tombstone, Ben Franklin was neither extremely religious nor serious. Living life as a Deist, he was not driven by religion as were some of his fellow countrymen, indeed he was viewed as extremely unorthodox and eccentric. One could argue that the fact that Franklin did not end up at Harvard training to join the clergy influenced his ability to approach science from a logical stance at a time when piety was still prevalent and puritanism literally ran through his veins; his aunt, Bethsheba Folger, was a major figure in the Salem Witch Trials and her accusations resulted in the execution of Martha Corey in 1692. Although not a staunchly religious man - he once said, 'A good example is the best sermon' - places of worship had been a constant throughout his life. He was born opposite the Old South Meeting House, a Congregational church founded by John Winthrop where the Boston Tea Party was partly organised in

1773. His father Josiah was also a well-known name in the Boston puritanical community and worked as a constable overseeing the tithingman (people who enforced church attendance). Like most Bostonians, the shadow of religion hanged heavy over Ben's life and the connection to religious hubs would not stop in London.

During Franklin's first visit to the city, he quickly found work as a compositor for master printer Samuel Palmer. Recalling the period in his autobiography, Franklin wrote, "I immediately got into work at Palmer's, then a famous printing house in Bartholomew Close and here I continued a year."[10] Palmer's was setup on the mezzanine of the Lady Chapel at The Priory Church of St Bartholomew the Great just off Cloth Fair in Smithfield. Now famous today for featuring in the 1994 film *Four Weddings and a Funeral*, Great St Bart's saw Franklin refine his already masterful skills, and aid with the printing of William Wollaston's second edition of the *Religion of Nature*.

After working for Palmer's for a year, Franklin scaled up to the bigger company of Watts's near Lincoln's Inn Fields. Describing Watt's as "still greater"[11] than his beloved Palmer's, the two-floor printing house in Wild Court would see Franklin experience significant othering from a number of the fifty-something workers. While working in the city he became known as the 'Water American' for his preference for water over ale. You couldn't blame the London workmen for choosing ale since there was a significant lack of clean water sources. Maybe Franklin's constitution could hold less-than-perfect water, or maybe he secretly discovered a clean water source for himself. Either way, his wholesome diet was mocked by his colleagues. While some tried his diet of porridge and water, others did not take kindly to his initial refusal to chip in for the price of the office ale. He was plagued by what he called 'a ghost' who would steal his ink from his desk and wreak havoc with his work. This mysterious form of blackmail stopped when he coughed up the shillings to pay for the boozy sustenance, he never himself drank.

COFFEE HOUSES

Rawthmell's Coffee House, Covent Garden | Pennsylvania Coffee House, Birchin Lane

In 1756, Franklin was made a member of the Royal Society. As a man who turned from slave owner to abolitionist; proved lightning to be electric, not divine; and who took such fervent interest in the furtherment of education, he illustrated the Enlightenment at its most potent moment. An integral facet of the Enlightenment movement was the coffee houses of London. Far more than places for refreshments, the coffee houses were social catalysts for change. Called Penny Universities for the wisdom they imparted sans the cost of a college education – and the beverages they provided for a mere penny - many were located in Covent Garden. Now a must-see place on vacation lists with a glorious market full of bars, restaurants, and designer shops, Covent Garden is a world away from its religious origins.

Previously a walled garden, possibly for monks or a convent – hence the etymological root of 'Covent' – a religious site had sat on the land since the Roman period. The embryotic design of the Covent Garden we know today was created in the 1630s by architect Inigo Jones. However, the area descended into poverty before Charles I committed to providing funds to gentrify the area. By the mid-seventeenth century, the arrival of the flower market attracted some of the city's undesirables. The year that Franklin arrived in London, a directory called *Harris's Book of Covent Garden Ladies* was first published. The creation of a guide to the prostitutes who frequented the area cemented the neighbourhood's reputation as a bawdy red-light district. Yet, despite the reputation, Covent Garden's brothels were frequented by some of the most illustrious figures in the upper echelons of society, including the brother of George III himself: William, Duke of Cumberland. William was a regular patron at the sumptuously decorated brothel of Jane Douglas, a madam who offered London's best prostitutes in a gilded setting and even provided contraception. Thus, as a result of its bawdy but liberal values, Covent Garden was known for its free-flowing thoughts. It was a place where one could meet with like-minded people to discuss ideas that were separate from the norm and erred away from the constraints of religion. As a result, a profusion of coffee houses sprang up.

The first coffee house in London was opened in 1652 by Pasqua Rosée. Rosée had worked as a servant for a British merchant in Turkey when he came across the dark, rich elixir which had been served in the Middle East for centuries. Exquisitely different from tea, Rosée began importing the bean to England where locals quickly developed a taste for the caffeine booster at his coffee house in the City of London. Rosée's idea quickly caught on and Britain became saturated with the establishments. By the early 1700s, there were around five hundred and fifty coffee houses in London. The Royal Society was born at Rawthmell's Coffee House on Henrietta Street before its permanent residence on John Adam Street was built in 1770. Thus, it's likely that Rawthmell's is one of a slew of establishments that saw Franklin interact with other key thinkers of the day on a cornucopia of topics including science, art, and, importantly, slavery. While it was to be another sixty or so years before Britain outlawed the Slave Trade, and another century before Abraham Lincoln issued the Emancipation Proclamation, abolitionist movements were already growing on both sides of the Atlantic. Although the concept of abolition was not a new idea, it was exacerbated by the Enlightenment period and succeeded in turning some people who had previously been involved in the trade into staunch anti-slavery campaigners: Benjamin Franklin was one of them.

Back in Philadelphia, Franklin's newspaper, the *Pennsylvania Gazette* had advertised slaves for sale. He also owned slaves himself and brought two to England with him: Peter, his own personal slave, and King, who was owned by William Franklin. King ran away while in London and was later found in the charge of a lady who was teaching him to read and write. While Britain was involved in the slave trade, it was not an unusual sight to see Black Britons on the streets of London - this possibly influenced King's decision to escape from the Franklins' ownership and seek his freedom. Although King was found, he was given his freedom and remained with the lady. Peter remained as Franklin's personal slave but was promised his freedom upon Franklin's death. Unfortunately, Franklin's longevity meant that Peter passed before the Founder.

After returning home in 1775, Franklin's actions began to shift and, if he had thought slavery an abhorrence beforehand, he was now turning those thoughts into deeds. Although he may never have lived up to the level of bigotry which is evidenced in a large cohort of his fellow Founders, he still partook in the facilitation of the slave trade, no matter how lenient he may have been towards the men he purchased. Famously, Franklin has been criticised for allowing the anti-slavery clause to be dropped from the Declaration of Independence in the hope that it would be adopted by the Continental Congress. Of course, the blame does not lie solely with him as the other members of the Committee of Five were also responsible for editing. Thomas Jefferson's original version of the declaration outlined in no uncertain terms George III's role in the transatlantic slave trade and attacked the institution as an abomination, describing it as an "assemblage of horrors."[12] Placing blame directly at the feet of the king, TJ had originally written:

> He has waged cruel war against human nature itself, violating its most sacred rights of life and liberty in the persons of a distant people who never offended him, captivating and carrying them into slavery in another hemisphere or to incur miserable death in their transportation thither.[13]

However, during the editing process, it was removed. In his autobiography, Jefferson explained the reason for doing so was two-fold. On one hand, they did not want to alienate the southern states who had shown no interest in eradicating slavery, and on the other, although they were not as heartily involved with the trade, the north relied on the institution of slavery for economic advancement:

> [The clause] reprobating the enslaving the inhabitants of Africa, was struck out in compliance to South Carolina and Georgia, who had never attempted to restrain the importation of slaves, and who on the contrary still wished to continue it. Our Northern brethren also I believe felt a little tender under these censures; for though their people have very few slaves themselves, yet they had been pretty considerable carries of them to others.[14]

Over the next decade, Franklin blossomed into an ardent abolitionist. Historians have suggested that his change of mind happened in London where he was not only influenced by the coffee houses, but also by Dr. Bray's school for Black children which Dr. Samuel Johnson – writer of the dictionary – took him to visit in 1758. Unlike Jefferson who, in his *Notes on The State of Virginia*, suggested that Black people were mentally inferior to White people, Franklin realised that the perceived lack of knowledge in Black people was not hereditary, but the result of poor education and terrible lives at the hands of bigotry. In 1787, at the age of eighty-one, he began his tenure as President of the Pennsylvania Society for Promoting the Abolition of Slavery. Franklin only had three more years to live but he dedicated the rest of his life to analysing the evils of slavery and petitioning for change. Benjamin Franklin's last act as a public servant was to send to congress a petition to end slavery. It was denied. However, it sparked a debate between pro and anti-slavery congressmen. Hamilton never owned slaves, was an abolitionist, and, despite growing up with slaves in her home, Eliza was also an anti-slavery proponent. Yet, like Franklin, his relationship with slavery is not clean-cut. Although he argued against slavery and belonged to the Manumission Society in New York (anti-slavery society founded by John Jay), he took some questionable actions in his life which would lead historians to question the bigger picture of Hamilton's relationship with slavery, including procuring slaves for Angelica and John Barker Church ready for their return from London.

While Covent Garden reigned supreme as the hub of coffee houses, a fair number also existed in the City of London, including the one frequented most often by Franklin with a rather fitting name: Pennsylvania Coffee House on Birchin Lane. By 1760, it was known as the Carolina and Pennsylvania Coffee House before dropping from records completely in 1822. It was from here that Franklin retrieved his mail from the American packets and scrawled off letters home. It seems that, before leaving America, Franklin was already familiar with the coffee house, informing his sister, Jane Mecom, to, "Direct your letters to be left for me at the Pennsylvania Coffee House in Birchin Lane, London."[15]

The wealth of figures Franklin wrote to from the Pennsylvania included Irish-born MP Edmund Burke. Burke held the seat for Wendover which John Barker Church would later represent. He was publicly critical of the government's actions towards the colonies and represented Hamilton's adopted home colony of New York in British parliament, however, he stopped short of supporting independence. Franklin wrote to him from the coffee house in December 1774 inviting him to meet his fellow North American agents at a meeting at Waghorn's Coffee House near the Houses of Parliament in Westminster. He also wrote to his printing business partner David Hall. He and Hall had a pecuniary arrangement which saw Hall handle the business while the retired Franklin received half of the profit, ensuring a comfortable life. More than anyone else though, he wrote to Deborah from the Pennsylvania, often composing a quick line to her before the next packet left for the coast. Like most of London's antique coffee houses, the original building no longer stands.

RIVER THAMES

In our collective public memory, we often think of Benjamin Franklin as the older man he was during the years that he achieved international prominence. Yet, in his younger years, he was still an exceptional man of learning, eccentricity, and physicality. During his time in London in the 1720s, he took up one of the loves he had nurtured since childhood in America: swimming. In Boston, he had shown glimpses of his future self when, at eleven years old, he created one of his first inventions: a pair of swimming fins made of two planks of wood which attached to the hands and allowed one to move faster in the water – a humanised fish for all intents and purposes. He also toyed with similar contraptions for the feet with less success. His feats in London and the U.S. led to him being posthumously inducted into the International Swimming Hall of Fame in 1968.

With the lack of swimming pools or, for many people, access to open swathes of water, swimming was not a widespread skill in eighteenth-century England, in fact, without correct tuition, it was – as it is today – an extremely hazardous pursuit. Yet, Franklin, taking advantage of the biggest vessel of water in his vicinity, took up swimming in London's River Thames. Wading into murky and unhygienic depths, the eighteen-year-old would swim around the curve of the Southbank from Chelsea to Blackfriars - one wonders how this excursion did not make the young American violently ill as the Thames was an extremely polluted water source. Although, by the time Franklin was in London the Thames had not even reached its most hazardous level, the events of the mid-nineteenth century illustrate the general extent of the Thames's unhygienic calibre.

For centuries, the river had been London's sewer - day after day the remnants of human waste thrown in the street would make its way to the Thames if it hadn't just been thrown in directly. By the sixteenth century, as the population grew, inroads had started to be made into creating specific sewer systems yet given the inadequacies of technology, these only worked so well. In summer 1858, London was plagued by an event called the Great Stink as the heat exacerbated the waste in the water. Not only was the city covered with an offensive odour, but outbreaks of cholera inundated the inhabitants. As a result of the Great Stink, the sewer systems known as the Victoria, Chelsea, and Albert Embankments were introduced by engineer Joseph Bazalgette who designed the intricate structure to improve the flow of sewage through the city and inhibit such toxication of the river. Interestingly, the Victoria Embankment runs along the bottom of Craven Street, thus during Franklin's time in London between 1757 and 1775, the river would have still been open at the bottom of the road. It is unknown whether he took up his old love of swimming during this time, yet one suspects that between his reading, dining, entertaining, and fighting for the rights of the colonies, swimming may have been put on the back burner – even though by the time Franklin arrived in London the second time, swimming pools had started to open.

As a young man, however, Franklin's swimming exploits had amazed Londoners and the tales of the young printer's aquatic skill reached the ears of some of the capital's most important figures. Having already taught one of his colleagues, a fellow printer called Wygate, to swim in only a few hours, Ben received further offers from men of stature. Recalling in his autobiography:

> A Sir William Wyndham...had heard by some means or other of my swimming from Chelsea to Blackfriars, and of my teaching Wygate and another young man to swim in a few hours. He had two sons, about to set out on their travels; he wished to have them first taught swimming, and proposed to gratify me handsomely if I would teach them.[16]

Sir William Wyndham – whom Franklin described as a "great man"[17] - had served in the illustrious roles of Secretary of War and Chancellor of the Exchequer. Even so, he declined the offer to become a swimming instructor. However, always one to consider pecuniary advantages, he pondered that, "I thought it likely, that if I were to remain in England and open a Swimming School, I might get a good deal of money; and it struck me so strongly that, had the overture been sooner made me, probably I should not so soon have returned to America."[18] Interestingly, this watery prowess could have been an area where the sage and Alexander Hamilton could have bonded had they not been fifty-odd years apart in age because, unlike many other Americans, Hamilton *could* swim. In 1777, he escaped an ambush along the Schuylkill River in Pennsylvania by swimming across it. His mortality had been assumed and when the young soldier turned up at Washington's camp, tired and dripping, his comrades were shocked as news of his death had already reached them.

ST. GEORGE'S CHURCH, HANOVER SQUARE

In the fall of 1762, Benjamin Franklin was crossing the Atlantic on his only journey home to Philadelphia during his London residence. Onboard, he was likely gathering evidence for the Gulf Stream which he was the chart seven years later in 1769. An issue back in London was likely keeping him occupied as well. He had left the city saddened and frustrated. His son, on the other hand, had stayed behind and was getting married. While this would usually be a joyous occasion for any father to see their son establish a family, Franklin was disappointed in William's choice of bride. He had desperately wanted William to marry Polly Stevenson, but the younger Franklin had chosen a fellow colonist as his new wife. On September 4, William married his first wife, Elizabeth Downes, at St. George Hanover Square - a beautiful Anglican church a ten-minute walk east of Grosvenor Square which, a century later, saw the wedding of future-president Theodore Roosevelt to Edith Kermit Carrow.

The youngest of three children, Elizabeth Downes was an heiress born in Barbados to a once-prosperous sugar planter called John Downes. Although not the richest heiress, and not the most sought-after spinster because of it, upon her father's death she inherited £1,200 (£357,432/$492,878), a yearly £70 (£14,717/$20,293) stipend, and two female slaves.

St. George's Church, Hanover Square.

By the time William married Elizabeth, he was already a father. Like his father before him, he had conceived an illegitimate son with an unknown mother in London. Named after his father and the Inn of Court where he had studied, William Temple Franklin was acknowledged and adopted by William senior after a period of living in foster care.

The wedding was a fracture in Ben and William's relationship which would only grow. While in London, William was named as the successor to Josiah Hardy in the post of Governor of New Jersey. He would be the last in the role to be appointed by the Crown. William would remain loyal to the king and was even imprisoned by the Americans during the Revolutionary War. Franklin disowned him but that did not stop suspicions growing within the older Franklin's circle towards his true alliances. After the Revolution, William Franklin fled into self-imposed exile in England. Father and son attempted to reconcile a number of times; however, no lasting stable relationship was ever formed again. The pair last saw each other when the elder Franklin briefly stopped in Britain during his journey home from France in 1785. William ended his days impoverished in Marylebone and is buried in St. Pancras Old Church in north London. Sadly, during the building of the neighbouring railway lines, the headstone was moved, and the location of his remains is unknown.

WESTMINSTER

Westminster Abbey | The Palace of Westminster

If one were to list all the figures whom they thought may have attended George III's coronation, Benjamin Franklin would be unlikely to crop up. However, the only man who signed all four documents which facilitated the creation of the United States

(Declaration of Independence 1776; Treaty of Alliance, Amity, and Commerce with France, 1778; Treaty of Paris, 1783; the United States Constitution, 1789) joined the throngs of people lining the streets outside the abbey to witness the emergence of the newly coronated monarch. William bagged himself a seat inside which George Goodwin suggests could have been a sign of successful social climbing in the city, a project which he had worked on since early in their visit and had nurtured during his tenure at the prestigious Middle Temple at the Inns of Court.

Being in London when King George II died on October 25, 1760, Benjamin Franklin would have known of the monarch's death months in advance of his countrymen across the Atlantic. George had outlived his first heir, Frederick, Prince of Wales, who died in 1751, and overlooked his next surviving son, Prince George William, as a potential heir. Thus, the line of succession skipped to his grandson, the future George III. The twenty-two-year-old George was coronated at Westminster Abbey on September 22, 1761. Steeped in tradition, the ceremony was an ostentatious display of British monarchy. George and his new wife, Princess Charlotte of Mecklenburg-Strelitz, whom he had only married two weeks earlier, proceeded through the streets on sedan chairs before entering the abbey for a six-hour-long ceremony where they were crowned, and George was anointed by the Archbishop of Canterbury.

Benjamin and William had made plans to travel in Europe immediately before the coronation date and the elder Franklin's anxiety to return to London in time for the ceremony is evident in letters written to Deborah: "We shall therefore, having little to do at present, set out in a few days for Harwich and possibly may take a trip over to Holland, but purpose to be again in London, God willing, before the coronation."[19] He even set out his plans to Polly, telling her that he had strategically planned when to travel to ensure he saw George III crowned. Polly and Margaret themselves also likely watched the parade from a nearby home, as opposed to inside like the haughty William, as Polly apologised to Franklin in

September 1761 for not writing for a while, "My mother wanted me to write another letter to you while I was with her, but my time was so taken up with seeking for places at the coronation that I had not leisure during my stay."[20]

While it seems a bizarre turn of history that the Founder made a robust effort to see the new king crowned, standing in the dirty, people-filled streets, the event represents a key facet of Franklin's beliefs and aims early in his mission. Benjamin Franklin was born in British America and spent three-quarters of his life as a proud Briton. Prior to the Revolution, America was not seen as 'international', rather as an extension of British land, albeit four thousand miles away. When Franklin originally arrived in Britain in the late 1750s, his disillusionment with Pennsylvania's proprietors caused him to eventually seek a royal alternative. Eight of the other thirteen colonies - Georgia, Massachusetts, New Hampshire, New Jersey, New York, North Carolina, South Carolina, and Virginia - were Royal Colonies under the direct rule of George II. Franklin, eager to find a solution to the colony's problems, wanted Pennsylvania to join them.

His strategy to see Pennsylvania escape from the deleterious hands of its proprietors never succeeded, yet his initial determination to see the colony comforted by a king illustrates the robust change in Franklin by 1775. Arriving before the end of the French and Indian War, no one could have foreseen the future for America. As is evidenced by his elongated stay, the problems that Franklin was originally in the city to address burgeoned into a wider issue of taxation in the colonies, rebellion, an intellectual and ideological battle between America and its mother country, and, eventually, all-out war. Indeed, as his role in Britain morphed from diplomat negotiating at a local level to America's representative during the War of Independence, his loyalties changed too. As he pushed back against the slew of acts passed in parliament during his time in England - the Sugar Act (1764), the Currency Act (1764), the Quartering Act (1765), the Stamp Act (1765), and the Townsend

Acts (1767) - he made enemies of people he once nurtured working relationships with.

The nail in the coffin for Franklin was the Hutchinson Letter Affair and the fallout from the Boston Tea Party. The Hutchinson Affair had roots in the colonies as far back as the late 1760s when letters were exchanged between Thomas Hutchinson, Governor of the Province of Massachusetts Bay who now lived on Sackville Street, Andrew Oliver, the Lieutenant Governor, and Thomas Whately, an MP. The correspondence concerned the outbreak of hostilities in the colonies and how to respond to it. Through a convoluted series of events which involved the letters changing hands several times after Whatley's death, the parchments somehow ended up on the doorstep of 36 Craven Street. Upon reading the correspondence, Franklin found evidence that Hutchinson and Oliver were suggesting the implementation of repressive measures, including sending more troops to the colonies. He thought that the two men were misleading parliament over the events in America and sent the packet to the Massachusetts Assembly with the order that they could be shown to other assembly members but not directly published. Yet, although the assembly sought to follow Franklin's direction, inevitable leaks to the press ensured that the letters' content was soon public knowledge. They were finally published in full in the *Boston Gazette* in summer 1773. The back-and-forth over who sent the letters to the Massachusetts Assembly toiled on and even led to a duel in London's Hyde Park in December 1773 between two men: William Whately (Thomas's brother who had handled his possessions following his death) and the man who Whately accused, John Temple. Neither was satisfied - even though the duel wasn't bloodless as Whately was wounded - and both demanded another chance to defend their honour. To avoid further bloodshed, or even death, Franklin publicly announced on Christmas Day in the *London Chronicle* that he was responsible for the letters:

Finding that two gentlemen have been unfortunately engaged in a duel, about a transaction and its circumstances of which both of them are totally ignorant and innocent, I think it incumbent on me to declare (for the prevention of farther mischief, as far as such a declaration may contribute to prevent it) that I alone am the person who obtained and transmitted to Boston the letters in question. Mr. W. could not communicate them, because they were never in his possession; and, for the same reason, they could not be taken from him by Mr. T. They were not of the nature of "private letters between friends:" They were written by public officers to persons in public station, on public affairs, and intended to procure public measures; they were therefore handed to other public persons who might be influenced by them to produce those measures: Their tendency was to incense the Mother Country against her colonies, and, by the steps recommended, to widen the breach, which they effected. The chief caution expressed with regard to privacy, was, to keep their contents from the colony agents, who the writers apprehended might return them, or copies of them, to America. That apprehension was, it seems, well founded; for the first Agent who laid his hands on them, thought it his duty to transmit them to his constituents.[21]

There was an outcry in the British government, yet unbeknownst to anyone, far more controversial news was steaming its way across the Atlantic: nine days earlier on December 16, the 'Destruction of the Tea', as John Adams called it, had taken place at Griffin's Wharf in Boston, Massachusetts. Spurred in part by the content of the Hutchinson letters, when news of the Boston Tea Party reached British shores on January 20, Franklin was again under the spotlight and called to the Privy Council. As a representative of America, he was accused of treason against the crown and given a thorough, public dressing down. Within the space of a few weeks, he had turned from nuisance to Public Enemy Number One in the eyes of Lord North's Tory government. Furthermore, Franklin himself had cemented in his own mind his re-birth as one of America's staunchest defenders of - and fighter for - independence. However, he was to stay in London for another year.

In the final few months of his stay, Franklin visited the Houses of Parliament to hear his friend, William Pitt the Elder, deliver one of his last speeches, fittingly on American independence. During the debate, as Franklin watched on, he was publicly demonised by Lord Sandwich, First Lord of the Admiralty, and his boss in the role of Postmaster General, who labelled the Founder as "One of the bitterest and most mischievous enemies (Britain) had ever known."[22] There was no making his way back into British affection now as any hopes of rapprochement floated away like the some three hundred and forty-two chests worth of tea in Boston Harbour. An excellent litmus test to measure the gelid feeling towards Franklin in his final months would be the *Times* newspaper article which translated America's – and thus Franklin's – treason into biblical proportions: rendering Mrs. Stevenson's opulent lodging house with its fourteen Italian Carrera marble fireplaces and plethora of servants into a den of sin, they designated it as 'Judas's office in Craven Street.'

Franklin left London on March 20, 1775, never to return to the city where he had spent almost a fifth of his life fighting for America.

Although more of a peripheral figure in the life of Alexander Hamilton, Benjamin Franklin was nonetheless a God-like elder the young politician possessed deep admiration for. At the Constitutional Convention, Hamilton honoured Franklin by seconding the sage's motion that those in the executive branch would have their expenses covered but receive "no salary, stipend fee or reward whatsoever"[23], though nothing came of this proposal.

Interestingly, Franklin's grandson, Benjamin Bache, detested Hamilton and founded the Jeffersonian newspaper the *Philadelphia*

Aurora, in which the treasury secretary was regularly admonished. However, that is not a reflection of Franklin's views on Hamilton, of which none really exist. Although both were Founding Fathers, Hamilton and Franklin's careers drove in two very different directions. While Hamilton had a one-track mind which focused on building the new government, Franklin's thoughts covered a multitude of subjects: science, philosophy, civics, humour, writing - he had a finger in every pie. Resultingly, the two did not cross paths often. Franklin also spent most of the war and Confederation Period in Europe as the first United States Minister to France, a position he held from 1779 to 1785. In fact, Lin-Manuel Miranda often sites Franklin's impressive curriculum vitae for his lack of presence in the musical, suggesting that it would have taken the show on several tangents and overwhelmed the crux of the story.

While Franklin and Hamilton passed almost like ships in the night through the Revolutionary and Confederation periods, since Franklin is remembered as a frontal figure in the American Revolution - despite never holding office in the executive branch or in the cabinet - his trail in London is worth noting.

Moreover, who's to know how large a part Franklin would have played in Hamilton's life had he lived. Alexander's actions in seconding the sage's quixotic motion at the Constitutional Convention may provide a small insight into how that relationship might have played out. Although Franklin warned against divisive political parties at the convention, noting that they would only serve to create factions in society, weaken the American cause, and create enemies within groups of Americans who were once brothers-in-arms, his political position - although an Independent - erred on the side of Federalism. The old Bostonian may have continued to have been a guiding hand for the rambunctious, young politician - especially in the aftermath of the convention and the dawn of the presidency as politicians butted heads over the correct path for the country, and Hamilton fought to keep eyes focused on the Constitution's sentiments. Hamilton may well have benefitted from heeding Franklin's facetious outlook on the Constitution, writing in 1789 he noted, "Our new Constitution is now established, everything seems to promise it will be durable; but, in this world, nothing is certain except death and taxes."

CHAPTER FIVE

———————

BENEDICT & PEGGY ARNOLD

In May 1781, the Marquis de Lafayette received a letter from his friend, Benjamin Franklin, in which the elderly statesmen summed up the sentiments of Patriots everywhere towards the turncoat Benedict Arnold: "Judas only sold one man, Arnold sold three millions."[1] For those who believed in the glorious cause, Arnold's treason was of biblical proportions, and rightly so, he had just carried out one of the greatest acts of betrayal in history. Indeed, had Arnold been successful, who knows what the world would look like today.

Benedict Arnold was, prior to 1780, one of the Continental Army's shining generals. He fought courageously and led his men in the Capture of Fort Ticonderoga, an offence which seriously weakened the British and allowed the Patriots to use the Anglo weapons to re-secure Boston. In October 1777, he led a winning charge at the Battle of Saratoga - a stunning turn in the Revolutionary War which, for the first time, showed that the Americans did have sufficient power to defeat the British. Resultingly, France publicly acknowledged America as an independent country. During the adrenaline-filled throws of battle, Arnold was shot in the leg. Wounded in the line of fire, the historian Joyce Lee Malcolm has said of Benedict Arnold that, had he died in the Battle at Saratoga, he would have been remembered as one of America's greatest heroes and an enduring patriot. However, Arnold did not die from the leg wounds he received, instead he went on to betray his country and forever sentence his name to synonymy with treachery.

Born in Connecticut on January 14, 1741, Arnold was a young man when the first shots were fired at Lexington and Concord, yet his rise to military prowess within Washington's ranks somewhat parallels Alexander Hamilton's. Like the boy from St. Croix, Arnold showed such valour and promise at a young age that he was appointed to the rank of major general and personally placed in charge of the army's most strategic fortress, West Point, by General Washington. Today, West Point is a military academy which includes President Eisenhower, Union Army General Custer, Confederate General Robert E. Lee, and astronauts Buzz Aldrin and Michael Collins among its alumni. Described by Washington as "the most important post in America,"[2] the logistical position of West Point along the Hudson River, approximately sixty miles north of New York City, marked it as the most valuable post for the Continental Army in the War of Independence as it allowed the Patriots to control the Hudson and thus inhibit the spread of British power. If West Point fell, the fate of independence would hang precariously in the balance, a fact that was more than evident to Arnold.

During the war, Arnold performed heroically. Not only did he seize Fort Ticonderoga, but he had shown gallantry from the start when he was a member of the Sons of Liberty and personally formed a militia following the fighting at Lexington and Concord - actions which he thought merited trust and accolades. Yet, when the Continental Army invaded Quebec in 1775, despite it being, in part,

West Point, from Phillipstown. W. J. Bennett, 1831.

Arnold's brainchild, Washington gave the command to Hamilton's future father-in-law, Philip Schuyler. Arnold, suffering wounded pride after he had risked his life to annex Ticonderoga - and provided a massive payoff for the Patriots by doing so - was riled by Schuyler's appointment to the top job. Thus, he convinced Washington to allow a second expedition to Quebec. However, the plan was stifled by major hiccups as Arnold suggested invading via the Canadian wilderness, a terrain that is hazardous by twenty-first-century standards. When the two expeditions rendezvoused, they suffered a calamitous defeat at the Battle of Quebec, which saw eighty-four men killed and four hundred and thirty-one captured. One of the expedition's leaders, Robert Montgomery, was killed and his aide-de-camp - a young soldier from New Jersey called Aaron Burr – tried, and failed, to repatriate his body to American lines.

Despite his faults, Arnold felt his patriotism and actions within the army were not getting the recognition they deserved. By spring 1779, he was also irked by the court-martial he received – and was later acquitted of – for spending beyond his means. Unlike his comrade Hamilton, who, in later years when riled, would adopt a pen name and let off some steam in a newspaper, the indignant Arnold decided to succour his vengeance by switching sides.

In 1779, Arnold married Margaret 'Peggy' Shippen, a Philadelphia-born socialite whose Loyalist father had studied at the Middle Temple in London. Two years prior, in the fall of 1777, the British had begun an eight-month occupation of Philadelphia, and Peggy met a dashing young British soldier named John André. Legend has it that Peggy and André may have been enmeshed in a romantic relationship, however, evidence to support the claims remains lacklustre. Yet, the two forged a strong friendship and kept up correspondence throughout the next three years. By the time Arnold was becoming disillusioned by his treatment in Washington's forces, André was far more than his wife's friend – he was General George Clinton's head of British spy operations in America. He was also Arnold's only real hope of carrying out a treacherous plan the American hero had been concocting.

By the time Arnold took over the command of West Point in the August of 1780, he had already been discreetly sending juicy titbits to the British side outlining strategic information, such as troop posts. By the following month, Arnold's conversion into America's Iscariot was complete and he was ready to hand West Point over to the British via Peggy's very debonair connection.

On September 20, 1780, the banks of the Hudson River transformed into the Garden of Gethsemane as André travelled north on the British sloop *Vulture* to meet with Arnold. At first, André's crossing into American lines went unnoticed. The next morning, however, saw heavy musket fire rain down on the ship after it was spotted resting on the waves. Arnold sent out a small boat with three men - all unaware of his plan and told they were carrying out actions in the American interest - to rescue André from the sloop and deliver him to the west bank near Stony Point. There, on the muddy ridge next to water, André's American counterpart sold West Point for £20,000 (£3.67 million/$5 million today) and the promise of a British military command.

After believing he had sealed the fate of America, Arnold had to smuggle André back to the British as the *Vulture* had rescinded back downstream. Dressing him as a civilian and providing false passes, the plan seemed somewhat foolproof and almost modern in its use of counterfeit documentation, yet Arnold could not control what André might say himself. Travelling across enemy territory, the British general encountered a group of Patriot soldiers whom he mistook for Loyalists and subsequently outed himself as a redcoat; the Americans famously found the all-important detailed plans of their West Point fortress hidden in his stockings and boots.

Washington and his aides, including Hamilton, hearing of André's capture but unaware of Arnold's involvement, hot-footed it to the turncoat's home to discuss the event which almost cost them the war. At this point, Arnold was not under suspicion and the visit was purely procedural as a member of the inner circle of Washington's forces. Yet, what awaited them at Arnold's house was worlds away from their wildest dreams. On arrival, they discovered the turncoat had fled to British lines, leaving nothing but a mass of evidence that pointed to his undeniable treason. Peggy - now accepted to have been a key component in Arnold's treason for her role connecting him to André - had remained at the home but disappeared upstairs and collapsed in perceived hysteria claiming that Hamilton and co were there to kill her baby; Hamilton described the incident as "the most affecting scene I ever was witness to."[3] Twenty years Benedict's junior, she was, at the time, believed to have been innocent of her husband's misdemeanours and was even given a pass by Washington to return home to her family in Philadelphia.

On her way to Pennsylvania, Peggy stopped at a mansion in New Jersey called the Hermitage, owned by one Theodosia Provost - the future wife of Aaron Burr and current wife of Jacques Marcus Provost, a British officer. According to Burr's memoirs, Peggy confessed to Theodosia her role in the plot, which many historians take to be truthful. Despite the major players in Washington's cabinet thinking Burr a perfidious man, writing of this tale years later would have had no significant benefit for Burr, thus historians accept his account of the event and support his story with the fact that George III later issued Peggy with a £500 ($121,165/£87,600 in today's money) stipend per annum, marking her as the highest-paid British spy of the American Revolution.

LONDON

In early December 1781, the Arnolds braved a winter Atlantic crossing and sailed for England. The British surrender at Yorktown only two months prior had exacerbated Arnold's desire to flee the states, which was evident as far back as his inaugural days at West Point when he had started to slowly trickle his assets to England. Settling in London, Benedict soon attempted to ingratiate himself in some kind of service to the British establishment. He aspired to work for the East India Company, or even become an advisor to George III, whom he had already pestered to re-spark the war in America. However, Arnold was looked upon as untrustworthy. Despite fighting for the British, he was deemed a man who would turn his foot and walk in the other direction as soon as he was wronged or unappreciated. In short, the government did not want a petulant child heading integral facets of their trade or military institutions. With London falling short of Arnold's expectations, after three years in the city, he, and his eldest son with his first wife, Richard, moved to Saint John, New Brunswick, where they involved themselves with trade with the West Indies. In 1786, Peggy and the rest of his family traversed back west and landed in Saint John to join their patriarch. But their time in New Brunswick soon turned as sour as their jaunt in London. Following a flurry of inopportune business and dissension with a former business partner, the Arnolds returned to

England after effigies of the turncoat were burned in the streets. As in America and Europe, Arnold, it seemed, was trusted by no one.

---

62 GLOUCESTER PLACE, MARYLEBONE

In 1791, the Arnolds returned to London. From 1796 to 1801, they lived at 62 Gloucester Place in the illustrious W1 postcode. Located a few blocks back from Oxford Street in the affluent Marylebone neighbourhood, the Georgian townhouse the treacherous family inhabited is presently a private dentist surgery. As Benedict quietly whiled away his final years after yet another chaotic period in his life - amongst other things, he was imprisoned by suspicious French forces in the Caribbean during the early years of the French Revolution, and he duelled with a British politician - the most scandalous Arnold-related event to happen at 62 Gloucester Place would be posthumous.

In 1987, a cast iron plaque dedicated to Arnold was erected on the side of the house. One may question the extent of the planning committee's eighteenth-century history knowledge as the plaque, which features both the Union Flag and the Stars and Stripes, reads:

> Major General Benedict Arnold, American patriot, resided here 1796 until his death June 14, 1801.

The plaque's insinuation that the epitome of a traitor was an American patriot went unnoticed for decades, aside from by those American history boffins or any U.S. tourists who found themselves in the backstreets of Marylebone. In 2014, however, that all changed when the then-American Ambassador to the UK, Matthew Barzun, asked for help investigating why the plaque was so historically inaccurate. After careful investigation, it appeared the provenance of the plaque was a Mr. Peter Arnold living in East London. Peter had found a distant ancestral link to Benedict while creating his family tree and began researching the turncoat's history. Enthralled by the story of the Son of Liberty-turned-traitor, Peter had first proposed the plaque to English Heritage in 1984 but the idea was swiftly denied. Instead, Peter Arnold took his request directly to Westminster City Council who were responsible for the plaque's creation.

Still, that did not answer why America's foremost traitor is labelled a patriot. It seems that Peter felt that Benedict was misunderstood. Speaking to NBC News, Peter said:

> His heart was in America, and he felt that what he was doing was in the interest of America as a country and the people who lived there. And at the end of the day, he didn't think we should be divorced from England and the king, so somebody loved us![4]

Unsurprisingly, Americans didn't share the sentiment. So much so, that Peter even started to receive death threats about the plaque, which had been up for over twenty-five years before it gained any widespread recognition.

Following Arnold's death, Peggy downsized drastically to the nearby Bryanston Street. Writing that she was "living in a very small house on Bryanston Street using furniture purchased from Carlow,"[5] she possessed worries that her more affluent friends in London society would refuse to be seen in such circumstances. However, it appears that her fears were soon alleviated as she happily reported there was "no reluctance in my friends in a superior line, to visiting me here."[6] Obviously, the duty she had done for England outweighed her meagre circumstances in the eyes of her illustrious social circle.

ST. MARY'S CHURCH, BATTERSEA

By early 1801, many around Arnold saw the old soldier growing ill and frail. He died of suspected oedema in June of the same year and Peggy followed him in 1804 after developing what is thought to have been cancer. They are buried together in St. Mary's Church in Battersea, West London. Their graves are not in the churchyard but beneath the church in a small crypt which is also used for the St. Mary's playschool. Bizarrely, while the children spend their day colouring, making friends, and learning, Benedict and Peggy lay at peace in a visible tomb next to a tropical fish tank. Their daughter, Sophia Matilda Phipps, is also with them.

In the main church is a stained-glass window dedicated to the building's Anglo-American connections, it features a profile of Arnold flanked by the Stars and Stripes and the Union Flag. The tomb itself has also attempted to resolve Arnold's life with a silver-lining – however, one does not think that it would have received the same homage in the United States – by highlighting the fact that the two countries he served are now enmeshed in a Special Relationship:

> Benedict Arnold, 1741-1801, Sometime general in the army of George Washington. The two nations whom he served in turn in the years of their enmity have united in enduring friendship.

Just under three miles away from Arnold's final resting place, his partner in crime, John André, lies in Westminster Abbey. The captured André was hanged in Tappan, New York, on October 2, 1780, and his remains were buried nearby. His execution was witnessed by Hamilton, who disagreed with General Washington on the fate that befell the twenty-nine-year-old soldier. Watching André climb the gallows and tighten the noose around his own neck, Hamilton felt it too extreme a punishment. For sure, he was a British general, but he had not betrayed his side as Arnold had done. After watching André's body swinging in the breeze, he penned a description of his death which one imagines was exactly what Hamilton would have wanted said of him had the roles been reversed – reminding those who read it of the bravery of the man in question.

> In going to the place of execution he bowed familiarly as he went along to all those with whom he had been acquainted in his confinement a smile of complacency expressed the serene fortitude of his mind…Upon being told the final moment was at hand and asked if he had anything to say he answered nothing but to request you will witness to the world that I die like a brave man.[7]

John André.

In 1821, Prince Frederick, Duke of York, ordered that André's body be exhumed and shipped to England. Legend has it that he was buried with a peach a lady had given to him as he made his journey to the gallows. Indeed, the roots of a peach tree had pierced André's coffin and the tree itself was dug up and taken along with him. Today, it is planted in the King's garden at the back of the grand Carlton House on the Mall.

In Westminster Abbey, André's remains are at rest in a large trunk. There is also a separate ostentatious marble monument erected in 1782 and paid for by George III with the inscription:

> Sacred to the memory of Major Jon André, who raised by his merit at an early period of life to the rank of Adjutant General of the British Forces in America, and employed in an important but hazardous enterprise fell a sacrifice to his zeal for his king and country on the 2nd of October AD 1780 Aged 29, universally beloved and esteemed by the army in which he served and lamented even by his foes. His gracious sovereign King George the Third has caused this monument to be erected.

André was venerated in Westminster Abbey, yet a visitor to the site soon after the monument was unveiled did not have quite the same outlook. During his tour of London in 1783, John Quincy Adams complained:

> I own I was struck with awe and veneration, at finding myself on the spot, where lay the remains of the greatest part of the sages, and heroes, which Great-Britain has produced, but I felt a painful sensation, at seeing a superb monument, erected to Major André, to reflect how much degenerated that nation must be, which can find no fitter objects for so great an honour, than a spy, than a man whose sad catastrophe, was owing to his unbounded ambition, and whose only excuse for his conduct, was his youth; as if

youth, gave a man the right to commit wicked and contemptible actions.[8]

Decidedly placed within the foe category in this anthology, Benedict and Peggy Arnold had the power to alter the history of the west forever and very nearly achieved it. Although they ventured back to North America after leaving the U.S., and their list of London links is not extensive, for seekers of Revolutionary traitors, Gloucester Place and St. Mary's Battersea are spots of pilgrimage. Not only had Hamilton known Arnold within Washington's coterie, but his arrival at the Arnold household following Benedict's flight and his subsequent witness to Peggy's faux hysteria links him inextricably to the unfolding of Arnold's treachery and, as a result, his consequential move to London.

CHAPTER SIX

JOHN JAY

John Jay is among the seven names that historian Richard B. Morris designated as the central Founding Fathers. Arguably though, he doesn't necessarily rank in the minds of Americans as being among the likes of Washington and Jefferson, but, then again, for over two centuries, neither did Alexander Hamilton. Like Hamilton, Jay is one of only three Founders on Morris's list that didn't ascend to the presidency. And, like Hamilton, and Benjamin Franklin, he held a number of influential positions within government for which he doesn't necessarily get credit for, including the Secretary of State, Governor of New York, and, most memorably, the first Chief Justice of the Peace. For the lovers of the musical, Jay is remembered as a part of the trio who wrote the Federalist Papers but suffered an attack of rheumatism meaning he could write only five, while Hamilton wrote fifty-one. Yet, his role in the making of the new nation was far more profound than that, especially in terms of the part he played in ensuring a continued peace with Britain in the two decades after independence was declared.

Born in New York City, John Jay's family had only recently arrived in America. His grandfather, Augustus Jay, washed up in the colonies as a French Huguenot immigrant in the late 1680s before expanding his family of wealthy merchants, including Jay's father, Peter. On his mother's side, he was Dutch and Belgian with his ancestors having lived in New Amsterdam. In 1774, Jay married Sarah Van Brugh Livingston, daughter of William Livingston: signer of the U.S. Constitution and succeeder of William Franklin as the first Governor of New Jersey in the new republic. Sarah's great-grandmother was Alida Schuyler van Rensselear, the sister of Eliza Hamilton's great-grandfather Johannes Schuyler, making the two wives of America's pre-eminent Founding Fathers third cousins by blood and relations by marriage through the Van Rensselear line.

Like Hamilton, Jay had attended King's College in New York and graduated in 1764. Entering the profession of law like nearly all other Founders, Jay founded his own practice in New York and started to involve himself in civil cases. As his juridical star grew, he served in both the First and Second Continental Congresses and supported the Declaration of Independence despite at first pursuing rapprochement and co-authoring the 1775 Olive Branch Petition along with John Dickinson, John Rutledge, Jefferson, and Franklin. The petition was quickly rebuffed by George III.

In another link between Hamilton and Jay, despite serving in the congress, Jay did not sign the Declaration of Independence as he had been recalled to New York. Similarly, Hamilton, like Washington, is not inked at the bottom of the parchment as both men were fighting in New York in July 1776. Although neither soldier was a delegate to the Continental Congress at that time (Washington had been from 1774 to 1775), many expect to see their names amongst the fifty-six signatures.

At the close of the Revolutionary War, Jay was instrumental in negotiating the Treaty of Paris. Alongside Franklin, Adams, and Henry Laurens, Jay would make contacts and procure a holistic knowledge of the treaty during this period which would be beneficial over a decade later when he would be sent to London to halt an Anglo-American war.

LONDON

On the evening of April 15, 1794, John Jay sat down after an exhausting day at court in Philadelphia to write to Sarah at home in New York:

> I expect, my dear Sally, to see you sooner than we expected. There is here a serious determination to send me to England, if possible, to avert a war. The object is so interesting to our country, and the combination of circumstances such, that I find myself in a dilemma between personal considerations and public ones. Nothing can be much more distant from every wish on my own account. I feel the impulse of duty strongly, and it is probable that if, on the investigation I am now making, my mind should be convinced that it is my duty to go, you will join with me in thinking that, on an occasion so important, I ought to follow its dictates, and commit myself to the care and kindness of that providence in which we have both the highest reason to repose the most absolute confidence. This is not of my seeking; on the contrary, I regard it as a measure not to be desired, but to be submitted to.[1]

Over the decade since the Treaty of Paris had been signed, the relationship between Britain and America had been growing into an obvious crescendo of discontent. As hard as John Adams had fought to woo Britain into friendship with his beloved U.S., and display attentive courtesy towards the king and court, outside the gates of

St. James's Palace, the real Anglo-American relationship was crumbling. From American eyes, Britain was not adhering to the terms agreed upon in the Treaty of Paris. It seemed almost as if Britain was agitating for war by being intentionally belligerent towards trade, which caused issues with establishing a stable U.S. economy. The export-import relationship between Britain and the U.S. was vital for both countries. America had the raw goods, meanwhile, Britain had the factories to turn those materials into products needed in the United States and around the world. In a true Hamiltonian fashion, the treasury secretary had attempted to massage American industry and gradually withdraw the U.S.'s reliance on British industry by stealing secrets from British manufacturers by procuring workers to move to America - passage paid - if they brought industry secrets along with them; however, the Industrial Revolution could not be mirrored across the Atlantic, meaning that the dependent trade relationship between the U.S. and Britain continued. In fact, nearly a century later when the American Civil War took place between 1861 and 1865, Queen Victoria allowed Confederate ships to be built in Liverpudlian shipyards, so extreme was her concern of a Union triumph which would mean an extreme decrease in the amount of cotton entering British factories.

By spring 1794, the tension between America and Britain was reaching a breaking point. Jay, inclined to believe that this would only be a cold war, but preparedness never hurt anyone, wrote to Sarah, "I am rather inclined to think that peace will continue, but should not be surprised if war should take place. In the present state of things, it will be best to be ready for the latter event in every respect."[2] Three days after his April 15 letter, the Senate confirmed Jay's mission to England. All but three senators voted for his election, one of them was Aaron Burr. President Washington bestowed upon him his new ostentatious title of Envoy Extraordinary from the United States of America to the Court of His Britannic Majesty, but Jay mourned to Sally that "No appointment ever operated more unpleasantly upon me."[3] As Jay was preparing to leave America, on May 12 he received further correspondence from Washington who asked him to consider remaining in London to succeed Thomas Pinckney as the Minister Plenipotentiary. The minister to France, Gouverneur Morris – who would eulogize at Hamilton's funeral - was returning to America and Washington hoped to replace him with Pinckney. Eventually, none of these appointments were ever made as Jay turned down Washington's offer to take up a permanent role in London. Having already written reams of ululating sighs to Sarah outlining his disdain at having to undertake the short mission, becoming minister plenipotentiary was not an offer Jay considered at length. Washington requested that if Jay decided to take up the role, he simply send the letter back to him, instead, the reply returned to Mount Vernon came with refusal but also a request to remain in service as the Chief Justice of the United States.

Landing at Falmouth on June 8 accompanied by his son Peter and Colonel John Trumball (the painter acting in an administrative capacity as Jay's secretary for the trip), Jay carried with him the weight of America, and a six-point list of instructions from Secretary of State Edmund Randolph. Opening with instructions to explain his specialised appointment to Pinckney as to avoid hurting the minister's sensibilities, Randolph enumerates the rest of the commands:

One: To air grievances with the British about trade. Moreover, Randolph mentions the topic of Francophilia in America:

> If the British ministry should hint at any supposed predilection in the United States for the French nation, as warranting the whole or any part of these instructions, you will stop the progress of this subject, as being irrelative to the question in hand. It is a circumstance which the British nation have no right to object to us; because we are free in our affections and independent in our government.[4]

Two: To draw to a conclusion all points of difference between the United States and Great Britain concerning the treaty of peace. Randolph noted that Jay would go armed with copies of the Treaty of Paris yet, being one of the original American negotiators and Chief Justice, he would be more than equipped for the negotiations without the document. In this point, Randolph includes the caveat that the British agents have been arming Native Americans in the Western Frontier and encouraging them to attack Americans.

Three: Negotiate a commercial treaty – after which Randolph lists nineteen points that should be agreed to, including sharing fishing waters.

Four: If nothing satisfactory and advantageous to America can be formed as a treaty, do not sign anything.

Five: If the British become belligerent, seek the ministers of Russia, Denmark, and Sweden who have also assigned themselves to neutrality.

Six: Randolph outlines that Jay had movement on these points in his negotiations as long as they remained in the American interest with the exceptions of two points:

> First. That, as the British ministry will doubtless be solicitous to detach us from France, and may probably make some overture of this kind, you will inform them that the Government of the United States will not derogate from our treaties and engagements with France, and that experience has shown that we can be honest in our duties to the British nation without laying ourselves under any particular restraints as to other nations; and second, that no treaty of commerce be concluded or signed contrary to the foregoing prohibition.[5]

By November, Jay had successfully negotiated the Jay Treaty and both the American Envoy Extraordinary and Lord Grenville, the Foreign Minister, had signed on the dotted line, ensuring both countries would avoid another costly and bloody war…at least until the War of 1812.

ROYAL HOTEL, PALL MALL

During his stay in London, John Jay lodged at the Royal Hotel on Pall Mall. Located directly behind St. James's Palace, Pall Mall existed as an early London road before being turned into a court on which to play the game 'pell-mell': a form of croquet which became popular in England in the seventeenth century. In the early 1660s, Charles II - grandson of James I, under whom the court was constructed - ordered the playing area to be rejuvenated into its prior incarnation as a road. Quickly, the area grew into an affluent residential street and shopping hub. It was home to several prominent individuals and private gentleman's clubs, such as the Travellers Club (established after Jay's visit in 1819) and was well known for its plethora of pricey retail outlets. One block north of the Mall – the avenue which runs from Trafalgar Square to Buckingham Palace – Pall Mall boasted opulent residential off-shoots, such as Cleveland Row, where John Adams had met the Secretary of State before visiting St. James's Palace and which was named in honour of Charles II's mistress, the Duchess of Cleveland.

The Royal Hotel opened in 1777 and was described in the early nineteenth century as "an extensive establishment for the reception and accommodation of gentlemen and families of distinction."[6] By the time Jay walked through its doors, the hotel already boasted links to the Revolution. One of the occupants, a decade before Jay arrived, was the Comte de Grasse. The Frenchman had commanded the French fleet at the Battle of the Chesapeake in 1781, however, he was captured by the British Admiral Reynolds and imprisoned –

'imprisoned' being used lightly here given the luxurious surrounds – at the Royal Hotel. Indeed, Jay was not shacking up in a lodging house as Jefferson had done during his short trip, but in a hotel which was grand enough to house guests of the Royal Family. In 1797, the hotel hosted the future Frederick I of Wurttemberg (then the duke) when he visited England to meet his future wife, Charlotte, the Princess Royal.

Above any other guest though, the history of one of the building's very specific former inhabitants may have been a lucky charm for Jay; maybe the forging of a successful Anglo-American alliance seeped into the New Yorker's bones while he slept in his lap of luxury. The hotel was the former residence of the M.P for Chipping Wycome, Thomas Fitzmaurice. Fitzmaurice's brother, the Whig politician William Petty Fitzmaurice, 1st Marquess of Lansdowne, had been the Prime Minister for the final months of the American Revolution. Succeeding the 2nd Marquess of Rockingham, who had held the post for less than one hundred days, William had only agreed to serve in his predecessor's government if George III recognised the United States as a legitimate country. William had been a friend of Benjamin Franklin during his stint in London and, while P.M., he was one of the principal figures in negotiating peace with the United States. Legend has it that he is said to have drafted part of the Treaty of Paris in the Round Room Cocktail Bar at the Lansdowne Club on Fitzmaurice Place in Mayfair (both the Lansdowne Club and Fitzmaurice Place are eponymous of William). Thus, here lies the irony of John Jay's stay at the Royal Hotel. In his role on the American side organising the treaty with Britain in 1783, Jay would have negotiated with William. He was now staying in William's brother's former home, trying to inhibit another costly war with the British.

Sadly, like most eighteenth-century hotels in London, the original building has been demolished. Until 1940, the site served as the Carlton Club, the original headquarters of the Conservative Party.

The Lansdowne Club.

Unlike the journeys of other figures mentioned in this anthology, Alexander Hamilton was instrumental in organising Jay's trip to Britain. From suggesting the ship on which to sail to England (the *Adriana*) to in-depth directions. On May 6, 1794 - the same day Edmund Randolph sent Jay his official letter of instruction - Hamilton also wrote a lengthy dispatch setting out his opinion on how to deal with the British. Outlining his beliefs of how the British operate regarding trade Hamilton wrote, "The principle of Great Britain is that a neutral nation ought not to be permitted to carry on in time of War a commerce with a Nation at war which it could not carry on with that nation in time of peace."[7] Hamilton, the man who was stealing British manufacturing secrets, was well aware of the extent to which the United States and Britain relied on each other for successful commerce:

> As a consumer the paper A will show that we stand unrivalled. We now consume of her exports from a million to [a] million and a half sterling more in value than any other foreign country & while the consumption of other countries from obvious causes is likely to be stationary that of this country is increasing and for a long, long, series of years, will increase rapidly. Our manufactures are no doubt progressive. But our population and means progress so much faster, that our demand for manufactured supply far outgoes the progress of our faculty to manufacture. Nor can this cease to be the case for any calculable period of time…How unwise then in Great Britain to suffer such a state of things to remain exposed to the hazard of constant interruption & derangement by not fixing on the basis of a good treaty the principles on which it should continue?[8]

Additionally, like Randolph, Hamilton enjoined Jay not to sign anything without consulting with colleagues in America:

> But you will discover from your instructions that the opinion which has prevailed is that such a Treaty of commerce ought not to be concluded without previous reference here for further instruction. It is desirable however to push the British Ministry in this respect to a result that the extent of their views may be ascertained.[9]

This could have elongated his stay to possibly six months just for one exchange of letters – not quite the short trip Jay was hoping for. Meanwhile, letters from Jay to Hamilton, all composed from the confines of the Royal Hotel, show the two Federalists to be in some form of private cahoots about the reality of Jay's trip - at least in the sense of soft diplomacy, if not full-frontal political gains. On July 18, Jay told Hamilton:

> Shortly after my arrival I dined with Lord Grenville; the cabinet minister were present, but not a single foreigner. On Monday next I am to dine with the Lord Chancellor, and on next Friday with Mr. Pitt. I mention these facts to explain what I mean by favourable appearances. I think it best that they should remain unmentioned for the present and they make no part of my communications to Mr. Randolph or others. This is not the season for such communications - they may be misinterpreted, though not by you.[10]

Some of Jay's most interesting connections to Hamilton while in London relate to the domestic news he imparted to his colleague. Jay wrote to Hamilton notifying him of his interactions with another pair of famous Americans in London: The Churches. Angelica and John were just a few blocks away on Sackville Street and made the effort to welcome Jay and his party. Writing to Sarah, he said that "Mr. and Mrs. Church are particularly kind and civil to us, and Peter has much reason to be pleased with the attentions which he has received from them."[11]

Meanwhile, his letter to Hamilton notes Angelica's yearning for the United States, as well as her charm, "Mr. and Mrs. Church are out of town. We are much indebted to their civilities and friendly attentions. She looks as well as when you saw her and thinks as much about America and her friends in it as ever. She certainly is an amiable agreeable woman."[12]

DOWNING STREET, WESTMINSTER

John Jay's correspondence during this period suggests he dealt chiefly with Lord Grenville, the Foreign Secretary who was to become Prime Minister in 1806. Their dispatches indicate that Jay was often invited to meet with Grenville in his office which, as his letter headers indicate, was on Downing Street. Built in the 1680s by Sir George Downing, Downing Street has been the official residence of British Prime Ministers since 1735. As the White House is for the U.S. President, Downing Street is now a poecilonym for the head of British government and their activities. A fifteen-minute walk from Pall Mall, Jay would have probably ambled along Horse Guards Road, wedged between St. James's Park and Horse Guards Parade, to finally arrive at Downing Street, likely lamenting his posting with every step in the chilly London winter.

Grenville became PM for just over a year in 1806 before being succeeded by the Duke of Portland. Interestingly, he had hereditary American connections as his maternal grandfather, William Wyndham, was the same William Wyndham who had sought out Benjamin Franklin for swimming lessons for his two sons. It is unlikely the two men knew this - or if they did, it's unlikely it was at the forefront of their minds during negotiations.

While in the city, Jay made an interesting observation regarding the opinions of British society. Writing to Tench Coxe, a fellow American politician who had served in the Continental Congress, in January 1795, Jay remarked:

> The best disposition towards us prevails here, and the indications and proofs of it daily increase. I do really believe that this government means to give conciliatory measures with the United States a full and fair trial. I wish it may be reciprocated on our part. It never can be wise to cast ourselves into the arms and influence of any nation; but

certainly, it is wise and proper to cherish the good-will of those who wish to be on terms of friendship and cordiality with us. It may seem strange, and yet I am convinced, that next to the king, our president is more popular in this country than any man in it.[13]

Despite his initial disdain at his British appointment, the perceived love for General Washington in English society may have been a silver-lining for Jay during his dreary residence in London.

John Jay was a man keen to avoid seasickness. Writing to Hamilton in November 1795, after informing him a treaty had been finalised – telling him, however "whether *finis coronat opus* [the end crowns the work], the president, senate, and public will decide"[14] – Jay said he was not fit for the fatigues of a winter voyage and would wait out the season in London and return in the spring. A wise choice many of his countrymen had failed to make over the years.

Jay's tenure in London came at a time when Hamilton was in full flow forging ahead in his role as the architect of the American economy. Yet, despite Hamilton's hand in the construction of the governmental infrastructure, his interactions with Jay during this time act as examples of some of the only diplomacy-orientated correspondence he sent to London – and more broadly, Europe - during his lifetime. While his letters streamed off the packet ships and into the city during the Churches' time in London, the topics discussed remained almost solely in a domestic sphere. Though Hamilton promulgated his views on how to contend with British manufacturing while safely on the west side of the Atlantic, his advice to Jay provides a fascinating insight into how he himself may have dealt with various issues had he ever been posted as a diplomat.

CHAPTER SEVEN

JOHN LAURENS

John Laurens was one of the last casualties of the War of Independence. Born in Charleston, South Carolina, in 1754, the eldest of thirteen children descended from Huguenots, he has come to prominent public attention in recent years due to his frontal role in Miranda's musical. Portrayed in theatre as he was in life – Hamilton's avid anti-slavery promoter friend who procured slaves to fight for the Continental Army in the hope that they too would gain their freedom - Laurens was a progressive young soldier who stood up for what was morally right, even amongst the backdrop of war and the constant threat of death.

Despite his American soul, Laurens spent much of his youth in Europe. His father, Henry, had taken John and his brothers east to ensure they received a high, classical standard of education. Henry himself had trained in London as a young adult under the watchful eye of Richard Oswald, a man who would later work with him again when he represented Britain in the negotiations for the Treaty of

Paris. John Laurens's moral compass, however, was far removed from that of his father. Henry was a rice planter and slave master in South Carolina. Although, beyond just owning slaves, he was also a major player in the transatlantic slave trade as a partner in Austin and Laurens – the largest slave-trading company in the colonies which oversaw the bondage of thousands of humans before the American Revolution even started. The firm's account books from 1750 - 1758 held at Yale University are absolutely saturated with records of human cargo arriving upon American shores along with other commodities of sugar, rum, and flour, making it easy to see how the company was the principal slave-trading organisation in North America at the time.

In John Laurens's short life, he stood as the antithesis of his father. He was also a complex man whose amorous exploits in London left him with responsibilities outside of fighting for his country. Friends with Alexander Hamilton for only a short time, the two men found kindred spirits in each other in their want of revolution and lust for battle. They have also been the cynosure of an intricate debate examining the nature of their relationship. Hamilton's supposed virile antics with women have been widely discussed, but there is also a range of historians who question whether he was bisexual and whether John Laurens, who is generally accepted to have been bisexual, was his lover.

LONDON

Like tides of Americans before them, John and his brother, Henry, entered England via Falmouth. Docking in the bay on October 9, 1771, John was to spend the next six years in Europe. Soon, Henry senior enrolled his sons at Reverend Richard Clarke's House for Carolina Boys. Clarke was a Winchester-born Oxford-educated man of the cloth who had an illustrious career in England before travelling to Carolina in the early-1750s. The clergyman had been working as a lecturer at Nicholas Cole Abbey in the City of London when St. Philip's Church in South Carolina sent word to London that they were in need of a replacement for the church's ageing commissary. Soon, Clarke was on board a ship, traversing the open waters and rolling towards the New World.

Clarke divided opinion in South Carolina. First established in 1681, St. Philip's history was immense, and the church had several prominent Revolutionary and Confederationary figures attached to it, including Charles Pinckney, a signer of the U.S. Constitution who eventually married John Laurens's sister, Mary.

Clarke was initially well-liked in the community and came with gleaming references that he was "a gentleman of great piety and learning."[1] Though, he began to be mocked when he avowed his belief in the prophecies of a shunned Presbyterian minister called Christopher Love which had been found in the chest of a deceased sailor. Love had predicted natural disasters and the downfall of the papacy. Thus, when an earthquake hit Portugal in the mid-1750s, around the same time Love had suggested other such events in Europe, Clarke became even more invested. He began to preach about the end of days, which led Governor William Lyttleton to describe him as "a clergyman of much learning but of an overheated imagination,"[2] and started to wax lyrical about the millennium. Clarke, although still highly regarded, had begun to err on the side of madness for the people of Charleston. He was soon eager to rid himself of the New World and requested to return home to England.

In March 1759, he was again rolling on the waves and planning his return to London. Amongst other feats, in 1770 he opened his Westminster home as a boarding school for young Carolinian men studying in London. While his sons studied under Clarke, Henry Laurens lodged on Fludyer Street - one road along from Downing Street on Whitehall. For those in search of Laurens's house today, only disappointment awaits as, in the 1860s, the street was destroyed in order to build the grand home of the Foreign Office designed by Sir George Gilbert Scott, famed in London for his work creating St.

Pancras Station. The Laurenses did not stay long at Clarke's establishment though as patriarch Henry soon became disillusioned with the clergyman. Reports that Clarke was letting standards slip, as well as neglecting to actually teach, reached the ears of Laurens who pulled his sons out of the boarding school and arranged for them to finish their pre-university education in Geneva. However, John would soon return to the British school system. Moreover, as we will see, for John Laurens, London would not only provide an education but a family.

MIDDLE TEMPLE, INNS OF COURT, TEMPLE

Following two years in Geneva, Laurens returned to London. Henry Laurens had already scouted the colleges of both Oxford and Cambridge for his son but found himself dissatisfied with the world's leading hubs of scholarship: "The two universities are generally, I might say universally censured. Oxford in particular is spoken of as a school for licentiousness and debauchery in the most aggravated heights."[3] Laurens was not wrong in this respect. Although Anglican in outlook, Oxbridge housed a coterie of louche clubs, some of which exist to this day, including the King Charles Club. Moreover, four years after Laurens returned to America, the world-famous Bullingdon Club was founded. The dining club of dissipation counts famous names amongst its alumni, including two British Prime Ministers - David Cameron and Boris Johnson - as well as a legion of other Conservative politicians: Winston Churchill's father, Randolph; Cecil Rhodes; and a wealth of royalty, including Edward VII.

A far more suitable alternative to the hallowed institutions was found in London. John had already studied civil law while in Geneva and, in November 1774, he was matriculated into Middle Temple – arguably the most prestigious and well-known college of the Inns of Court - to train further in the judicial field. Located on the north

Middle Temple, c.1830.

bank of the River Thames - next to a building aptly named Hamilton House - Middle Temple had served in antiquity as the headquarters of the Knights Templar. By the time Laurens arrived, it was the hub for Carolinians pursuing law. Laurens would work for three weeks at a time over the year's four terms, meanwhile pursuing private study.

During his time at the Middle Temple, he lodged with renowned solicitor Charles Bicknell on Chancery Lane, a pleasant ten-minute walk north of the Inns of Court. Laurens found Charles to be a rather dull and conservative companion, yet he befriended his brother, John, who shared his abolitionist beliefs and had co-written the 1773 anti-slavery tome *The Dying Negro: A Poetical Epistle*. However, as we will see, the Bicknells were not the only London-based family John Laurens would spend time with.

ST. ANDREW UNDERSHAFT CHURCH, ST. MARY AXE

In October 1774, Henry Laurens returned to Charleston. Upon his departure, a local man called William Coventry Manning - a Caribbean colonist and plantation-owning patriarch who, like Hamilton, had been born on St. Kitts and Nevis - took on the role of John's unofficial guardian. William took John under his wing, and the young American began spending an ample amount of time at the Manning family home in the parish of St. Mary Axe located in the City of London. Manning was well connected and had inherited plantations in Negro Bay, St. Croix, which had once belonged to his father-in-law, John Ryan. A common pattern in the lives of figures in the American Revolution is that the six degrees of separation linking people together are not hard to decipher: Interestingly, one of Manning's daughters, Sarah, was married to Benjamin Vaughan, the same man who negotiated the Treaty of Paris with Henry Laurens and who had organised the visit to the British Museum for Jefferson and the Adams family in 1786.

Laurens grew close to the entire family, but, in April 1776, his connection to the family became genetic. Martha Manning, another of William's daughters, became pregnant by the dashing young American. John and Martha did not marry until she was around five to six months pregnant – possibly around the time when a pregnancy could no longer be disguised by a late eighteenth-century dress. The wedding was quietly held at St. Andrew Undershaft Church in the Manning's parish of St. Mary Axe on Saturday, October 26, 1776.

Some have suggested that John possibly slept with Martha to 'cure' him of bisexuality or homosexuality. During the eighteenth century, pseudo-scientific ideas surrounding homosexuality could easily have led Laurens to believe that he could have been cured by having sexual intercourse with a woman. The idea that John Laurens was bisexual, or homosexual, is an integral argument made in Ron

Chernow's *Hamilton* where the author analyses letters sent between the Laurens and Hamilton. Resultingly, Chernow probes the question of whether Alexander Hamilton too was bisexual and whether the pair had a relationship during the American Revolution. On one hand, Chernow suggests that indeed the duo's correspondence does brim with homoerotic imagery. Nevertheless, Hamilton had several close friendships with whom he would exhibit flirtatious conversation in correspondence. Some could say that his correspondence with Angelica Church is a key example of a platonic relationship in which Hamilton felt comfortable writing in a kittenish manner.

Both Chernow and historian Gregory D. Massey also point to the idea of Hamilton and Laurens engaging in enthusiastic homosociality (surrounding oneself with friends largely of the same sex), since both men mainly chose other men with whom to have their closest friendships. Nonetheless, historians are convinced that Laurens was at least bisexual, if not gay. Resultingly, he has become an enduring LGBTQ icon.

John and Martha's only child, a daughter named Frances Eleanor Laurens, was born three months after the wedding, and baptized on February 18, at the same church her parents married in. By that time, however, her father had returned to America to fight for the patriot cause. John, devoted to the thought of American independence, witnessed the surrender of General Cornwallis at Yorktown but was killed in the final days of the war when he was shot at the Battle of the Combahee River on August 27, 1782. Martha had planned to join Laurens in South Carolina but Henry Laurens was worried both about her passage and arrival during the war. John Laurens wrote to his father-in-law begging him not to send her, and luckily for him, plans she made fell through after her travelling companions decided to stay loyal to the king and did not sail to America. Supporting claims that Laurens had entered into his marriage to take responsibility for his venereal actions as opposed to love, Massey points out that Laurens neglected Martha. Indeed, her father-in-law seems to have been more concerned with her life and welfare than her husband, who was probably happy that his family wanted to inhibit her journey so he did not have to see her. Upon learning of Laurens's appointment as a special minister to France in 1780, Martha travelled to the continent in an attempt to be reunited with her husband and finally form a family unit. Alas, they were never to meet, and Martha died in France that autumn. Frances, known as Fanny, was returned to London but eventually moved to her father's native colony of South Carolina where she was raised by his sister, Martha Laurens Ramsey.

Although John Laurens's time in London did not impact Alexander Hamilton directly, the South Carolinian's actions regarding Martha Manning and the child they conceived feeds inextricably into the wider questions surrounding the nature of Laurens and Hamilton's relationship. It was also in London where Laurens's desire to return to his native country and fight for the American cause – Hamilton's beloved movement – grew.

An enjoyable yet melancholic snippet in the life of Alexander Hamilton, his friendship with Laurens, although short, was intense, whether they were brothers-in-arms whose bond was strengthened by the spirit of the Revolution, or lovers caught in the midst of war.

Like Jefferson's travels in the city, Lauren's time in the capital is little known, thus following his trail around the metropolis's alleyways, churches, backstreets, and law schools, keeps the London life of one of Hamilton's most cherished friends alive.

CHAPTER EIGHT

AARON BURR

The one other Founder synonymous with Hamilton's story above that of Washington, Adams, or even Jefferson, is Aaron Burr: the man who killed him. Like Hamilton, Burr's story was largely muted for centuries. Whether that was because he didn't make it to the presidency or sign the major founding documents, or maybe just because he lacked the political bravado that could be seen in other Revolutionary characters, one cannot say that he didn't cunningly try to make his mark on American history. Instead, his attempts to seal his name on the rollcall of the great men of the Founding Era plonked him, shamed and alone, right in the middle of London.

Born in Newark, New Jersey, in early 1756, his greatness was premeditated. His father, who died when he was only one year old, was president of what would be Burr's alma mater: the College of New Jersey (Princeton), one of the best universities in the world. His mother, Esther Edwards, was the daughter of Jonathan Edwards,

Governor John Winthrop

the Yale-educated theologian who also held the position of President of the College of New Jersey. Grandfather Edwards died two years after Burr was born as a result of having a smallpox inoculation. Furthermore, Burr's great-great-grandmother was Mary Downing, sister of Sir George Downing, the namesake of the British Prime Minister's residence of Downing Street. The Downings moved to Salem, Massachusetts, in 1638 to be near Governor John Winthrop, the four-times Governor of Massachusetts Bay Colony who delivered the 'City Upon a Hill' sermon and who also happened to be Sir George's uncle.

Burr entered his family's castle of Princeton in 1769 before being admitted to the bar in Albany in 1782. In the same year, he met and married the recently widowed Theodosia Provost whom he'd first encountered at her house, the Hermitage, in New Jersey. Despite being married to a British officer, Theodosia allowed the Continental

Army, including Washington and his men, to use the house as a base. Theodosia's home witnessed her wedding to Burr, but it was also an integral facet in one of the most scandalous tales in American history which questions her loyalty to the American cause (see *Chapter Five: Benedict Arnold*).

The couple had one child, Theodosia, born in 1783. However, Aaron Burr is said to have fathered at least eight children, including the half-Indian abolitionist John Pierre Burr, whom the Founder had conceived with Mary Emmons, a Calcutta-born servant working at the Hermitage. During his time in European exile, Burr is thought to have conceived two illegitimate children and a further two acknowledged daughters after his return to America, who were aged only two and six at the time of his death.

Burr fulfilled the destiny offered to him by the fresh slate the Revolution created. Steadily climbing through the ranks from soldier to lawyer to member of the New York State Assembly, then onto Attorney General of New York, senator, and finally vice-president. What was to stop him from attaining the presidency following Jefferson's time in office? The answer: an amalgamation of ambition, conceit, and one man who ultimately played a larger role in Burr's story in death than he did in life: Alexander Hamilton.

On July 11, 1804, Burr wounded Hamilton in a duel on the Weehawken duelling grounds in New Jersey (see *Chapter One: Angelica Schuyler Church* for a more in-depth discussion of the duel itself). The next day, the crime's repercussions would grow greater as Hamilton died in the early afternoon; Aaron Burr was now a murderer.

Duelling was illegal in New Jersey but dealt with less harshly than in New York, nonetheless, Burr fled the scene – and state – of the crime. While he did not immediately go into hiding, spending almost a month in New York before anything serious happened, by August 2 he was wanted by the state for murder and the misdemeanour of duelling and later wanted in New Jersey. Fleeing to the south, the vice-president hid in a number of locations, including the Georgia plantation of Irish senator and fellow Founder, Pierce Butler. Burr's future as vice-president seemed uncertain, however, the charges were soon abandoned, and Burr returned to the seat of power to continue in his role. However, Jefferson dropped him from the ticket in the 1804 election. He was replaced by the Governor of New York, George Clinton, once a Hamilton supporter but now a passionate anti-Federalist. The murder of Hamilton and the loss of his vice-presidency were not the end of Burr's troubles, instead, they were the tumultuous start of irrevocable descent into ignominy and ostracism.

LONDON

The final nail in the coffin for Aaron Burr's tumultuous career was the Burr Conspiracy. The parameters of the conspiracy are a hazy mess of he-said-she-said with disputed ideas over what the final outcome of the whole affair was meant to be. Yet, whatever the intentions, the plan ended with Burr retreating into exile in Europe.

In 1806, President Thomas Jefferson received a letter from General James Wilkinson, General of the United States Army and Governor of the Louisiana Territory which Jefferson had bought from the French three years earlier. In the parchment that arrived at the White House, Wilkinson handed Jefferson evidence that Burr was attempting to annex Mexico for himself. Some even suggested later that he was planning to take over Washington D.C. Burr, who saw an opportunity to seize the territory and gift it to England, with the added possibility of a slice of territory in the West, had been working on his plan since he was in office.

Evidence uncovered indicated that he had already been preparing for possible conflict by compiling arms and assembling men on Blennerhassett Island near West Virginia. The president immediately issued a warrant for Burr's arrest. The sly politician was initially discovered along the Bayou Pierre on his way to New Orleans. Although, while under arrest, he escaped only to be found again and subsequently put on trial in Richmond, Virginia, with Judge John Marshal presiding. Despite Wilkinson's letter and the overwhelming context of Burr being unreliable and untrustworthy, the jury acquitted him. He evaded imprisonment due to the simple fact that the prosecution lacked sufficient evidence to convict him. Although the claims against him showed conspiracy to commit treason, he had carried out no actions that would be deemed overtly treasonous acts of war. Despite speaking out about his dissatisfaction with the government, his words, as they would be today, were protected under the Constitution's First Amendment right to free speech which was ratified only sixteen years earlier in 1791. The John-Adams-inflicted Alien and Sedition Acts, which had warped free speech for a period, had also expired in the first years of the 1800s and thus did not have repercussions for Burr.

Yet, it would be wrong to suggest that Burr got off scot-free. While he was never convicted, his already dying career flatlined. Disgraced for the conspiracy – as well as for the lingering fact that he murdered New York hero Hamilton - and with few amiable acquaintances left, nine months after the end of the trial, Burr paid $60 ($1,294/£936 today) for a cabin on the *Clarissa Ann* and departed from New York on June 9. He was not to return to America for four years. Keeping a detailed journal of his time in Europe, which included travels in England, Scotland, Germany, Holland, France, and Sweden, it is possible to follow almost exactly in his footsteps. A sickly being since birth, while away in Europe, Burr was plagued with insomnia, migraines, and indigestion. He also made friends with society figures, including Jeremy Bentham; complained endlessly about London and Londoners; spent hours trying to force the British to support his plan to annex Mexico; and was even softly imprisoned in an official's home for one night. The London life of Aaron Burr was one of a once-great man scrambling to have those he once fought against see things his way and, ultimately, never succeeding.

30 CRAVEN STREET, CHARING CROSS

Docking at Falmouth on July 13, Burr spent a couple of days on England's west coast before setting off for London. Travelling through Exeter, the disgraced former vice-president arrived in the capital city on June 16 and spent a night at Gloucester Coffee House in Piccadilly. The coffee house was a hub for coaches travelling to and from England's West Country, which includes Somerset, Exeter, and Gloucester, hence it was a practical lodging stop for those who had docked at Falmouth. In 1897, it was reincarnated into the ostentatious hotel, The Berkley – the name derived from its original location at the intersection of Piccadilly and Berkley Street. In the early 1970s, it was moved to the far more affluent Knightsbridge neighbourhood.

Burr notes how he arrived at the establishment at 6:30 a.m. and took breakfast in his rooms at 9 a.m. Burr's diary leaps, as did his speech annoyingly for those who weren't bilingual, between English and French, often in the same sentence. He ends his first entry in London with, "Soir – opera – galere,"[1] meaning that in the evening he attended the opera and watched from a gallery. Sadly, for us historians, he does not specify where. He could, however, be referencing the Royal Opera House in nearby Covent Garden which burnt down nearly two months to the day later.

Lodging at other establishments, such as The Ship Inn (possibly The Ship owned by a Mr. James Wild located on Bow Street in Covent Garden), sometime before August 10, Burr found a more permanent residence a few doors along from where the now-deceased Benjamin Franklin had lived during his time in the city. On his declaration to John Reeves, an official at the British Alien Office, Burr answered the question, 'Where you now reside and have resided since your last arrival?' with, 'London, Craven Street, Number 30.'[2]

At Number 30, his landlady was one Madame Wilken. Interestingly, Craven Street seemed to be somewhat of a magnet for Americans staying in London. In 1815, John Quincy Adams set up his offices at Number 13 while following in his father's footsteps as the American Minister to Britain. Later in the century, the author of Moby-Dick, Herman Melville, also lived on the road while writing the White-Jacket the year before he published his iconic American Novel about whaling in Nantucket.

Burr did not leave a detailed opinion of his lodgings as he was often out and spent elongated periods at Queen's Square Place (more about anon). A sufferer of insomnia and frequent illness, Burr's description of his activities at Number 30 tend to largely focus on a list of sleeping habits, headaches, and dietary complaints while only once mentioning a visitor by name who called on him at Craven Street: a Captain Sinclair who left a note to call on him at the Virginia Coffee House, yet he does mention at length apparent reams of visitors whom 'Madame W' told him he had missed. To be fair, life did not start positively for the new-born Aaron Burr, who was premature and suffering from diphtheria. Throughout his life, he relied on cream of tartar to while away his nights dealing with stomach upsets - not surprising when his diet was so poor, one defining dinner in the city was ice cream and a bottle of wine - and would spend days in bed in London suffering from debilitating migraines.

QUEEN'S SQUARE PLACE, WESTMINSTER

Whatever one thinks of Burr - killer, liar, fraudster, conceited - you must also include, to an eighteenth-century extent, progressive. Arguably, Burr ranked among the most progressive in the theological standings of the Founding Fathers. Beyond the usual stand of opposition to slavery, which is the usual litmus test by which to divide the Founders between progressive or not, Burr also stood up for women's rights. Described by Lin-Manuel Miranda as "an ardent feminist,"[3] in a time when women were thought of as their husband's property upon matrimony, Burr's feminism shines in the letters to his wife and through the measures he took to ensure his daughter obtained an education above and beyond what other American women would have received. Theodosia Burr could read and write by three years old, younger than most educated children can in the twenty-first century. He was also an admirer of Mary Wollstonecraft, the author of the ground-breaking *A Vindication of the Rights of Women*, which he described as a "work of genius"[4] - in fact, while in London in 1812, he attended a talk by the son of William Godwin who had been married to the late Wollstonecraft. In the same entry, he mentions William's sister, Mary, who would have been fifteen at the time. The daughter of William senior and Mary Wollstonecraft, she would go on to be known as Mary Shelley, the author of Frankenstein. Interestingly, Mary had a half-sister called Fanny Imlay who was born as the result of an affair between her mother and Gilbert Imlay, an American diplomat who was born less than fifty miles away from Burr in New Jersey and who had also served in the American Revolution.

Early on in his tenure in London, Burr met with one of the day's most progressive individuals: social reformer Jeremy Bentham. A jurist by trade and philosopher in his soul, Bentham inspired the founding of one of the world's top universities, University College London, which opened in 1826 and offered a non-religious alternative to attending England's only other two universities at the time - the Anglican institutions of Oxford and Cambridge. Later, in 1878, UCL became the first British university to admit women to degrees on the same terms as men. Almost prophetically, in his journal, Burr mentions walking along Gower Street where UCL is located.

Bentham was an ardent utilitarian and is remembered as the father of modern utilitarianism. His collegiate brainchild lists some of history's most formidable characters amongst its alumni, including Mahatma Gandhi, David Attenborough, and Alexander

Jeremy Bentham by Henry William Pickersgill.

Graham Bell. Bentham's progressive beliefs went beyond what we would even label liberal for the time. For example, he argued that homosexuality should be de-criminalised. Bentham's views of homosexuality – which he did not believe to be unnatural, as was the mindset of the day – were published posthumously since they were seen as far too scandalous for public consumption during his lifetime, pointing to how radical a man he really was. Like Benjamin Franklin, Bentham found notoriety in his later years and thus portraits of him have affected the national mindset for us to remember him as an older, almost paternalistic figure for Burr, whose portraits show him in his young pre-exile years. In reality, there was only an eight-year age gap between Bentham and Burr.

Burr, though not having outwardly spoken on homosexuality in either direction, is remembered as being one of the only Founding Fathers who supported emancipation. Although, he cannot be thought of progressive to a John Adams extent. Akin to Jefferson, Burr was a dichotomy in that he wanted to end slavery but owned slaves himself. And, like Jefferson - who many have chosen to remember with the juxtaposing title of a 'kind master' - Burr is thought to have treated his slaves with more leniency than other southern slave owners. He, for example, ensured his slaves were educated and fought for the destruction of the system that had placed them in his household but, like Benjamin Franklin, he still subscribed to the abhorrent institution of owning human beings. He even defended slaves in court, but hypocritically refused the argument that they should have voting rights.

Despite Burr's hypocritical nature, the two men bonded over the affairs of the day, and Bentham became a constant figure during the American's time in London. He is first mentioned in his journal on August 21, when Burr notes, "Received invitation from Jeremy Bentham inviting me to pass some days chez lui."[5] Upon his father's death in 1763, Bentham had inherited a house on Queen's Square Place. Overlooking St. James's Park to the southwest of Buckingham Palace, Bentham moved into the property in the early 1790s and kept it as his London residence until his death in 1832. Burr became so close to Bentham and Bentham's secretary, John Herbert Koe, that his frequent visits to Queen's Square Place escalated into Burr being allowed to use the residence even when its owner was not home, often noting that Bentham's housekeeper, Mrs. Stocker, had let him in.

On the other hand, Bentham was a surprising ally for Aaron Burr. As part of the British reaction to the colonies declaring their independence in 1776, the government had enlisted barrister and pamphleteer – and close family friend of Jeremy Bentham - John Lind, to compile a series of essays refuting the document. Historians have suspected Bentham of having authored the treatise called a

Short Review of the Declaration in which he mocks the Americans, their understanding of government, and attempts to form a new nation. He even compares the Declaration of Independence to the Salem Witch Trials arguing:

> The opinions of the modern Americans on government, like those of their good ancestors on witchcraft, would be too ridiculous to deserve any notice, if like them too, contemptible and extravagant as they be, they had not led to the most serious evils.[6]

Bentham was an ideological turncoat, however. Born into a Tory family and attending the most elite schools England had to offer: Westminster School and Queens' College, Oxford, before being admitted to Lincoln's Inn at the Inns of Court to read law, it is easy to understand why Bentham would have come down on the British side during the Revolution. Later in life, however, he took inspiration from America as a political model when attempting to reform the British Constitution. Once describing the Patriots as having "outdone the utmost extravagance of all former fanatics,"[7] Bentham now championed the phrase 'Look to America' to convince his countrymen of the benefit of expanded democracy and suffrage.

Jeremy Bentham's home no longer stands, however, in its place is the Home Office, complete with a commemorative plaque marking Bentham's long residence at 50 Queen Anne's Gate. It was erected as part of the UCL Bentham project in 2004 - it fails to mention Burr though. In his will, Bentham requested that his body be preserved. For years, the severed, mummified head of Burr's buddy was on display at University College London. Now, one can only view the auto-icon which holds his skeleton in the entrance to the UCL Student Centre.

———————————

WAR OFFICE, WHITEHALL

Despite being tried for treason, Burr's aspirations to carry through with plans seeded during the Burr Conspiracy were not dampened. On his departure, he left his daughter, Theodosia, with a list of names which translated to a number so his correspondence would be, at least in part, coded. He also referred to his plans relating to Mexico as 'X'.

Furthermore, he frequently visited the War Office to meet with General Hope. General John Hope was a Scotch-born Lieutenant General in the British Army who became well acquainted with Burr during his time in the city. Born in 1765, Hope played a small role in the War of Independence when he served in the Royal American Regiment, however, he is best remembered for the Peninsula War. Burr likely hung around the War Office attempting to befriend members of the British military establishment in the hopes that he could convince them of his plans to annex Mexico. In the early stages of the Burr Conspiracy, the lawyer from New Jersey had tried to convince the British to join in his quest by corresponding with Anthony Merry, the British Minister to the United States, who would pass on his plans to London to no avail.

While Burr was flagrantly trying to pursue his Mexican ambitions, he aroused such intense suspicion at the War Office that he was taken into a lax form of custody for a day at the home of an official at 31 Stafford Place, near Buckingham Palace, which Burr called his "prison":

> At 1 o'clock [British officials] came in, without knocking, four coarse-looking men, who said they had a state warrant for seizing me and my papers; but refused to show the warrant. I was peremptory, and the warrant was produced, signed Liverpool; but I was not permitted to read the whole. They took possession of my trunks, searched every part of the room for papers, threw all the loose articles into a sack,

called a coach, and away we went to the Alien Office. Before going I wrote a note to Reeves, q.v, and on our arrival sent it in. Waited one hour in the coach, very cold, but I refused to go in. Wrote in pencil to Reeves another note. He came out. We had a little conversation. He could not then explain but said I must have patience. After half an hour more orders came that I must go with one of the messengers (Hughes) to his house. On this order I first went into the office to see Brooks, the under-secretary, whom I knew. You may recollect the transaction in July, which must have fixed me in his memory. He did not know me except that I was Mr K. None of them knew me, though every devil of them knew me as well as I know you. Seeing the measure was resolved on and having inquired of the sort of restraint to which I was doomed, I wrote a note to Koe, which Brooks took to show Lord Liverpool for his approbation to forward it. Arrived at my prison, 31 Stafford Place, at 4.[8]

Reeves was the same John Reeves to whom Burr had declared himself as an Alien shortly after his arrival. Reeves was a conservative anti-republican who had connections to North America having served as the first Chief Justice of Newfoundland and Labrador in the early 1790s. With his dislike of republicanism and having served His Majesty's Government overseas in the empire, it is unlikely that Burr and Reeves were ever on the same footing despite Burr's attempts to expand British stakes in America. The War Office itself, as well as Reeves's office block, was located on Whitehall. Now a metonym for the British Government, Whitehall is an expansive avenue running parallel to the River Thames in Westminster from Trafalgar Square in the north to the Palace of Westminster in the south. Scattered along the route is many a touristic hotspot, including 10 Downing Street, Banqueting House, and Horse Guards Parade (which Burr used as an alternative name for Whitehall). On the road once sat the Palace of Whitehall. Bigger than Versailles, it had straddled both sides of the street from 1530 until 1698. Built at the behest of Henry VIII, the palace was the main royal residence in London and even saw a visit by Pocahontas and her husband, Virginia planter John Rolfe, who were introduced to James I at the Banqueting House (which is the only remaining component of the palace) in January 1617 at the Twelfth Night masque.

It was because of his ambitions relating to Mexico and the shady way in which he conducted himself – a trademark Burr trait - that he was eventually elbowed out of England. It seems that, despite Burr's admirable commitment to his cause, hanging around the War Office only served to shoot himself in the foot.

COFFEE HOUSES

Virginia Coffee House | Storey's Gate Coffee House | Salopian Coffee House | Tower Coffee House

Aaron Burr delineates in detail his trips to London's coffee houses where he often dashed off correspondence to America or met with prominent acquaintances. In fact, Burr mentions more coffee houses than any other visitor to the city in this anthology. Aside from his first night in London at the Gloucester Coffee House, he was also a frequenter of the Virginia, Storey's Gate, Salopian, and Tower coffee houses. While Burr did not use the establishments for quite the same reason Benjamin Franklin had done during his residence in London – the former vice-president was not a fervent attendee of Enlightenment meetings – he often met his acquaintances for dinner at the coffee houses, such as fellow American, Captain John Percival.

The Virginia Coffee House, one of Burr's regular haunts, had – as the name suggests - American connections. Established in 1744 with the full name the Virginia and Baltick Coffee House, the coffee house, located at 61 Threadneedle Street in the City of London, was an important hub for trade in the eighteenth century, with merchants from the southern colony meeting at the establishment to flog their wares and network.

West Country Mail at the Gloucester Coffee House by James Pollard. Burr stayed at the Gloucester on his first day in London.

On November 13, 1808, Burr dined with a Sir Mark A. Gerrard at Storey's Gate Coffee House located next to an entrance to St. James's Park on Great George Street, Westminster. Unlike the coffee houses in the City of London with eponymous American names, the establishments around Westminster and Charing Cross had a far less American feel but were still integral to Americans in London in terms of networking and being able to deliver letters for the packets. Burr later made plans to meet Gerrard again at the Salopian Coffee House in Charing Cross on November 20. Not far from his Craven Street lodgings or the War Office on Whitehall, Burr waited for Gerrard only for Captain Percival – known as Mad Jack Percival – to turn up in his stead.

Massachusettson "Captain Percival of the Marines,"[9] as Burr referred to him, was twenty-three years Burr's junior and had been a fellow traveller on the *Clarissa Ann*. Gallingly, Burr does not delineate at length about social excursions, except to note that they happened. Thus, we do not know the content of Percival's conversations with Burr, nor his conversations with Gerrard. However, given their kindred blood as Americans, talk may have turned to the political temperament the two men had left behind four thousand miles away or even the rising Anglo-American tensions which would lead to another cross-Atlantic fight called the War of 1812, in which Captain Percival was to receive great recognition for his actions.

Burr's most visited coffee house is one he refers to as 'Tower Coffee House'. Vexatiously, this coffee house has an air of mystery as a number of London coffee houses during this period began with 'Tower'. On one hand, it could have been Lloyd's Coffee House which originated near the Tower of London but, by the time Burr arrived, had relocated to Cornhill near the Royal Exchange. Lloyd's was founded in 1688 by Edward Lloyd and primarily served seafarers coming off the Thames and those who wanted to discuss maritime affairs and trade. On the other, Burr refers to a coffee house on Bond Street in the same breath as discussing meetings at the 'Tower.'

While the location remains an enigma, it was at the Tower Coffee House that Burr continued networking with those in the British military establishment and dined with General Thomas Picton, a British Army officer who had seen action in the Caribbean and was later killed at the Battle of Waterloo in 1815.

Not only did Burr frequent coffee houses, but also a fair share of London's coaching inns. In a section wedged in his journal called *The Adventures of Gil Blas Moheagungk of Manhattan* – a parody of French author Alain-René Lesage's early eighteenth-century novel *The Adventures of Gil Blas of Santillane* – Burr recounts travels in and out of London, including a slew of inns. One of note was The Black Lion on Water Street (now renamed Whitefriars Street with almost no eighteenth-century buildings left due to damage inflicted on the City during the Blitz) which stuck out to him for its "very dirty bed."[10]

THE TOWER OF LONDON, THE CITY OF LONDON

Like several other Americans mentioned in this book, Burr noted his visit to the Tower of London. On November 27, 1808, Burr whiled away the afternoon on a walking tour of London. He passed over Westminster Bridge from the north side of the river to the south. He perused Southwark and London Bridge before finally arriving at the Tower of London which he had not yet laid his eyes on despite having been galivanting around the city for four months. His descriptions of the Tower make it seem that he was less than impressed. Instead of describing the majesty of the medieval fortress, Burr showed his inner revolutionary and former soldier when he wrote this description of the Tower, "It is surrounded by a ditch, through which the Thames water flows; but it would not resist an enemy provided with heavy cannon for twenty-four hours. It may do very well to keep the lions and state prisoners."[11] Had Washington D.C. had its own version of the Tower of London, Burr may likely have very well had found himself a state prisoner at the behest of Tom J.

The Tower of London, 1737.

HAYMARKET, PICCADILLY

Burr's journal namedrops several locations in London: Charing Cross; Tottenham Court Road; Oxford Street etc, are all mentioned in passing. The New Jerseyan also discusses his consumer habits, he bought a peruke in Covent Garden, for example. He also goes off on several tangents about flagrant bootmakers, complains tediously about printers, and notes how he went to extreme lengths to avoid walking home via the Strand where Abigail Adams had frequently shopped as it was "forever so crowded and so dirty."[12] He even visited Grosvenor Square to call on the Earl of Bridgwater and the Viscount Grimston (in a coincidental turn of events, Grimston's daughter married into the Craven family, see *Chapter Four:* Benjamin Franklin), both members of the British establishment but neither were home to greet him.

However, Haymarket is the location that stands out against the other names. On December 7, 1808, Burr remarks, "Rose at ten. Such is the mode in London. Sor [*go out*] at 1. Going up Haymarket,

Met Madame O., and walked with her half an hour."[13] Was Burr to have known that he passed the very store where Angelica and John Church had chosen the duelling pistols which he later used to kill Hamilton? Likely not. However, the cyclical nature of his trip in bringing him back to the same spot where the stem of his duelling nightmare began cannot escape the delight of historians who revel in the coincidences of the past.

In July 1812, Aaron Burr returned to the United States and began operating under the name of his matrilineal line, Edwards. For years in Europe, he had been trying to obtain a passport to return home to Theodosia. Yet, the father and daughter never saw each other again. Theodosia was living in South Carolina and, due to the death of her son, had decided not to venture north to meet her father until the winter. Boarding the vessel *Patriot* on New Year's Eve, Theodosia sailed out of a Georgetown harbour and was never seen again. Multiple conspiracy theories exist about Theodosia's disappearance including stories of her walking the plank, being captured and or murdered by pirates, and a fairytale-esque story of being found naked and half-dead on a shipwreck by a chief of the Karankawa people to whom she gave a golden locket inscribed with 'Theodosia' to be shown to Burr if he ever searched for her. The most likely scenario was that Theodosia perished in a violent storm which is recorded in weather logs of British sailors.

Burr was heartbroken but managed to quietly return to his work as a lawyer in New York City. In 1833, he married a fifty-eight-year-old widow called Eliza Jumel. They divorced after three years having only been together for four months after the wedding when Eliza discovered that Burr was dwindling her finances and left him. The divorce took three years to play out, and who represented Eliza in the proceedings? None other than Alexander Hamilton Jr., who surely approached the case with more vengeance than a standard divorce trial.

Burr's tumultuous life finally came to a discreet end on Staten Island on September 14, 1836, where he died broke and shamed in a boarding house – the same day his second marriage official ended. Far from the ostentatious and heroic grave Hamilton has in the grounds of Trinity Church, Burr's body was returned to New Jersey to be buried in a simple plot in Princeton Cemetery near the father he barely knew.

While Aaron Burr's stint in London came after the Hamilton's death, the path and legacy he left in the city for Hamilton lovers is, for many, the most important. Even though one can trace other intensely potent links to Hamilton in London - such as John Adams's home, Benedict Arnold's grave and the birthplace of the duelling pistols – Burr's connections are fascinating as he was not visiting the city for education like Laurens, or for business like Franklin, Jefferson or Jay; Burr was there because, in part, his duel with Hamilton had forcibly put him there. Tracing the roots of his exile to the amalgamation of events which led Burr to set sail on the *Clarissa Ann* that June, it is undeniable that Hamilton is at the heart of Burr's time in London.

EPILOGUE

LONDON'S BUT A DREAM

Eliza had time to travel; she lived for fifty years after Hamilton died. Yet, she dedicated herself to preserving her husband's legacy and undertaking philanthropic work. On January 20, 2021, her effort to ensure America did not forget what her husband had done was finally complete. While the forty-sixth president of the United States was being sworn in on the steps of the Capitol Building, a speedy team of workers renovated the Oval Office ready for its new occupant. Out of storage came John Trumball's 1806 portrait of her husband. Painted after Hamilton's death, Trumball had searched his memory to capture the young, dashing politician with his trademark upturned nose, looking into the distance with ideas brimming from his dark eyes, before the Reynolds Affair and Philip's death turned his hair grey, and a dark cloud brewed over his once rollicking life. Hanging over the Oval's fireplace – over Thomas Jefferson's portrait to be exact, a fact which would have the Virginian turning in his grave – parallel to Gilbert Stuart's portrait of George Washington, Alexander Hamilton's legacy was restored; justice had finally been done to the memory of her Hamilton. Although Eliza would have adored traveling outside of her beloved New York, dedicating herself to Hamilton's memory was undeniably more important, despite the fact she had once so intensely "cried 'Atlantic.'"

Although Alexander, Eliza, and their brood of mini Hamiltons never docked at Falmouth - it was just another dream in Hamilton's short life that went unfulfilled – the potential trail they may have left had they sojourned creates a wealth of possibilities and questions:

Where would they have stayed? That could be dependent on time. If they arrived during Angelica's tenure, one can imagine the whole family shacked up on Sackville Street while Alex and Eliza swooned around her older sister, cousins played, and the vacationing Americans threw questioning, disapproving looks at the company kept.

What would they have done? A student of history, Hamilton would have certainly soaked up the city's museum, as well as perusing Stockdale's and other Piccadilly booksellers. Eliza would probably have enjoyed an afternoon's entertainment at the theatre with her sister, and the whole family likely could have been seen taking long walks through the neighbouring parks, and maybe even called on the new minister plenipotentiary in Grosvenor Square.

Who else would they have visited? Would Hamilton have been tempted to meet with British politicians and courtiers, even George III himself? Maybe they would have headed out of the city to see the booming hub of the Industrial Revolution in England's north which Alexander was so keen to replicate, or possibly travelled even further to his ancestral homeland of Scotland. Would they have crossed the English Channel to visit America's beloved Frenchman, the Marquis de Lafayette?

All these questions will remain unanswered, lost to a history that was never meant to be. Yet, through the travels of his contemporaries - whether they were in London for six weeks or sixteen years – historians eager to follow in the footsteps of some of the most preeminent figures of the Revolutionary or Confederation eras, who had consequential effects on the life of Alexander Hamilton, can do so. Not only that, but Hamilton's imprint is also so obviously weaved all the way through the London stories of his broad milieu of coevals, that it almost does not matter that he never visited, his story is as much part of London's tapestry in his absence as it would have been had he physically paced the city's cobbled streets with the bravado, excitement, and sense of profoundness that only an American can bring.

CHAPTER NOTES

Prologue: Betsey Cries "Atlantic!"

1. From Alexander Hamilton to Angelica Church, [31 January 1791]. *The Papers of Alexander Hamilton*, vol. 7, *September 1790–January 1791*, ed. Harold C. Syrett. New York: Columbia University Press, 1963, p. 608.
2. From Alexander Hamilton to Angelica Church, [2 October 1791]. *The Papers of Alexander Hamilton*, vol. 9, *August 1791–December 1791*, ed. Harold C. Syrett. New York: Columbia University Press, 1965, pp. 266–267.
3. The Obama White House (2009), *Lin-Manuel Miranda Performs at the White House Poetry Jam*. [Online video] [Accessed September 11 2021] Available at: <https://www.youtube.com/watch?v=WNFf7nMIGnE>
4. BroadwayInHD (2016), *70ᵗʰ Annual Tony Awards 'Hamilton'*. [Online video] [Accessed September 11 2021] Available at: <https://www.youtube.com/watch?v=b5VqyCQV1Tg>
5. Chernow, Ron. *Alexander Hamilton*. London: Head of Zeus, 2020. p. 12-13
6. Ibid.
7. From Alexander Hamilton to The Royal Danish American Gazette, [6 September 1772], *The Papers of Alexander Hamilton*, vol. 1, *1768–1778*, ed. Harold C. Syrett. New York: Columbia University Press, 1961, pp. 34–38.
8. *The Papers of Alexander Hamilton*, vol. 21, *April 1797–July 1798*, ed. Harold C. Syrett. New York: Columbia University Press, 1974, pp. 238–267.
9. Chernow, Ron. *Alexander Hamilton*. London: Head of Zeus, 2020. Elizabeth Hamilton Holly to John C. Hamilton, February 27, 1855.
10. Atlantic Monthly, August 1896. p. 3.
11. Hamilton, John C. .*The Life of Alexander Hamilton*. (New York, 1840) p. 126
12. Widenor, William. C. *Henry Cabot Lodge and the Search for an American Foreign Policy*. London: University of California Press, 1980, p. 28.
13. Abigail Adams to Mary Smith Cranch, [11 September 1785], *The Adams Papers*, Adams Family Correspondence, vol. 6, *December 1784–December 1785*, ed. Richard Alan Ryerson. Cambridge, MA: Harvard University Press, 1993, pp. 357–360.

Chapter One: Angelica Schuyler Church

1. From Thomas Jefferson to Angelica Schuyler Church, [17 February 1788], *The Papers of Thomas Jefferson*, vol. 12, *7 August 1787–31 March 1788*, ed. Julian P. Boyd. Princeton: Princeton University Press, 1955, pp. 600–601.

2. To Thomas Jefferson from Maria Cosway, 25 December [1787], *The Papers of Thomas Jefferson*, vol. 12, *7 August 1787–31 March 1788*, ed. Julian P. Boyd. Princeton: Princeton University Press, 1955, pp. 459–460.

3. Miranda, Lin-Manuel. 2015. Non-stop. Performed by: Lin-Manuel Miranda, Phillipa Soo, Christopher Jackson, Renée Elise Goldsberry and the Original Broadway Cast of "Hamilton". *Hamilton: An American Musical (Original Broadway Cast Recording)*. New York: Atlantic.

4. From Alexander Hamilton to Angelica Church, [8 November 1789]," *The Papers of Alexander Hamilton*, vol. 5, *June 1788–November 1789*, ed. Harold C. Syrett. New York: Columbia University Press, 1962, pp. 501–502.

5. Chernow, Ron. *Alexander Hamilton*. London: Head of Zeus, 2020. p.

6. Hamilton, Allan Mclane. *Alexander Hamilton: Illustrated Biography Based on Family Letters and Other Personal Documents*. Madison & Adams Press, 2019.

7. From Alexander Hamilton to Angelica Church, [8 November 1789] *The Papers of Alexander Hamilton*, vol. 5, *June 1788–November 1789*, ed. Harold C. Syrett. New York: Columbia University Press, 1962, pp. 501–502

8. From Angelica Church to Alexander Hamilton, [15 August 1793], *The Papers of Alexander Hamilton*, vol. 15, *June 1793–January 1794*, ed. Harold C. Syrett. New York: Columbia University Press, 1969, p. 247.

9. From Angelica Church to Alexander Hamilton, [2 October 1787] *The Papers of Alexander Hamilton*, vol. 4, *January 1787–May 1788*, ed. Harold C. Syrett. New York: Columbia University Press, 1962, pp. 279–280.

10. Historic Royal Palaces. *George III*. [Accessed September 9, 2021]. <https://www.hrp.org.uk/kew-palace/history-and-stories/george-iii/#gs.ayj2wf>

11. Letter of Angelica Church to HRH George, the Prince of Wales [March 25, 1811], University of Virginia Library. [Accessed September 9, 2021]

<https://explore.lib.virginia.edu/exhibits/show/church/kings/kings>

12. From Alexander Hamilton to Angelica Church, [2 October 1791], *The Papers of Alexander Hamilton*, vol. 9, *August 1791–December 1791*, ed. Harold C. Syrett. New York: Columbia University Press, 1965, pp. 266–267.

13. Ibid.

14. Chernow, Ron. *Alexander Hamilton*. London: Head of Zeus, 2020. Angelica Church to Elizabeth Hamilton, January 23, 1792.

15. Scott, Susan Holloway (2017). *A History Mystery Solved: Rediscovering a Lost Portrait of Angelica Schuyler Church*. [Accessed September 9, 2021] <https://susanhollowayscott.com/blog/2017/2/26/history-mystery-is-this-a-forgotten-portrait-of-angelica-schuyler-church>

16. From Angelica Church to Alexander Hamilton, [4 February 1790], *The Papers of Alexander Hamilton*, vol. 6, *December 1789–August 1790*, ed. Harold C. Syrett. New York: Columbia University Press, 1962, p. 245.

17. Chernow, Ron. *Alexander Hamilton*. London: Head of Zeus, 2020. p. 681.

Chapter Two: John Adams

1. From John Adams to Benjamin Rush, 25 January 1806. *Founders Online,* National Archives, [Accessed September 15 2021] <https://founders.archives.gov/documents/Adams/99-02-02-5119>

2. Letter from Alexander Hamilton, Concerning the Public Conduct and Character of John Adams, Esq. President of the United States, [24 October 1800], *The Papers of Alexander Hamilton*, vol. 25, *July 1800–April 1802*, ed. Harold C. Syrett. New York: Columbia University Press, 1977, pp. 186–234.

3. Ibid.

4. *The Adams Papers*, Diary and Autobiography of John Adams, vol. 3, Diary, 1782–1804; Autobiography, Part One to October 1776, ed. L. H. Butterfield. Cambridge, MA: Harvard University Press, 1961, pp. 175–178.

5. Abigail Adams to John Adams [31 March 1776], *The Adams Papers*, Adams Family Correspondence, vol. 1, *December 1761–May 1776*, ed. Lyman H. Butterfield. Cambridge, MA: Harvard University Press, 1963, pp. 369–371.

6. *The Adams Papers*, Diary and Autobiography of John Adams, vol. 3, *Diary, 1782–1804; Autobiography, Part One to October 1776*, ed. L. H.

Butterfield. Cambridge, MA: Harvard University Press, 1961, pp. 175–178.

7. Ibid.

8. Abigail Adams to Elizabeth Smith Shaw, [28 – 30 July 1784] *The Adams Papers*, Adams Family Correspondence, vol. 5, *October 1782– November 1784*, ed. Richard Alan Ryerson. Cambridge, MA: Harvard University Press, 1993, pp. 402–408.

9. Abigail Adams to Cotton Tufts [26 April 1785], *The Adams Papers*, Adams Family Correspondence, vol. 6, *December 1784–December 1785*, ed. Richard Alan Ryerson. Cambridge, MA: Harvard University Press, 1993, pp. 103–109.

10. John Adams to Abigail Adams Smith, [27 July 1784], *The Adams Papers*, Adams Family Correspondence, vol. 5, *October 1782–November 1784*, ed. Richard Alan Ryerson. Cambridge, MA: Harvard University Press, 1993, pp. 400–401.

11. Ibid.

12. From John Adams to Boston Patriot, [14 February 1812], *Founders Online,* National Archives, [Accessed September 11 2021] <https://founders.archives.gov/documents/Adams/99-02-02-5757>

13 *The Adams Papers*, Adams Family Correspondence, vol. 6, *December 1784–December 1785*, ed. Richard Alan Ryerson. Cambridge, MA: Harvard University Press, 1993, pp. 186–194.

14 Ibid.

15 Chernow, Ron. *Alexander Hamilton*. London: Head of Zeus, 2020. p. 525.

16 John Adams Diary 44, 27 March - 21 July 1786.

13 *The Adams Papers*, Adams Family Correspondence, vol. 6, December 1784–December 1785, ed. Richard Alan Ryerson. Cambridge, MA: Harvard University Press, 1993, pp. 169–173.

13. *The Adams Papers*, Papers of John Adams, vol. 17, *April–November 1785*, ed. Gregg L. Lint, C. James Taylor, Sara Georgini, Hobson Woodward, Sara B. Sikes, Amanda A. Mathews, and Sara Martin. Cambridge, MA: Harvard University Press, 2014, pp. 160–161.

14. Thomas Jefferson: Autobiography, [6 Jan.-29 July 1821, 6 January 1821], *Founders Online,* National Archives, [Accessed September 11 2021] <https://founders.archives.gov/documents/Jefferson/98-01-02-1756>

15. "From John Adams to John Jay, [2 June 1785], *The Adams Papers*, Papers of John Adams, vol. 17, *April–November 1785*, ed. Gregg L. Lint, C. James Taylor, Sara Georgini, Hobson Woodward, Sara B. Sikes, Amanda A. Mathews, and Sara Martin. Cambridge, MA: Harvard University Press, 2014, pp. 134–145.

16. Ibid.
17. Ibid.
18. Ibid.
19. Ibid.
20. Ibid.
21. Ibid.
22. Ibid.
23. Abigail Adams to John Quincy Adams, [26 June 1785], *The Adams Papers*, Adams Family Correspondence, vol. 6, *December 1784– December 1785*, ed. Richard Alan Ryerson. Cambridge, MA: Harvard University Press, 1993, pp. 194–197.
24. Abigail Adams to Mary Smith Cranch, [24 June 1785], *The Adams Papers*, Adams Family Correspondence, vol. 6, *December 1784– December 1785*, ed. Richard Alan Ryerson. Cambridge, MA: Harvard University Press, 1993, pp. 186–194.
25. Abigail Adams to John Quincy Adams, [26 June 1785], *The Adams Papers*, Adams Family Correspondence, vol. 6, *December 1784– December 1785*, ed. Richard Alan Ryerson. Cambridge, MA: Harvard University Press, 1993, pp. 194–197.
26. Abigail Adams Smith to John Quincy Adams, [4 July 1785 – 11 August 1785], *The Adams Papers*, Adams Family Correspondence, vol. 6, *December 1784–December 1785*, ed. Richard Alan Ryerson. Cambridge, MA: Harvard University Press, 1993, pp. 204–223.
27. Abigail Adams to Mary Smith Cranch, [24 June 1785], *The Adams Papers*, Adams Family Correspondence, vol. 6, *December 1784– December 1785*, ed. Richard Alan Ryerson. Cambridge, MA: Harvard University Press, 1993, pp. 186–194.
28. vol. 6, *December 1784–December 1785*, ed. Richard Alan Ryerson. Cambridge, MA: Harvard University Press, 1993, pp. 194–197.
29. Abigail Adams to Mary Smith Cranch, [24 June 1785], *The Adams Papers*, Adams Family Correspondence, vol. 6, *December 1784– December 1785*, ed. Richard Alan Ryerson. Cambridge, MA: Harvard University Press, 1993, pp. 186–194.
30. Abigail Adams to John Quincy Adams, [26 June 1785], *The Adams Papers*, Adams Family Correspondence, vol. 6, *December 1784– December 1785*, ed. Richard Alan Ryerson. Cambridge, MA: Harvard University Press, 1993, pp. 194–197.
31. Abigail Adams Smith to John Quincy Adams, [4 July 1785 – 11 August 1785], *The Adams Papers*, Adams Family Correspondence, vol. 6, *December 1784–December 1785*, ed. Richard Alan Ryerson. Cambridge, MA: Harvard University Press, 1993, pp. 204–223.
32. Abigail Adams to Mary Smith Cranch, [24 June 1785], *The Adams Papers*, Adams Family Correspondence, vol. 6, *December 1784–

December 1785, ed. Richard Alan Ryerson. Cambridge, MA: Harvard University Press, 1993, pp. 186–194.

33. Abigail Adams to Cotton Tufts, [18 August 1785]," *The Adams Papers*, Adams Family Correspondence, vol. 6, *December 1784–December 1785*, ed. Richard Alan Ryerson. Cambridge, MA: Harvard University Press, 1993, pp. 283–287.

34. "Enclosure: Extracts from Newspapers", [6 June 1785], *The Adams Papers*, Adams Family Correspondence, vol. 6, *December 1784–December 1785*, ed. Richard Alan Ryerson. Cambridge, MA: Harvard University Press, 1993, pp. 173–174.

35. From John Adams to Thomas Jefferson, [7 June 1785], *The Adams Papers*, Papers of John Adams, vol. 17, *April–November 1785*, ed. Gregg L. Lint, C. James Taylor, Sara Georgini, Hobson Woodward, Sara B. Sikes, Amanda A. Mathews, and Sara Martin. Cambridge, MA: Harvard University Press, 2014, pp. 160–161.

36. Ibid.

37. From John Adams to Boston Patriot, [17 February 1812], *Founders Online,* National Archives, [Accessed September 9, 2021] <https://founders.archives.gov/documents/Adams/99-02-02-5759>

38. John Quincy Adams to Elizabeth Cranch, [18 April 1784], *The Adams Papers*, Adams Family Correspondence, vol. 5, *October 1782–November 1784*, ed. Richard Alan Ryerson. Cambridge, MA: Harvard University Press, 1993, pp. 322–324.

39. From John Adams to Boston Patriot, [17 February 1812], *Founders Online,* National Archives, [Accessed September 9, 2021] <https://founders.archives.gov/documents/Adams/99-02-02-5759>

40. John Quincy Adams to Elizabeth Cranch, 18 April 1784," *Founders Online,* National Archives, https://founders.archives.gov/documents/Adams/04-05-02-0177. [Original source: *The Adams Papers*, Adams Family Correspondence, vol. 5, *October 1782–November 1784*, ed. Richard Alan Ryerson. Cambridge, MA: Harvard University Press, 1993, pp. 322–324.

41. Ibid.

42. Abigail Adams to Thomas Welsh, [25 August 1785], *The Adams Papers*, Adams Family Correspondence, vol. 6, *December 1784–December 1785*, ed. Richard Alan Ryerson. Cambridge, MA: Harvard University Press, 1993, pp. 297–299.

43. Abigail Adams to Mary Smith Cranch, [15 August 1785], *The Adams Papers*, Adams Family Correspondence, vol. 6, *December 1784–December 1785*, ed. Richard Alan Ryerson. Cambridge, MA: Harvard University Press, 1993, pp. 276–280.

44. Abigail Adams Smith to John Quincy Adams, [4 July 1785 – 11 August 1785], *The Adams Papers*, Adams Family Correspondence, vol. 6, *December 1784–December 1785*, ed. Richard Alan Ryerson. Cambridge, MA: Harvard University Press, 1993, pp. 204–223.

45. Abigail Adams to Thomas Welsh, [25 August 1785], *The Adams Papers*, Adams Family Correspondence, vol. 6, *December 1784– December 1785*, ed. Richard Alan Ryerson. Cambridge, MA: Harvard University Press, 1993, pp. 297–299.

46. Abigail Adams to Mary Smith Cranch?, [July – August 1785], *The Adams Papers*, Adams Family Correspondence, vol. 6, *December 1784– December 1785*, ed. Richard Alan Ryerson. Cambridge, MA: Harvard University Press, 1993, pp. 240–242.

47. Abigail Adams to Thomas Welsh, [25 August 1785], *The Adams Papers*, Adams Family Correspondence, vol. 6, *December 1784– December 1785*, ed. Richard Alan Ryerson. Cambridge, MA: Harvard University Press, 1993, pp. 297–299.

48. Abigail Adams to John Quincy Adams, [26 June 1785], *The Adams Papers*, Adams Family Correspondence, vol. 6, *December 1784– December 1785*, ed. Richard Alan Ryerson. Cambridge, MA: Harvard University Press, 1993, pp. 194–197.

49. Published in the Philadelphia literary magazine Port Folio.

50. *The Memoirs of Madison Hemings*. Pike County Republican, 1873.

51. Abigail Adams to Thomas Jefferson, [27 June 1787], *The Adams Papers*, Adams Family Correspondence, vol. 8, *March 1787–December 1789*, ed. C. James Taylor, Margaret A. Hogan, Jessie May Rodrique, Gregg L. Lint, Hobson Woodward, and Mary T. Claffey. Cambridge, MA: Harvard University Press, 2007, pp. 93–94.

52. Abigail Adams to Thomas Jefferson, [6 July 1787], *The Adams Papers*, Adams Family Correspondence, vol. 8, *March 1787–December 1789*, ed. C. James Taylor, Margaret A. Hogan, Jessie May Rodrique, Gregg L. Lint, Hobson Woodward, and Mary T. Claffey. Cambridge, MA: Harvard University Press, 2007, pp. 107–109.

53. Ibid.

54. Abigail Adams to Thomas Jefferson with a Memorandum of Purchases, [10 July 1787], *The Adams Papers*, Adams Family Correspondence, vol. 8, *March 1787–December 1789*, ed. C. James Taylor, Margaret A. Hogan, Jessie May Rodrique, Gregg L. Lint, Hobson Woodward, and Mary T. Claffey. Cambridge, MA: Harvard University Press, 2007, pp. 109–112.

55. "Phocian No.II", *Gazette of the United States*, [October 21, 1796].

56. To Thomas Jefferson from Abigail Adams, with Enclosure, [6 June 1785], *The Papers of Thomas Jefferson*, vol. 8, *25 February–31 October*

1785, ed. Julian P. Boyd. Princeton: Princeton University Press, 1953, pp. 178–181.

57. "[October 1783]," *The Adams Papers*, Diary of John Quincy Adams, vol. 1, *November 1779–March 1786*, ed. Robert J. Taylor and Marc Friedlaender. Cambridge, MA: Harvard University Press, 1981, pp. 195–198.

58. From John Adams to Charles Francis Adams, [25 June 1816]," *Founders Online,* National Archives, <https://founders.archives.gov/documents/Adams/99-03-02-3126>

59. Correspondence, vol. 6, *December 1784–December 1785*, ed. Richard Alan Ryerson. Cambridge, MA: Harvard University Press, 1993, pp. 260–262.

60. Abigail Adams to Thomas Jefferson, [12 August 1785], *The Adams Papers*, Adams Family Correspondence, vol. 6, *December 1784–December 1785*, ed. Richard Alan Ryerson. Cambridge, MA: Harvard University Press, 1993, pp. 262–266.

61. Abigail Adams to William Stephens Smith, [18 September 1785]," *The Adams Papers*, Adams Family Correspondence, vol. 6, *December 1784–December 1785*, ed. Richard Alan Ryerson. Cambridge, MA: Harvard University Press, 1993, pp. 365–369.

62. Abigail Adams to Elizabeth Smith Shaw, [4 March 1786], *The Adams Papers*, Adams Family Correspondence, vol. 7, *January 1786–February 1787*, ed. C. James Taylor, Margaret A. Hogan, Celeste Walker, Anne Decker Cecere, Gregg L. Lint, Hobson Woodward, and Mary T. Claffey. Cambridge, MA: Harvard University Press, 2005, pp. 80–85.

63. Ibid.

64. Levin, Phyllis Lee. *The Remarkable Education of John Quincy Adams*. New York: St. Martin's Press, 2015. John Quincy Adams to Peter Jay Munro.

65. "Tuesday. 28th.," *The Adams Papers*, Diary of John Quincy Adams, vol. 1, *November 1779–March 1786*, ed. Robert J. Taylor and Marc Friedlaender. Cambridge, MA: Harvard University Press, 1981, p. 197.

66. From John Adams to François Adriaan Van der Kemp, [3 January 1803]," *Founders Online,* National Archives, <https://founders.archives.gov/documents/Adams/99-02-02-5003>

67. "Monday [24 April.]," *The Adams Papers*, Diary and Autobiography of John Adams, vol. 3, *Diary, 1782–1804; Autobiography, Part One to October 1776*, ed. L. H. Butterfield. Cambridge, MA: Harvard University Press, 1961, p. 191.

68. Abigail Adams to John Quincy Adams, [26 June 1785], *The Adams Papers*, Adams Family Correspondence, vol. 6, *December 1784–*

December 1785, ed. Richard Alan Ryerson. Cambridge, MA: Harvard University Press, 1993, pp. 194–197.

69. Abigail Adams to Elizabeth Storer Smith, [29 August 1785], *The Adams Papers*, Adams Family Correspondence, vol. 6, *December 1784– December 1785*, ed. Richard Alan Ryerson. Cambridge, MA: Harvard University Press, 1993, pp. 314–316.

70. Thomas Jefferson to John Adams, [7 July 1785], *The Adams Papers*, Papers of John Adams, vol. 17, *April–November 1785*, ed. Gregg L. Lint, C. James Taylor, Sara Georgini, Hobson Woodward, Sara B. Sikes, Amanda A. Mathews, and Sara Martin. Cambridge, MA: Harvard University Press, 2014, pp. 220–223.

71. Abigail Adams to Elizabeth Smith Shaw, [28 – 30 July 1784], *The Adams Papers*, Adams Family Correspondence, vol. 5, *October 1782– November 1784*, ed. Richard Alan Ryerson. Cambridge, MA: Harvard University Press, 1993, pp. 402–408.

72. From John Adams to Boston Patriot, [17 February 1812], *Founders Online,* National Archives, [Accessed September 9, 2021] <https://founders.archives.gov/documents/Adams/99-02-02-5759>

73. John Adams to George III, [20 February 1788], *The Adams Papers*, Papers of John Adams, vol. 19, *February 1787–May 1789*, ed. Sara Georgini, Sara Martin, R. M. Barlow, Amanda M. Norton, Neal E. Millikan, and Hobson Woodward. Cambridge, MA: Harvard University Press, 2016, p. 276.

74. "Abigail Adams' Diary of her Return Voyage to America, [30 March– 1 May 1788], *The Adams Papers*, Diary and Autobiography of John Adams, vol. 3, *Diary, 1782–1804; Autobiography, Part One to October 1776*, ed. L. H. Butterfield. Cambridge, MA: Harvard University Press, 1961, pp. 212–217.

Chapter Three: Thomas Jefferson

1. Thomas Jefferson: Autobiography, [6 Jan.-29 July 1821, 6 January 1821], *Founders Online,* National Archives, <https://founders.archives.gov/documents/Jefferson/98-01-02-1756>

2. Rouan, Rick. *Fact check: No, Alexander Hamilton did not tell Thomas Jefferson he wanted to hit him with a chair*. USA Today. [Accessed September 11 2021] <https://eu.usatoday.com/story/news/factcheck/2021/04/08/fact-check-hamilton-didnt-threaten-hit-jefferson-chair/7144226002/>

3. From John Adams to Thomas Jefferson, [17 February 1786], *The Adams Papers*, Papers of John Adams, vol. 18, *December 1785–January 1787*, ed. Gregg L. Lint, Sara Martin, C. James Taylor, Sara Georgini,

Hobson Woodward, Sara B. Sikes, Amanda M. Norton. Cambridge, MA: Harvard University Press, 2016, pp. 165–167.

4. Dickens, Charles. *Nicholas Nickleby.* Ware: Wordsworth Editions, 1995.

5. Memorandum Books, 1786, *The Papers of Thomas Jefferson*, Second Series, *Jefferson's Memorandum Books*, vol. 1, ed. James A Bear, Jr. and Lucia C. Stanton. Princeton: Princeton University Press, 1997, pp. 605–649.

6. Declaration of Independence, 1776. [Accessed September 14 2021] <https://www.archives.gov/founding-docs/declaration-transcript>

7. Thomas Jefferson: Autobiography, [6 Jan.-29 July 1821, 6 January 1821], *Founders Online,* National Archives, [Accessed September 11 2021] <https://founders.archives.gov/documents/Jefferson/98-01-02-1756>

8. Adams, Charles F, and John Quincy. *John Adams, Volume 2.* New York: Cosimo Press, 2005. p. 102.

9. Ritcheson, Charles R. *Fragile Memory* [Accessed September 11 2021] <https://www.americanheritage.com/fragile-memory>

10. "[In Congress, May–July 1776], *The Adams Papers*, Diary and Autobiography of John Adams, vol. 3, *Diary, 1782–1804; Autobiography, Part One to October 1776*, ed. L. H. Butterfield. Cambridge, MA: Harvard University Press, 1961, pp. 335–337.

11. From Thomas Jefferson to Hugh Paul Taylor, [4 October 1823], *Founders Online,* National Archives, [Accessed September 11 2021] <https://founders.archives.gov/documents/Jefferson/98-01-02-3789>

12. Randall, Henry Stephens. *The Life of Thomas Jefferson.* New York: Derby and Jackson, 1858. Vol. 3, p. 336.

13. The contents of the Magna Carta. UK Parliament. [Accessed September 14 2021] < https://www.parliament.uk/about/living-heritage/evolutionofparliament/originsofparliament/birthofparliament/overview/magnacarta/magnacartaclauses/>

14. Brammer, Robert (2020). *Henry Laurens, the Founding Father who was imprisoned at the Tower of London.* Library of Congress. [Accessed September 15 2021] <https://blogs.loc.gov/law/2020/05/henry-laurens-the-founding-father-who-was-imprisoned-in-the-tower-of-london/>

15. Thomas Jefferson to Thomas Jefferson Randolph, [24 November 1808], *Founders Online,* National Archives, [Accessed September 11 2021] < https://founders.archives.gov/documents/Jefferson/99-01-02-9151=>

16. Jefferson, Isaac. *Memoirs of a Monticello Slave.* 1847. Charlottesville: University of Virginia Press, 1951.

17. *On This Day: July 4, 1826, Thomas Jefferson and John Adams die.* History. [Accessed on September 15 2021] <https://www.history.com/this-day-in-history/thomas-jefferson-and-john-adams-die>

18. Cerami, Charles A. *Dinner at Mr. Jefferson's: Three Men, Five Great Wines, and the Evening That Changed America.* United States: JW, 2009.

19. William Short to John Trumball [10 September 1788]. [Accessed September 14 2021] <https://founders.archives.gov/documents/Jefferson/01-14-02-0146> (*In post script notes*).

20. Thomas Jefferson, William Stephens Smith, and Richard Peters to John Adams [21 March 1786], *The Adams Papers*, Papers of John Adams, vol. 18, *December 1785–January 1787*, ed. Gregg L. Lint, Sara Martin, C. James Taylor, Sara Georgini, Hobson Woodward, Sara B. Sikes, Amanda M. Norton. Cambridge, MA: Harvard University Press, 2016, p. 217.

21. "Notes of a Tour of English Gardens", [2–14 April 1786], *The Papers of Thomas Jefferson*, vol. 9, *1 November 1785–22 June 1786*, ed. Julian P. Boyd. Princeton: Princeton University Press, 1954, pp. 369–375.

22. Ibid.

23. Thomas Jefferson to John Page, [4 May 1786], *The Papers of Thomas Jefferson*, vol. 9, *1 November 1785–22 June 1786*, ed. Julian P. Boyd. Princeton: Princeton University Press, 1954, pp. 444–446.

24. Ibid.

Chapter Four: Benjamin Franklin

1. Chernow, Ron. *Alexander Hamilton.* London: Head of Zeus, 2020. p. 229.

2. Goodwin, George. *Benjamin Franklin in London.* London: Weidenfield & Nicolson, 2017. p. 10.

3. *The Papers of Benjamin Franklin,* vol. 7, *October 1, 1756 through March 31, 1758*, ed. Leonard W. Labaree. New Haven: Yale University Press, 1963, p. 243.

4. From Benjamin Franklin to Deborah Franklin, [5 May 1774], *The Papers of Benjamin Franklin,* vol. 21, *January 1, 1774, through March 22, 1775*, ed. William B. Willcox. New Haven and London: Yale University Press, 1978, pp. 208–209.

5. Letter from John Adams to Abigail Adams, 9 January 1797 [electronic edition]. *Adams Family Papers: An Electronic Archive.* Massachusetts Historical Society. [Accessed September 9, 2021] <http://www.masshist.org/digitaladams/>

6. Isaacson, Walter. *Benjamin Franklin: An American Life.* New York: Simon & Schuster, 2004. p. 242

7. Labaree, Leonard W. *Benjamin Franklin's British Friendships.* Proceedings of the American Philosophical Society, Vol. 108, No. 5 (Oct. 20, 1964), p. 424.

8. Ferling, John. *John Adams: A Life.* New York: Henry Holt, 1996.

9. Isaacson, Walter. (2003) *Benjamin Franklin Joins the Revolution.* Smithsonian Magazine [Accessed September 9, 2021]. <https://www.smithsonianmag.com/history/benjamin-franklin-joins-the-revolution-87199988/>

10. Franklin, Benjamin. *The Autobiography and Other Writings.* New York: Penguin Books, 2003. p. 42.

11. Ibid, p. 45.

12. Williams, Yohuru. *Why Thomas Jefferson's Anti-Slavery Passage Was Removed from the Declaration of Independence.* History [Accessed September 9, 2021] <https://www.history.com/news/declaration-of-independence-deleted-anti-slavery-clause-jefferson/>

13. Ibid.

14. Ibid.

15. From Benjamin Franklin to Jane Mecom, [19 April 1757], *The Papers of Benjamin Franklin,* vol. 7, *October 1, 1756 through March 31, 1758,* ed. Leonard W. Labaree. New Haven: Yale University Press, 1963, pp. 190–191.

16. Franklin, Benjamin. *The Autobiography and Other Writings.* New York: Penguin Books, 2003. p. 49-50.

17. Ibid, pg. 49.

18. Ibid, pg. 50.

19. From Benjamin Franklin to Deborah Franklin, [7 August 1761], *The Papers of Benjamin Franklin,* vol. 9, *January 1, 1760, through December 31, 1761*, ed. Leonard W. Labaree. New Haven: Yale University Press, 1966, p. 337.

20. To Benjamin Franklin from Mary Stevenson, [10 September 1761], *The Papers of Benjamin Franklin,* vol. 9, *January 1, 1760, through December 31, 1761*, ed. Leonard W. Labaree. New Haven: Yale University Press, 1966, pp. 354–356.

21. Franklin's Public Statement about the Hutchinson Letters, [25 December 1773], *The Papers of Benjamin Franklin,* vol. 20, *January 1 through December 31, 1773,* ed. William B. Willcox. New Haven and London: Yale University Press, 1976, pp. 513–516.

22. Goodwin, George. *Benjamin Franklin in London.* London: Weidenfield & Nicolson, 2017. p. 10

23. "Constitutional Convention. Second of Benjamin Franklin's Motion that Proposed Executive Serve Without Pay", [2 June 1787], *The Papers of Alexander Hamilton,* vol. 4, *January 1787–May 1788*, ed.

Harold C. Syrett. New York: Columbia University Press, 1962, pp. 176–177.

24. National Constitution Centre. (2020) *Benjamin Franklin's last great quote and the Constitution.* [Accessed September 9, 2021] <https://constitutioncenter.org/blog/benjamin-franklins-last-great-quote-and-the-constitution>

Chapter Five: Benedict Arnold

1. From Benjamin Franklin to the Marquis de Lafayette, [14 May 1781], *The Papers of Benjamin Franklin,* vol. 35, *May 1 through October 31, 1781*, ed. Barbara B. Oberg. New Haven and London: Yale University Press, 1999, pp. 64–67.

2. From George Washington to William Heath, [21 March 1781], *Founders Online,* National Archives, <https://founders.archives.gov/documents/Washington/99-01-02-05145.>

3. Alexander Hamilton to Elizabeth Schuyler, [September 25, 1780], *Papers of Alexander Hamilton*, Vol. 2, p. 442.

4. NBC News, 2014, *Why Benedict Arnold is an 'American Patriot'...in London*, [Accessed September 9, 2021] <https://www.nbcnews.com/news/world/why-benedict-arnold-american-patriot-london-n48691>

5. Arnold, M, and Goodfriend, Joyce D. *The Widowhood of Margaret Shippen Arnold: Letters from England, 1801 -1803.* The Pennsylvania Magazine of History and Biography, Vol. 115, No. 2 (April 1991), p. 226.

6. Ibid.

7. *Papers of Alexander Hamilton*, vol. 2, p. 468.

8. John Quincy Adams to Elizabeth Cranch, [18 April 1784], *The Adams Papers*, Adams Family Correspondence, vol. 5, *October 1782–November 1784*, ed. Richard Alan Ryerson. Cambridge, MA: Harvard University Press, 1993, pp. 322–324.

Chapter Six: John Jay

1. John Jay to Sarah Jay, *The Correspondence and Public Papers of John Jay*, ed. Henry P. Johnston, A.M. (New York: G.P. Putnam's Sons, 1890 – 93). Vol 4 (1794 – 1826) p. 3.

2. Ibid, John Jay to Sarah Jay, p. 2.

3. Ibid, John Jay to Sarah Jay, p. 5.

4. Ibid, Edmund Randolph to John Jay, p. 14.

5. Ibid, p. 20.

6. *The Epicure's Almanack*, 1815, pp. 206–7.

7. *The Papers of Alexander Hamilton*, vol. 16, *February 1794–July 1794*, ed. Harold C. Syrett. New York: Columbia University Press, 1972, pp. 381–385.
8. Ibid.
9. Ibid.
10. *The Correspondence and Public Papers of John Jay*, ed. Henry P. Johnston, A.M. (New York: G.P. Putnam's Sons, 1890 – 93). Vol 4 (1794 – 1826) p. 30.
11. Ibid, John Jay to Sarah Jay, p. 24.
12. "*The Papers of Alexander Hamilton*, vol. 16, *February 1794–July 1794*, ed. Harold C. Syrett. New York: Columbia University Press, 1972, pp. 608–610.
13. *The Correspondence and Public Papers of John Jay*, ed. Henry P. Johnston, A.M. (New York: G.P. Putnam's Sons, 1890 – 93). Vol 4 (1794 – 1826) p. 153.
14. Ibid, John Jay to Alexander Hamilton, p.135.

Chapter Seven: John Laurens

1. Tyler, Lyon G. *The Gnostic Trap: Richard Clarke and His Proclamation of the Millennium and Universal Restoration in South Carolina and England.* Anglican and Episcopal History Vol. 58, No. 2 (June 1989), p. 147.
2. Ibid, p. 152.
3. Massey, Gregory D. *John Laurens and the American Revolution.* South Carolina: University of South Carolina Press, 2016. p. 26.

Chapter Eight: Aaron Burr

1. *The private journal of Aaron Burr, reprinted in full from the original manuscript in the library of Mr. William K. Bixby of St. Louis, Mo., with an introduction, explanatory notes, and a glossary.* New York: The Post Express Printing Co., 1903.
2. Ibid, p. 3.
3. Asleson, Robyn. *Aaron Burr: Forgotten Feminist.* Smithsonian. [Accessed September 9, 2021] <https://npg.si.edu/blog/aaron-burr-forgotten-feminist>
4. Wallace, Carey (2016). *Forget Hamilton, Burr is the Real Hero.* Time [Accessed September 14 2021] <https://time.com/4292836/forget-hamilton-burr-is-the-real-hero/>
5. *The private journal of Aaron Burr, reprinted in full from the original manuscript in the library of Mr. William K. Bixby of St. Louis, Mo., with an introduction, explanatory notes, and a glossary.* New York: The Post Express Printing Co., 1903. p. 3.

6.   *The Correspondence of Jeremy Bentham,* Volume 1: 1752 to 1776: UCL Press, 2017.
7.   Ibid, p. 343.
8.   Pjb. p. 93.
9.   Ibid, p. 10.
10. Ibid, p. 40.
11. Ibid, p. 20.
12. Ibid, p. 34.
13. Ibid, p. 30.

BIBLIOGRAPHY

Adams, Charles Francis, and John Quincy. *John Adams, Volume 2*. New York: Cosimo Press, 2005.

Arnold, M, and Goodfriend, Joyce D. *The Widowhood of Margaret Shippen Arnold: Letters from England, 1801 -1803*. The Pennsylvania Magazine of History and Biography, Vol. 115, No. 2 (April 1991), pp. 221- 255.

Atkinson, Rick. *The British Are Coming*. London: William Collins, 2019.

Blight, David W. *Frederick Douglass: Prophet of Freedom*. New York: Simon & Schuster, 2018.

Cerami, Charles A. *Dinner at Mr. Jefferson's: Three Men, Five Great Wines, and the Evening That Changed America*. United States: JW, 2009.

Chernow, Ron. *Alexander Hamilton*. London: Head of Zeus, 2020.

Chernow, Ron. *George Washington*. New York: Penguin Books, 2011.

'Craven Street and Hungerford Lane', in *Survey of London: Volume 18, St Martin-in-The-Fields II: the Strand*, ed. G H Gater and E P Wheeler (London, 1937), pp. 27-39. *British History Online* [Accessed 9 September 2021] <http://www.british-history.ac.uk/survey-london/vol18/pt2/pp27-39>

Epstein, Daniel Mark. *The Loyal Son: The War in Ben Franklin's House*. New York: Ballantine Books, 2017.

Foner, Eric. *Give Me Liberty! An American History*. New York: W. W. Norton and Company, 2014.

Franklin, Benjamin. *The Autobiography and Other Writings*. New York: Penguin Books, 2003.

Fraser, Rebecca. *The Mayflower Generation*. London: Vintage, 2018.

Gill, Stephen. *The Cambridge Companion to Wordsworth*. Cambridge: Cambridge University Press, 2003.

'Golden Square Area: Introduction', in *Survey of London: Volumes 31 and 32, St James Westminster, Part 2*, ed. F H W Sheppard (London, 1963), pp. 138-145. *British History Online* [[Accessed 9 September 2021] <http://www.british-history.ac.uk/survey-london/vols31-2/pt2/pp138-145>

Goodwin, George. *Benjamin Franklin in London*. London: Weidenfield & Nicolson, 2017.

Gordon-Reed, Annette. *The Hemingses of Monticello*. New York: W. W. Norton and Company, 2008.

Gordon-Reed, Annette. *Thomas Jefferson and Sally Hemings: An American Controversy*. Virginia: University of Virginia Press, 1998.

'Grosvenor Square: Individual Houses built before 1926', in *Survey of London: Volume 40, the Grosvenor Estate in Mayfair, Part 2 (The Buildings)*, ed. F H W Sheppard (London, 1980), pp. 117-166. *British History Online* [Accessed 9 September 2021] <http://www.british-history.ac.uk/survey-london/vol40/pt2/pp117-166>>

Hamer, Philip M. *Henry Laurens of South Carolina: A Man and His Papers*. Proceedings of the Massachusetts Historical Society. Third Series, Vol. 77 (1965), pp. 3-14.

Hamilton, Allan Mclane. *Alexander Hamilton: Illustrated Biography Based on Family Letters and Other Personal Documents*. Madison & Adams Press, 2019.

Hart, L. M. A. *Bentham and the United States of America*. The Journal of Law & Economics. Vol. 19, No. 3, 1776: The Revolution in Social Thought (Oct. 1976), pp. 547-567.

Havil, Julian. John Napier: *Life, Logarithms, and Legacy*. New Jersey: Princeton University Press, 2014.

'Henrietta Street and Maiden Lane Area: Henrietta Street', in *Survey of London: Volume 36, Covent Garden*, ed. F H W Sheppard (London, 1970), pp. 230-239. *British History Online* [Accessed 9 September 2021]. <http://www.british-history.ac.uk/survey-london/vol36/pp230-239>

Herman, Eleanor. *Sex with Presidents*. New York: HarperCollins, 2020.

Holton, Woody. *Abigail Adams: A Life*. New York: Atria Books, 2010.

Humphreys, Mary Gay. *Catherine Schuyler.* United States: C. Scribner's Sons, 1897.

Isaacson, Walter. (2003) *Benjamin Franklin Joins the Revolution.* Smithsonian Magazine [Accessed September 9, 2021] <https://www.smithsonianmag.com/history/benjamin-franklin-joins-the-revolution-87199988/>

Isaacson, Walter. *Benjamin Franklin: An American Life.* New York: Simon & Schuster, 2004.

Isenberg, Nancy. *Fallen Founder: The Life of Aaron Burr.* New York: Penguin Group, 2008.

Labaree, Leonard W. *Benjamin Franklin's British Friendships.* Proceedings of the American Philosophical Society, Vol. 108, No. 5 (Oct. 20, 1964), pp. 423 – 428

Levin, Phyllis Lee. *The Remarkable Education of John Quincy Adams.* New York: St. Martin's Press, 2015.

Limbird, John. *Limbird's Handbook Guide to London.* London, The Strand, 1851.

Massey, Gregory D. *John Laurens and the American Revolution.* South Carolina: University of South Carolina Press, 2016.

Mazzeo, Tilar. J. Eliza Hamilton: *The Extraordinary Life and Times of the Wife of Alexander Hamilton.* New York: Gallery Books, 2019.

McCullough, David. *1776.* London: Penguin Books, 2005.

McCullough, David. *Abigail in Paris.* Massachusetts Historical Review. Vol. 3 (2001), pp. 1-18.

McCullough, David. *John Adams.* New York: Simon & Schuster, 2001.

Meacham, Jon. *Thomas Jefferson: The Art of Power.* New York; Random House Trade Paperbacks, 2013.

Memorandum Books, 1786, *The Papers of Thomas Jefferson*, Second Series, *Jefferson's Memorandum Books*, vol. 1, ed. James A Bear, Jr. and Lucia C. Stanton. Princeton: Princeton University Press, 1997, pp. 605–649.

Middlekauff, Robert. *The Glorious Cause: The American Revolution, 1763 – 1789*. New York: Oxford University Press, 2005.

Nagel, Paul. *John Quincy Adams: A Public Life, a Private Life*. Cambridge: Harvard University Press, 1999.

'Pall Mall', in *Survey of London: Volumes 29 and 30, St James Westminster, Part 1*, ed. F H W Sheppard (London, 1960), pp. 322-324. *British History Online* [Accessed 9 September 2021] <http://www.british-history.ac.uk/survey-london/vols29-30/pt1/pp. 322-324>

'Pall Mall, South Side, Past Buildings: Nos 92-93 Pall Mall, The Royal Hotel', in *Survey of London: Volumes 29 and 30, St James Westminster, Part 1*, ed. F H W Sheppard (London, 1960), p. 352. *British History Online* [Accessed 9 September 2021] <http://www.british-history.ac.uk/survey-london/vols29-30/pt1/p352>

Philbrick, Nathaniel. *Mayflower: A Voyage to War*. New York: Harper Perennial, 2011.

Price, David A. *Love and Hate in Jamestown*. New York: Vintage Books, 2005.

Randall, Henry Stephens. *The Life of Thomas Jefferson*. New York: Derby and Jackson, 1858. Vol. 3

Reynolds, David. *America: Empire of Liberty*. London: Penguin Books, 2010.

Roberts, Cokie. *Founding Mothers*. New York: William Morrow, 2004.

Ronald, D. A. B. *The Life of John André: The Redcoat Who Turned Benedict Arnold*. Philadelphia: Casemate Publishers, 2019.

'Sackville Street', in *Survey of London: Volumes 31 and 32, St James Westminster, Part 2*, ed. F H W Sheppard (London, 1963), pp. 342-366. *British History Online* [Accessed 9 September 2021] <http://www.british-history.ac.uk/survey-london/vols31-2/pt2/pp342-366>

Stahr, Walter. *John Jay: Founding Father*. New York: Diversion Books, 2017.

The Correspondence and Public Papers of John Jay, ed. Henry P. Johnston, A.M. (New York: G.P. Putnam's Sons, 1890 – 93). Vol 4 (1794 – 1826)

The Correspondence of Jeremy Bentham, Volume 1: 1752 to 1776: London, UCL Press,

The Papers of Alexander Hamilton. ed. Harold C. Syrett. New York: Columbia University Press [Accessed September 14 2021] <https://founders.archives.gov/content/volumes#Hamilton/> *The private journal of Aaron Burr, reprinted in full from the original manuscript in the library of Mr. William K. Bixby of St. Louis, Mo., with an introduction, explanatory notes, and a glossary.* New York: The Post Express Printing Co., 1903.

'The Theatre Royal: Management', in *Survey of London: Volume 35, the theatre Royal, Drury Lane, and the Royal Opera House, Covent Garden*, ed. F H W Sheppard (London, 1970), pp. 9-29. *British History Online* Accessed 9 September 2021] <http://www.british-history.ac.uk/survey-london/vol35/pp9-29>

Tyler, Lyon G. *The Gnostic Trap: Richard Clarke and His Proclamation of the Millennium and Universal Restoration in South Carolina and England.* Anglican and Episcopal History Vol. 58, No. 2 (June 1989), pp. 146-168.
Walford, Edward. 'Westminster: Buckingham Palace', in *Old and New London: Volume 4 Online* (London, 1878), pp. 61-74. *British History* [Accessed 9 September 2021] <http://www.british-history.ac.uk/old-new-london/vol4/pp61-74>

Williams, Yohuru. *Why Thomas Jefferson's Anti-Slavery Passage Was Removed from the Declaration of Independence.* History [Accessed September 9, 2021] < https://www.history.com/news/declaration-of-independence-deleted-anti-slavery-clause-jefferson>

ILLUSTRATION INDEX

Jacket illustrations (front)

1. *A plan of the cities of London and Westminster, and borough of Southwark.* John Roque, 1746.
2. *Mrs John Barker Church with her son, Philip, and a servant.* John Trumball, c. 1785.
3. *John Adams.* John Singleton Copley, 1783.
4. *Thomas Jefferson.* Mather Brown, 1786.
5. *Benjamin Franklin.* Joseph Duplessis, 1788.
6. *Margaret Arnold and child*, Daniel Gardner. C. 1783-1789.
7. *Aaron Burr,* John Vanderlyn, 1802.
8. *Alexander Hamilton.* John Trumball, 1806. (As seen on the $10 bill).

Jacket illustrations (back)

9. *A plan of the cities of London and Westminster, and borough of Southwark.* John Roque, 1746.
10. *Benedict Arnold,* Thomas Hart, 1776.
11. *Abigail Adams.* Benjamin Blythe, 1766.
12. *John Jay.* Gilbert Stuart, 1794.
13. *John Laurens,* Charles Willson Peale, 1780.

Inside

1. *Alexander Hamilton.* John Trumball, 1792.
2. *Alexander Hamilton.* John Trumball, 1806.
3. *Eliza Hamilton.* Ralph Earl, c. 1787.
4. *Mrs John Barker Church with her son, Philip, and a servant.* John Trumball, c. 1785.
5. *John Adams.* Gilbert Stuart, c. 1800-1815.
6. *Abigail Adams.* Benjamin Blythe, 1766.
7. *Thomas Jefferson.* Rembrandt Peale, 1800.
8. *Benjamin Franklin.* Joseph Duplessis, 1788.
9. *Benedict Arnold,* Thomas Hart, 1776.
10. *Margaret Arnold and child*, Daniel Gardner. C. 1783-1789.
11. *John Jay.* Gilbert Stuart, 1794.
12. *John Laurens,* Charles Willson Peale, 1780.
13. *Aaron Burr,* John Vanderlyn, 1802.
14. *Sackville Street.* Hannah Ryan, 2021.
15. *St. James's Church, Piccadilly,* Hannah Ryan, 2021.
16. *Angelica Schuyler Church.* Samuel Shelley, 1784-1794.

ABOUT THE AUTHOR

Hannah Ryan lives in North London and is currently studying for her Master's degree in American History and Politics at University College London. She received her Bachelor's degree in American and Canadian Literature, History and Culture from the University of Nottingham in 2019. Alongside working in London's American heritage sector, she also writes a blog about American history in Britain called the *Anglo-American Almanac.*